IMAGES
of America

BRIDESBURG

IMAGES
of America

BRIDESBURG

Frederick Siegle and Teresa Pyott
for the Bridesburg Historical Society

ARCADIA
PUBLISHING

ISBN 978-0-7385-3605-7

Published by Arcadia Publishing
Charleston, South Carolina

Printed in the United States of America

Library of Congress Catalog Card Number: 2004103580

For all general information contact Arcadia Publishing at:
Telephone 843-853-2070
Fax 843-853-0044
E-mail sales@arcadiapublishing.com
For customer service and orders:
Toll-Free 1-888-313-2665

Visit us on the Internet at www.arcadiapublishing.com

Contents

ACKNOWLEDGMENTS

A book like this is created not by one, two, or even three individuals; rather, it is created by the memories and collectibles of the community's longtime residents. To that end, we must acknowledge, with great appreciation, the following people, whose generosity and contributions were of such help in putting together this history of Bridesburg: Russell F. Bush, W. Bruce Beaton, Ronald R. Gurczynski, Alfred Dombrowski, Catherine Bendler, Viola Chalfont, Donald Rosenberg, William Kearney, Edward Ludwig, H. Slykoff, Harry Silcox, and Jim Smart.

We would also like to thank the members of the Bridesburg Historical Society, the Rohm and Haas Company, Sunoco, Third Federal Savings, Earthstar Bank, the Ellis Coffee Company, and other neighborhood businesses, and the Bridesburg Civic Association, without whose dedication and help we would not be able to carry out our work.

Enough cannot be said for the Pennsylvania Historical Society, the Pennsylvania Genealogical Society, the Library Company of Philadelphia, and the Free Library of Philadelphia. Their collections and information sources were of extreme value.

We have the greatest appreciation for William Sliker and his son Charles Sliker, for the magnificent photographic record they created. Their Sliker Studio is responsible for nearly 80 percent of the nearly 1,000 photographs in the Bridesburg Historical Society's collection.

Finally, we are deeply grateful for the patience and support of their spouses—Pat Siegle and Stretch Pyott.

INTRODUCTION

This book is about Bridesburg, a neighborhood in northeast Philadelphia that is bound by the Delaware River and the Frankford Creek. From the very beginning, these two waterways shaped the lives of the people who lived here. The earliest known inhabitants were members of the Lenni Lenape tribe. The first European settlers in the area were the Swedes. By 1681, William Penn had received from the king of England a land grant that he called Pennsylvania.

The name for the village of Point No Point was derived from a natural phenomenon apparent from the river when nearing by boat. What seemed to be a point of land jutting into the river disappeared upon approach but reappeared once passed. Eventually the name of the area was shortened to the Point.

By 1795, Joseph Kirkbride was operating a ferry across the Frankford Creek. In January 1800, he purchased the Point Farm and laid out plots for 22 homes. The village took its name, Kirkbridesburg, from its founder. In time, the name of the town was shortened to Bridesburg.

In 1816, the Bridesburg Arsenal was established on the Frankford Creek. Inside the stone walls, officers' quarters and enlisted men's barracks still stand. In 1819, after 10 years of manufacturing cotton machinery in Holmesburg, Alfred Jenks moved his building to Bridesburg and established the Bridesburg Manufacturing Company.

One of the first schools was housed in the old town hall, which was built on land donated by the Kirkbride family. In 1848, the Irving Consolidated Grammar School was opened on Haworth Street, just east of Thompson.

Before the 19th century, residents traveled to churches in nearby communities. The Methodist Society, formalized in 1833, was the first church to be chartered in Bridesburg, holding services in the old town hall before building a church in 1851. A group of Presbyterians held their first services in the old town hall in 1829 and built their first church in 1837.

In 1842, Charles and Frederick Lennig purchased land at the junction of the creek and the river to establish a new home for their Tacony Chemical Works.

Bridesburg was incorporated as a borough on April 1, 1848. With the passage of the Act of Consolidation in 1854, Bridesburg became a part of the city of Philadelphia.

As the German population grew, the first religious services for German Protestants were held in the old town hall in 1859. The German Reformed congregation dedicated their new church building in 1864. The German Roman Catholics formed the parish of All Saints, and six months later, in 1861, the original church building was dedicated. This stands today as Marion Hall, on Edgemont Street at Buckius.

Like all communities in the nation, Bridesburg was affected by the Civil War. The growth of the Frankford Arsenal, the Bridesburg Manufacturing Company, and the Charles Lennig Company brought a great number of people to live here. During the Civil War, the arsenal served as a depot. In 1861, 29 boys between the ages of 13 and 16 left the Irving School to volunteer for the Union army. The Bridesburg Manufacturing Company, internationally known for its production of machinery for the textile industry, made 95,000 muskets for the Union forces.

After the Civil War, industry in Bridesburg continued to grow. The Lennig Company prospered. In 1884, the H. W. Jayne Company started operations as one of the earliest producers of coal chemicals. In 1896, the Jayne Company was absorbed by the Barrett Manufacturing Company.

Polish immigrants met in 1892 to organize a Roman Catholic parish to serve their community. They first held services in All Saints' original church building. In 1893, the new parish of St. John Cantius had erected their first church, the building now used as their chapel. One more church was added to the community in 1899, when a Baptist congregation began holding meetings in Holly Hall. Their present church building was dedicated in 1901.

When the Irving School could no longer accommodate all of the children, a new Bridesburg School was built in 1899 on the east side of Richmond Street, between Jenks and Ash Streets.

During World War I, millions of rounds of artillery ammunition were manufactured, loaded, and shipped from the Frankford Arsenal.

Just before the depression of 1921, the Rohm and Haas Company purchased the stock from the estate of the late John B. Lennig and began its expansion to become one of the major industries in the community. In 1930, the Philadelphia Coke Company opened to sell Kopper's coke, a domestic solid fuel.

In 1937, Ed Ludwig, a postman and a Bridesburg resident, organized Old Home Week. This led to the formation of the Bridesburg Civic Association.

During World War II, Bridesburg once again rallied to the country's call. Small arms and ammunition were manufactured and tested at the arsenal. The firing of guns could be heard throughout Bridesburg.

After World War II, Bridesburg was famous for its Fourth of July celebrations. Daylong games, refreshments, and contests in the park were followed by dazzling fireworks displays at dusk. The Memorial Day parade, sponsored by Bridesburg veterans' groups, is still an annual event.

In the aftermath of World War II, the Bridesburg Civic Association was successful in having the city dump at the south end of town closed. The creek and the river had become polluted from industry along the waterways. With environmental awareness, efforts have cleared the air and the river. The two chemical companies have undergone major changes. What was once known as Barrett's is now part of Sunoco, and Rohm and Haas has dramatically downsized its operation here, relocating many of its operations. Both companies, however, continue to support the community and, together with the Bridesburg Business Association, sponsor the biannual Pride Week, an event that highlights the very best of the neighborhood.

The Frankford Arsenal was closed by the government and is now known as the Arsenal Business Center. Developers now eye the riverfront as a potential site for new homes, and environmentalists work for a "green belt" along the Delaware. Perhaps the river, which has been dear to the hearts of so many residents, will once again be accessible to the community.

One

Around Town

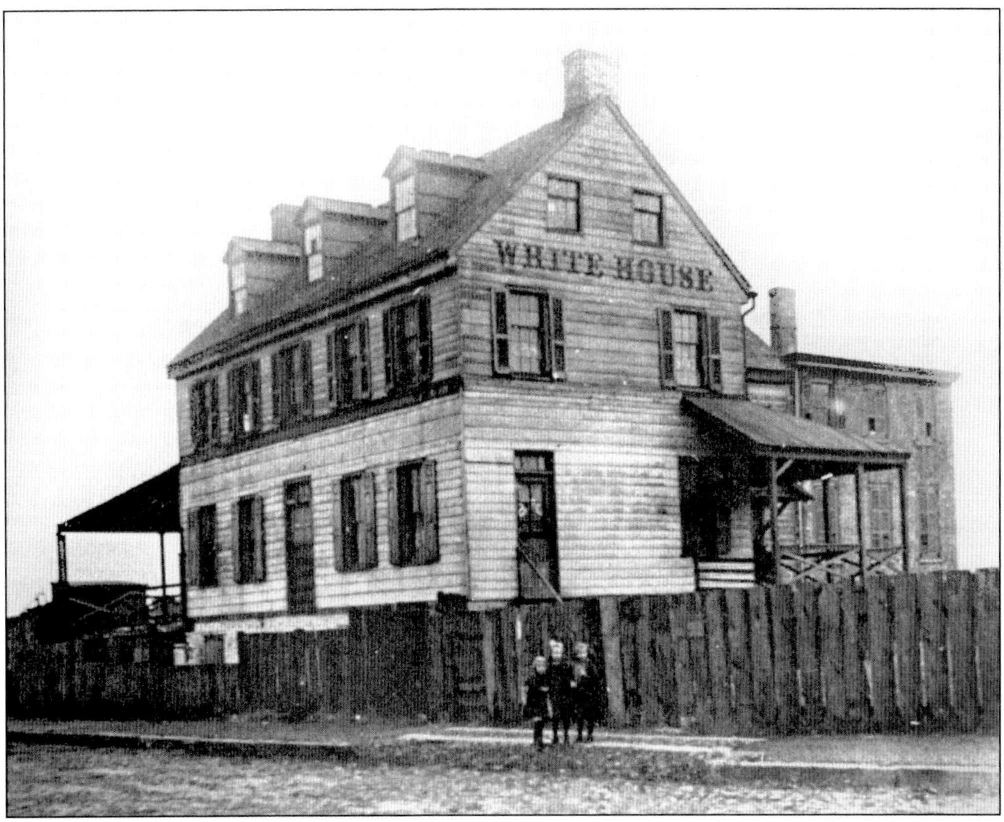

The White House Hotel was a favorite stopover for travelers and visitors to Bridesburg. Its location on Bridge Street was convenient to the steamer service to and from Philadelphia.

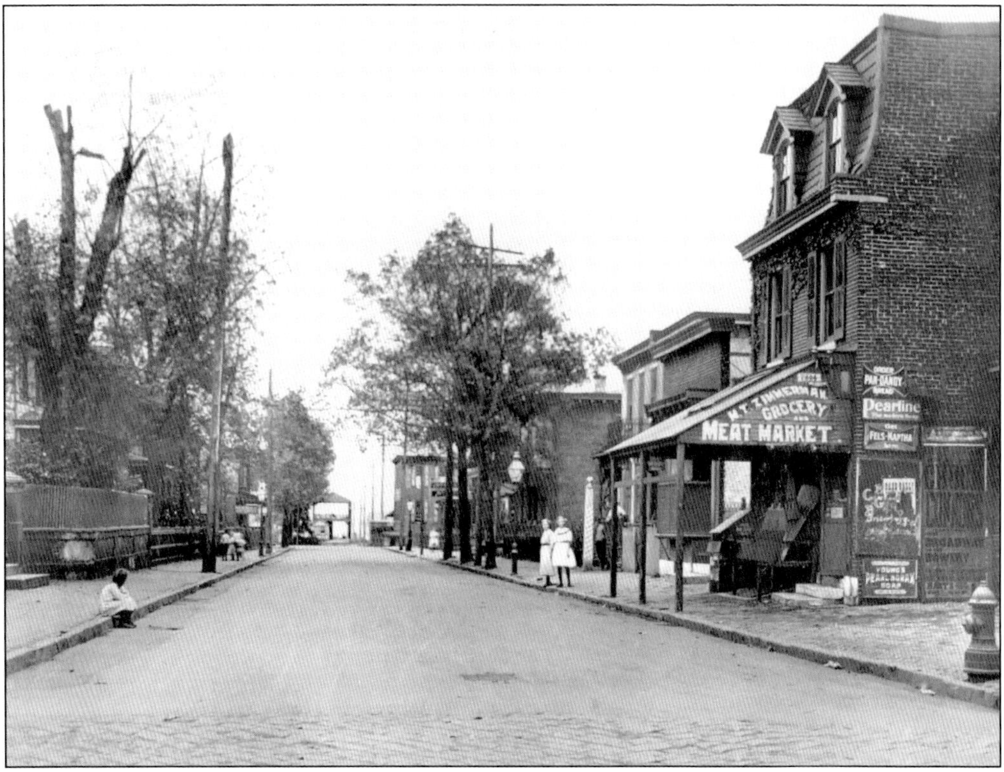

This view looks east on Bridge Street from Richmond, toward the river. To the right is Zimmerman's, one of the many shops located throughout Bridesburg. In the distance is the wharf where the paddle-wheel boats docked for their trip to the city.

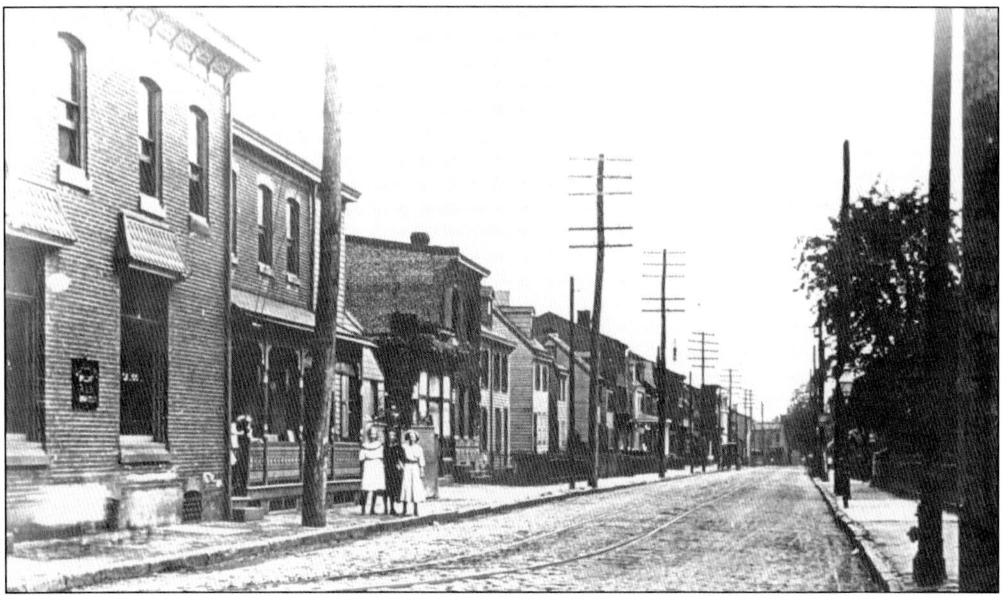

This photograph, taken in the middle of the 19th century, looks west on Bridge Street from Richmond toward Thompson Street. Notice the dress of the young people and the recently installed streetcar tracks.

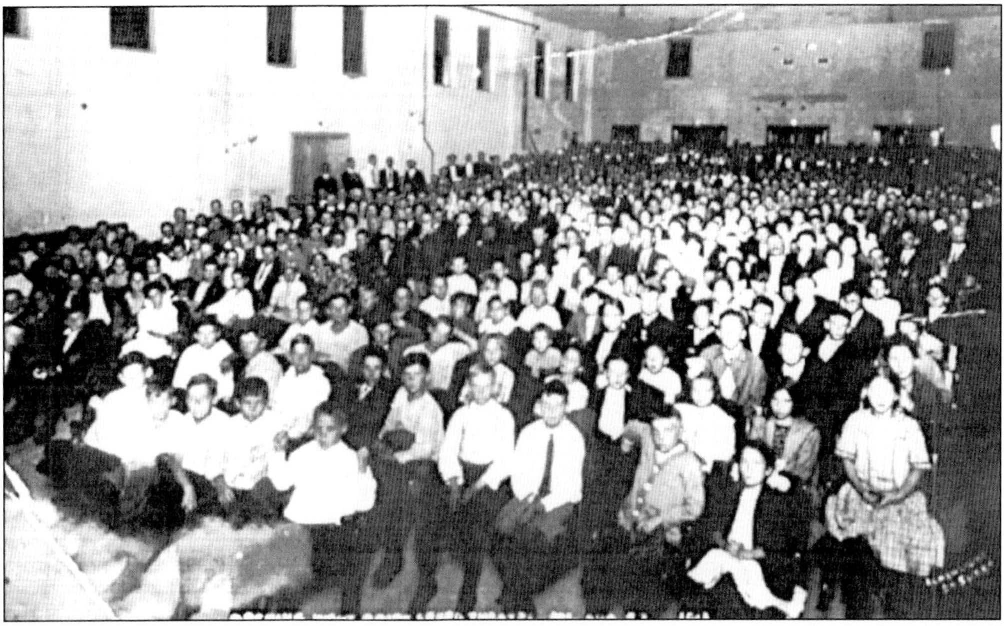

The new Elm Theater, an early movie house, was located at the corner of Bridge and Richmond Streets. This photograph, taken on opening night, August 22, 1913, shows the standing-room-only crowd in the 498-seat theater. The building was razed in 1957.

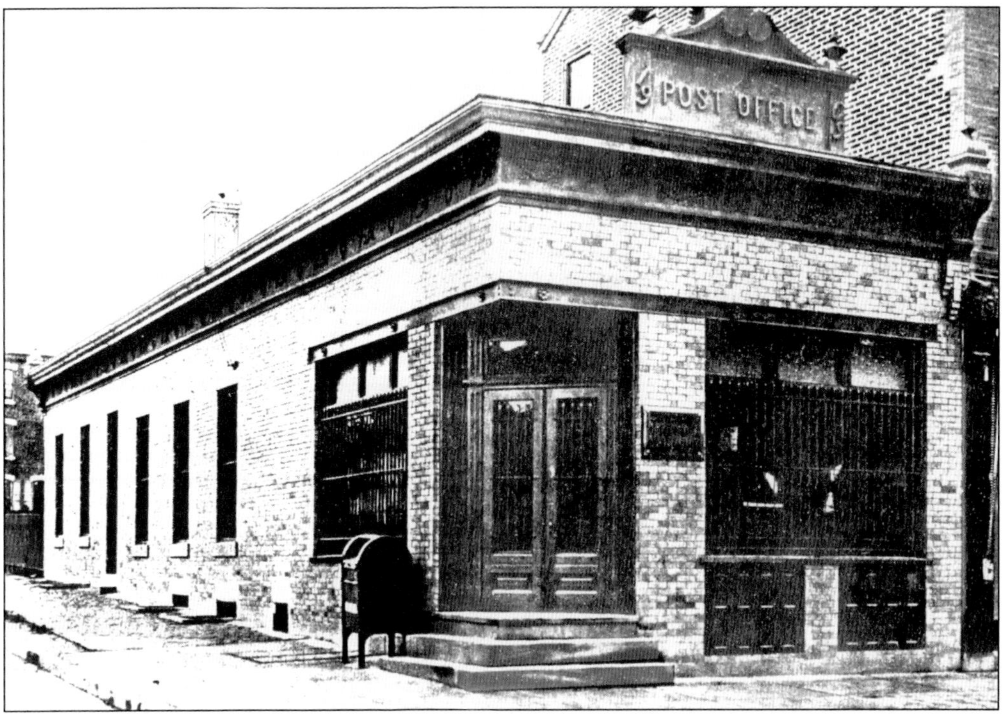

Throughout history, Bridesburg's post offices have been at four different locations. The one shown here was the second, on the corner of Bridge and Salmon Streets. It is now the well-known Post Office Café.

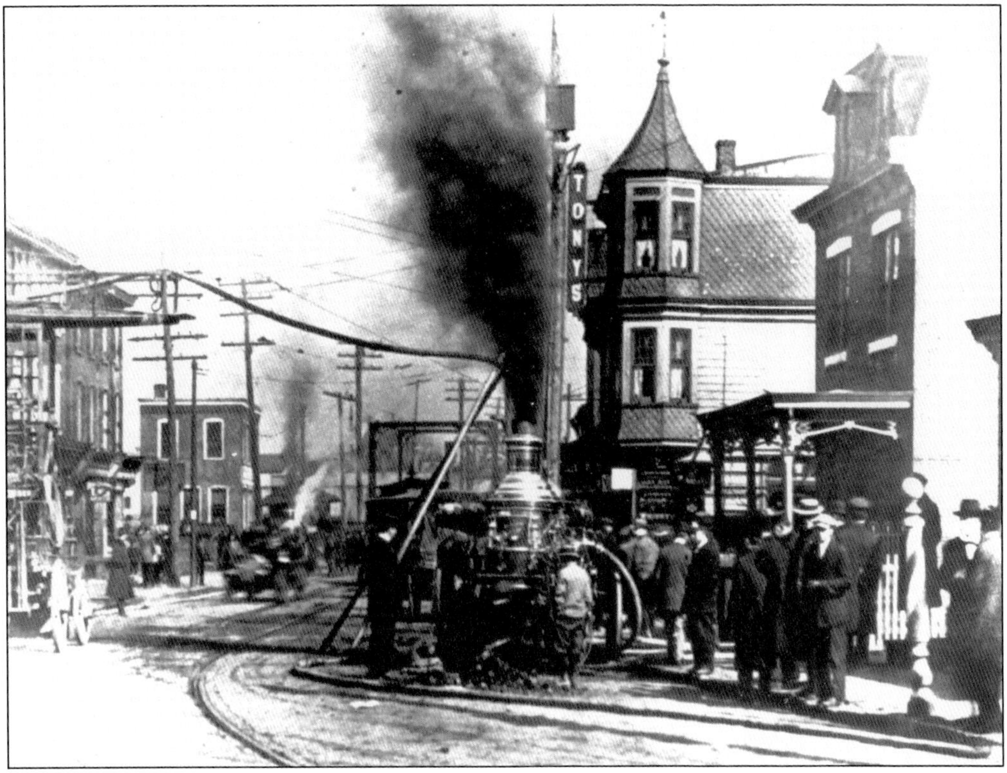

Bridesburg's Engine Company No. 33 is in action at the corner of Bridge and Thompson Streets. It is interesting to note that there seems to be more smoke coming from the fire engine than from the apparent actual fire across the street. Also of interest is the barber pole in the lower right corner.

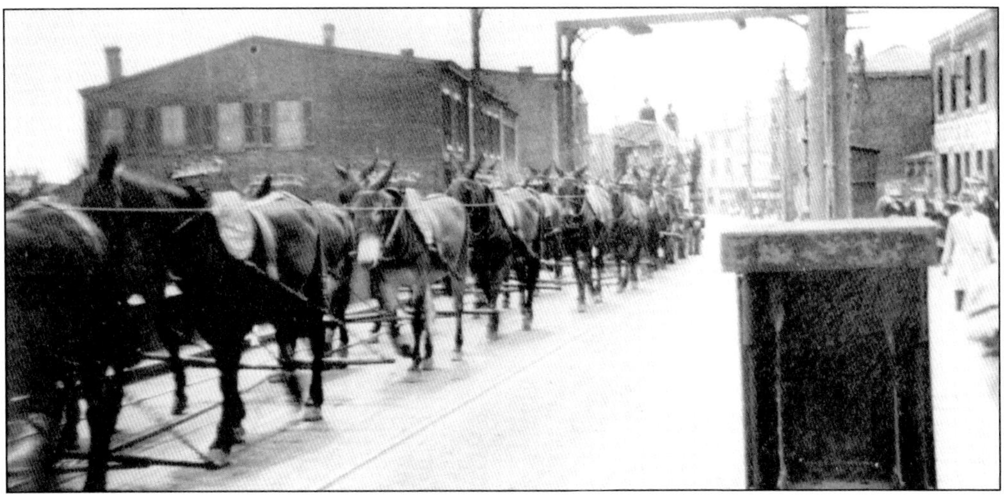

While this scene displays streetcar tracks and overhead wiring, it also shows that mule teams were still being used for hauling. The view looks east from the west side of the bridge over Frankford Creek.

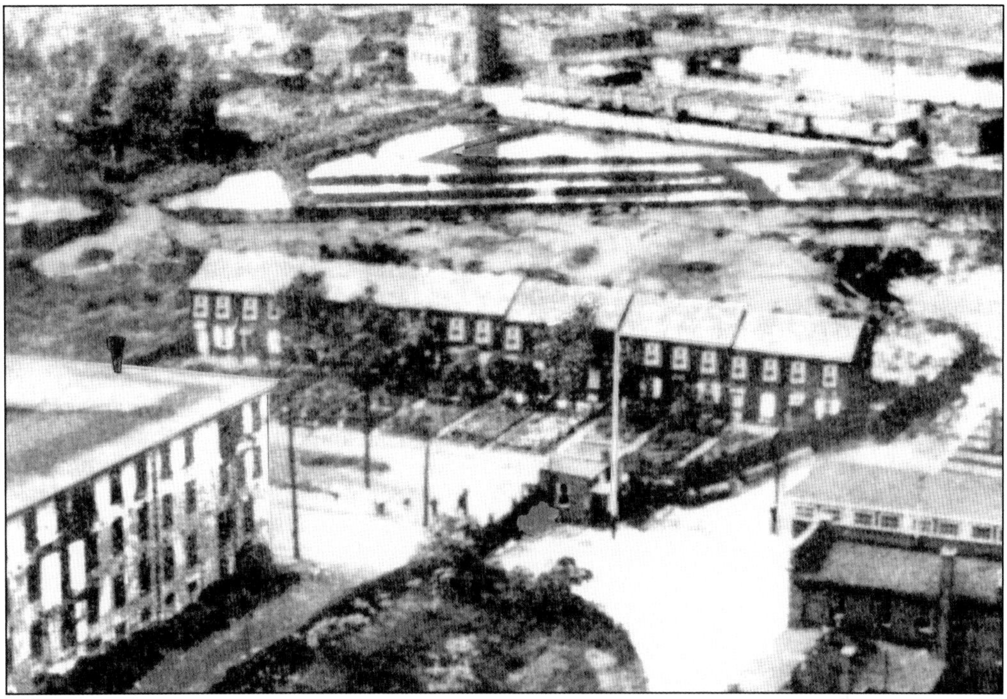

One of the best-known rows of homes in Bridesburg was Old Dutch Row. These houses were built by the Tacony Chemical Works to house chemists brought to the United States to work in the company's plant. The homes have since been removed to make way for company expansion.

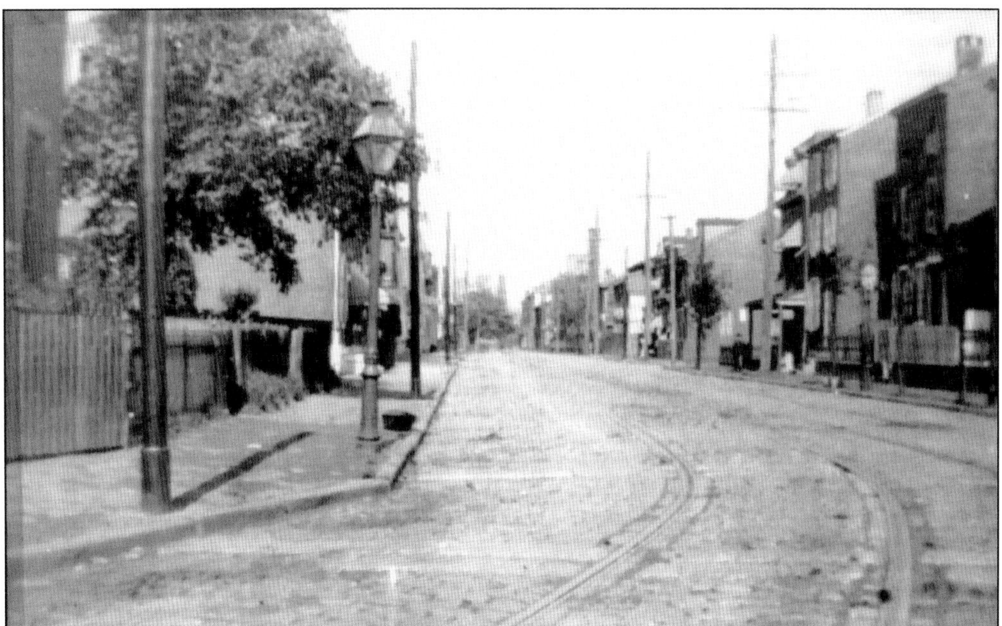

This view looks north at the bend on Richmond Street at Reynolds. In early Colonial days, Reynolds Street, which connected to the riverfront, marked the northern end of Point Road (now Richmond Street).

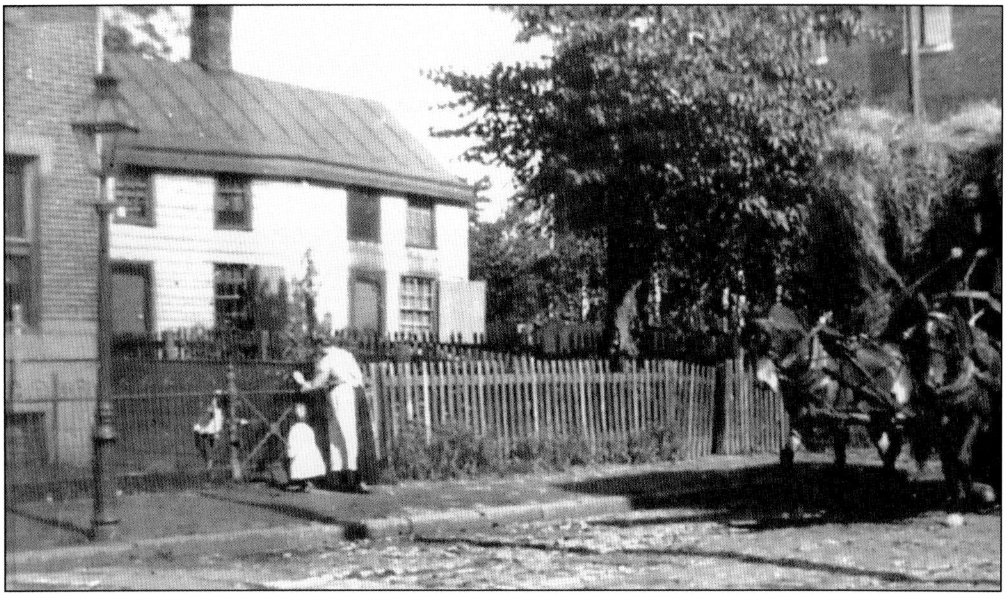

Taken at the Richmond Street location seen on the previous page, this photograph looks west from Reynolds. At this spot were two of the very early homes built in Bridesburg. The design was very similar to a number of other homes built in the early to mid-1800s. Unfortunately, these homes fell into disrepair over the years and were torn down and replaced with a grocery store and candy shop.

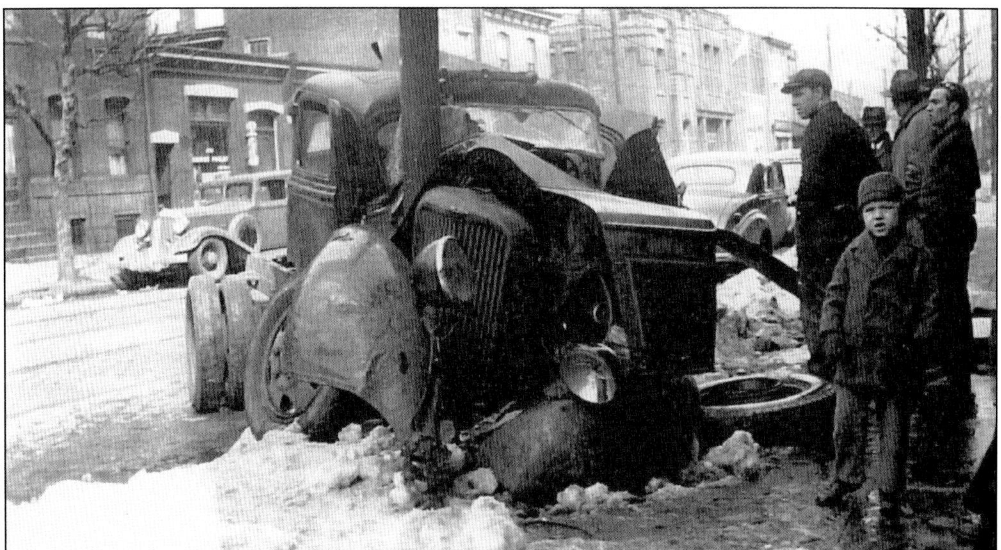

While the primary focus in this photograph is the truck accident, the image also offers a rare glimpse of Frank's Barbershop and of the laundry next door.

This beautiful and well-kept house at 4670 Richmond Street provided not only a home for its owners but also a workspace; they operated a tailor shop on the first floor.

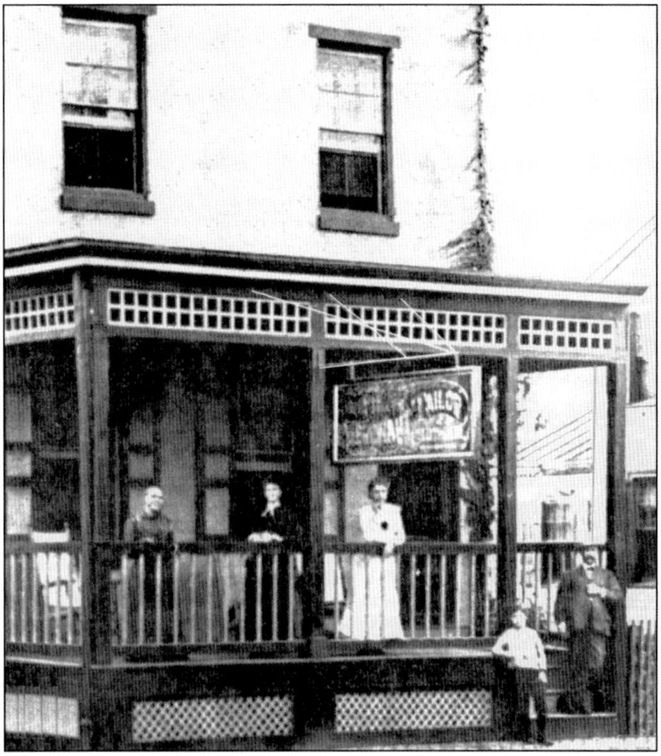

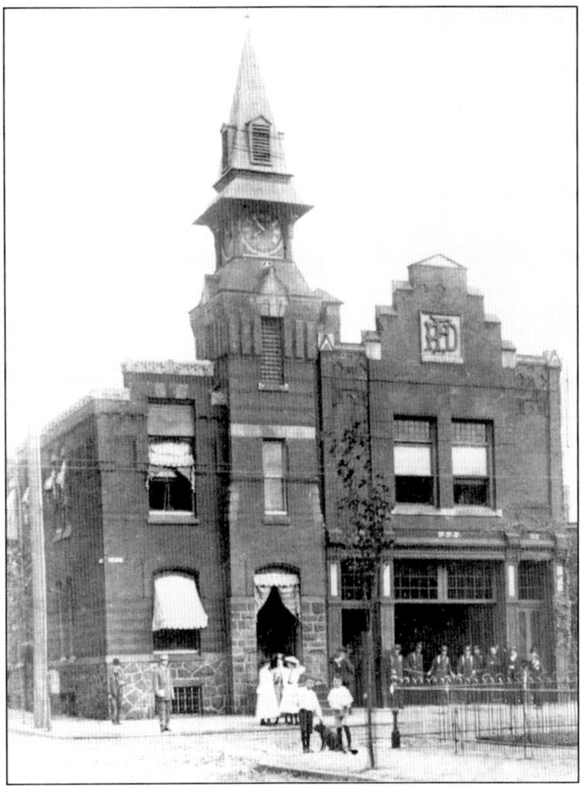

The old borough hall housed both the police and fire stations and served the community for many years before being replaced with a modern fire station. During World War II, it held the offices of the local draft board.

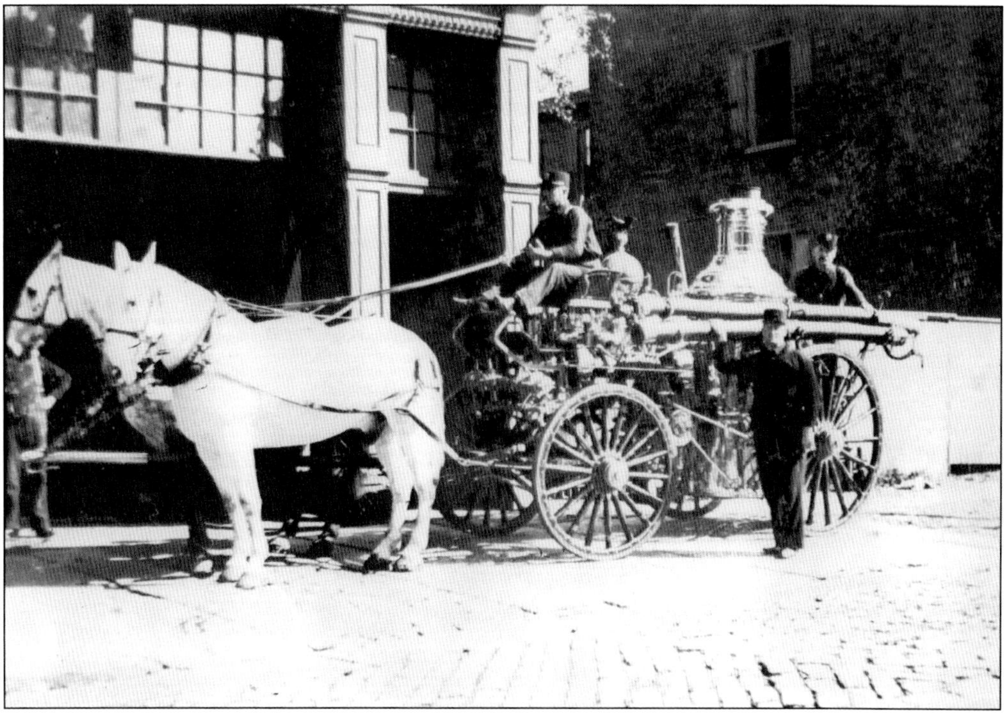

Taken in front of the original Firehouse No. 33 on Richmond Street, this photograph displays an early piece of firefighting equipment. Before the firehouse had engines, horses and steam-driven pumps got water to the fire.

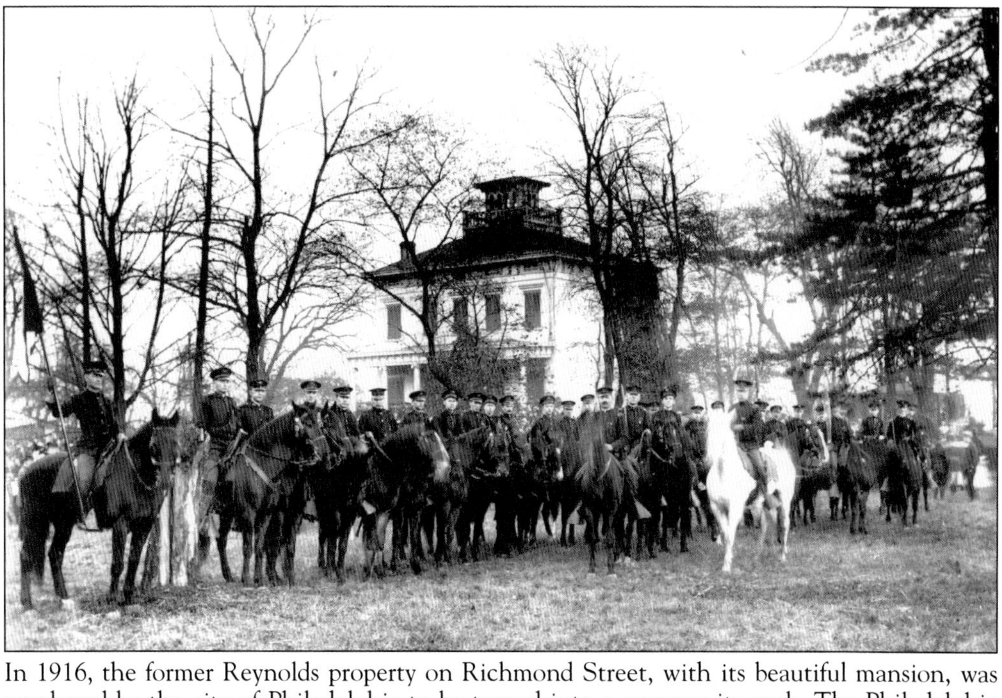

In 1916, the former Reynolds property on Richmond Street, with its beautiful mansion, was purchased by the city of Philadelphia to be turned into a community park. The Philadelphia horse-mounted police honor guard is shown here during the park's opening ceremonies.

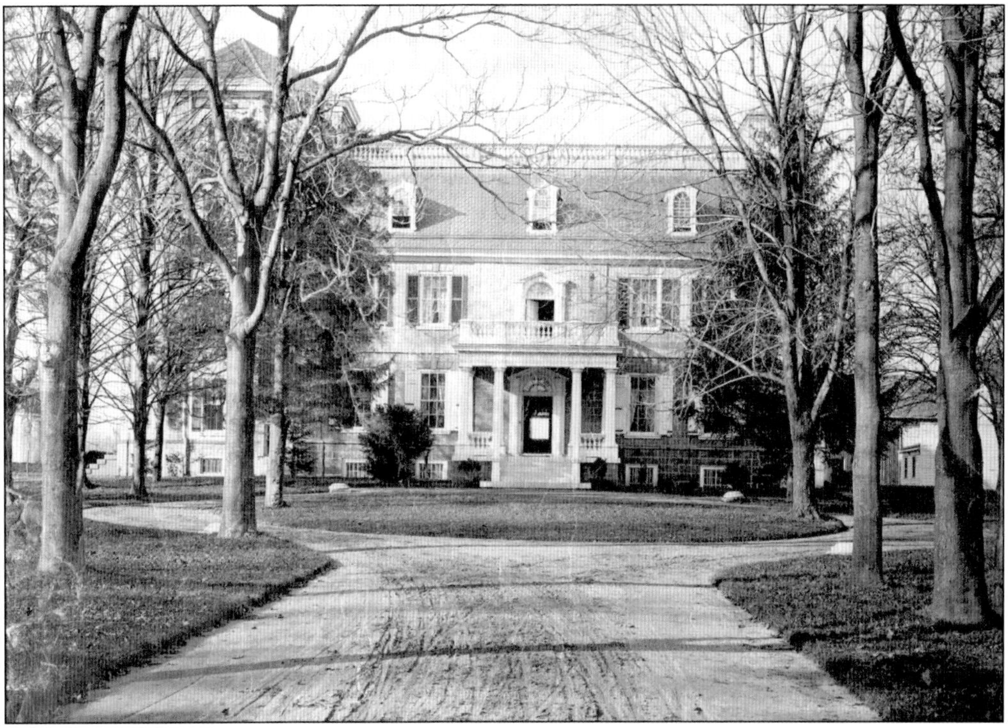

One of the most renowned mansions in Bridesburg was Holly Hall. Built in the mid-1700s, it was so named because of the many holly trees on the property. It served as General Howe's staff headquarters for the British occupation of Philadelphia during the American Revolution. It was later renamed Nugent Hall and was the home of Barton Jenks. In 1906, the building was torn down, and the property became known as Nugent Park.

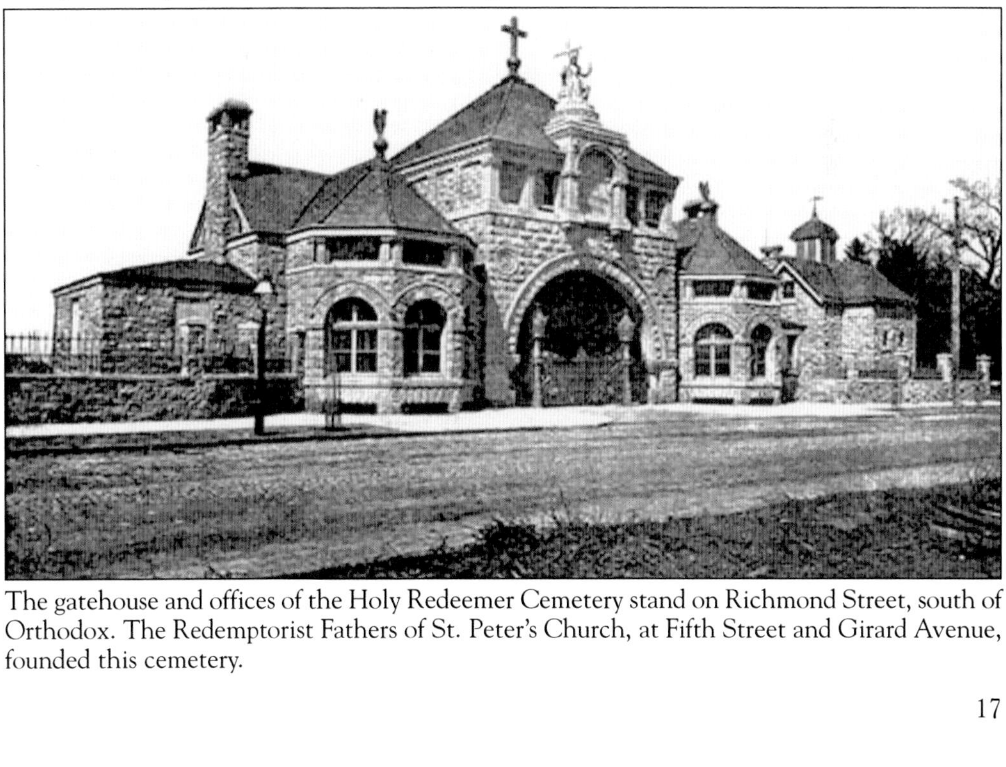

The gatehouse and offices of the Holy Redeemer Cemetery stand on Richmond Street, south of Orthodox. The Redemptorist Fathers of St. Peter's Church, at Fifth Street and Girard Avenue, founded this cemetery.

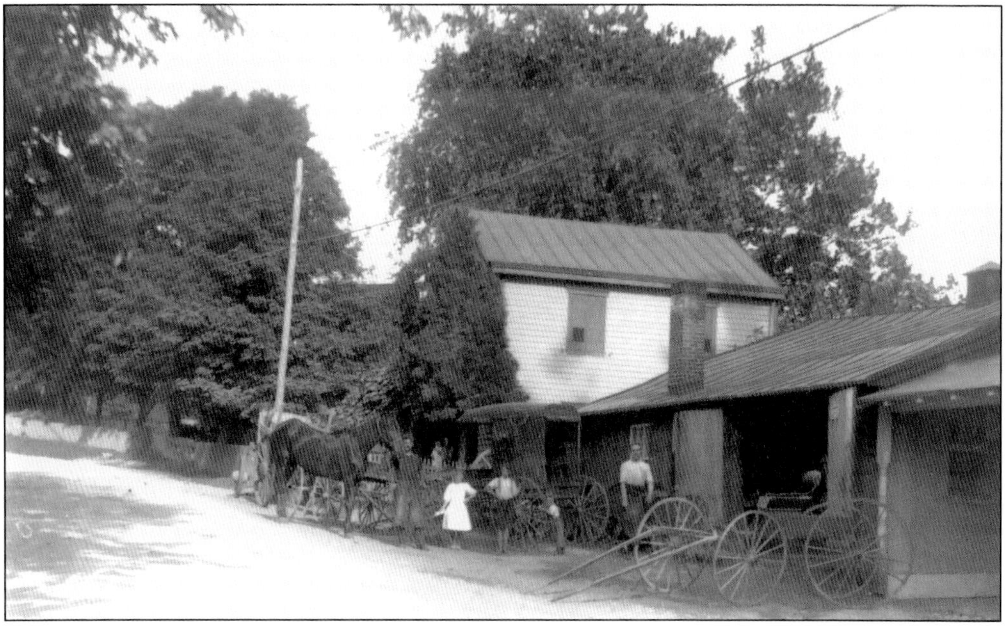

This is an interesting view of the "village smithy," which was likely located at the southern end of Bridesburg, somewhere near Wheatsheaf Lane.

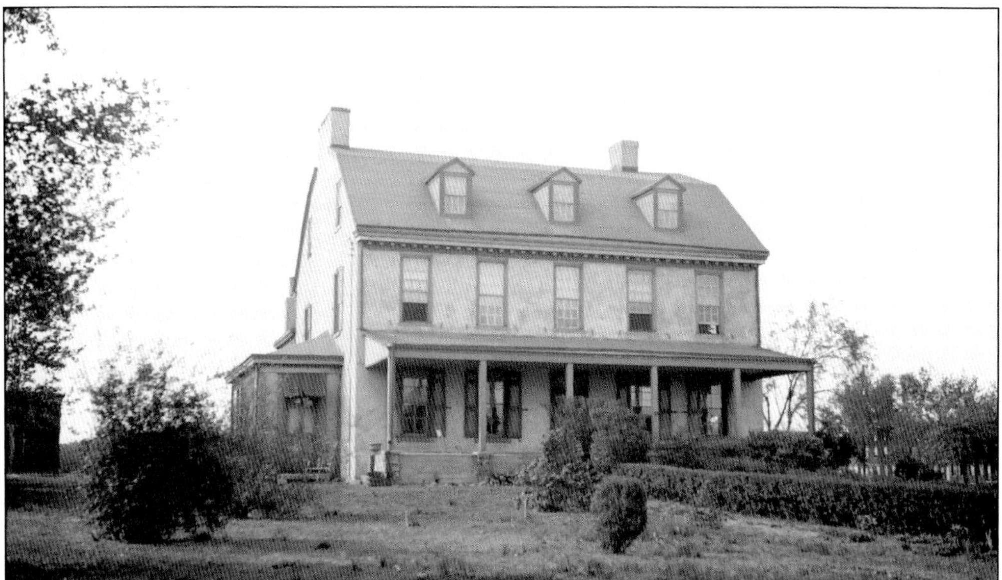

Situated on the west side of Richmond Street near Luzerne, this farmstead was home to the Harrison family. The Harrisons owned a large tract of land here. The row of homes on Berkshire Street was built on part of their holdings and was known as Harrison Row.

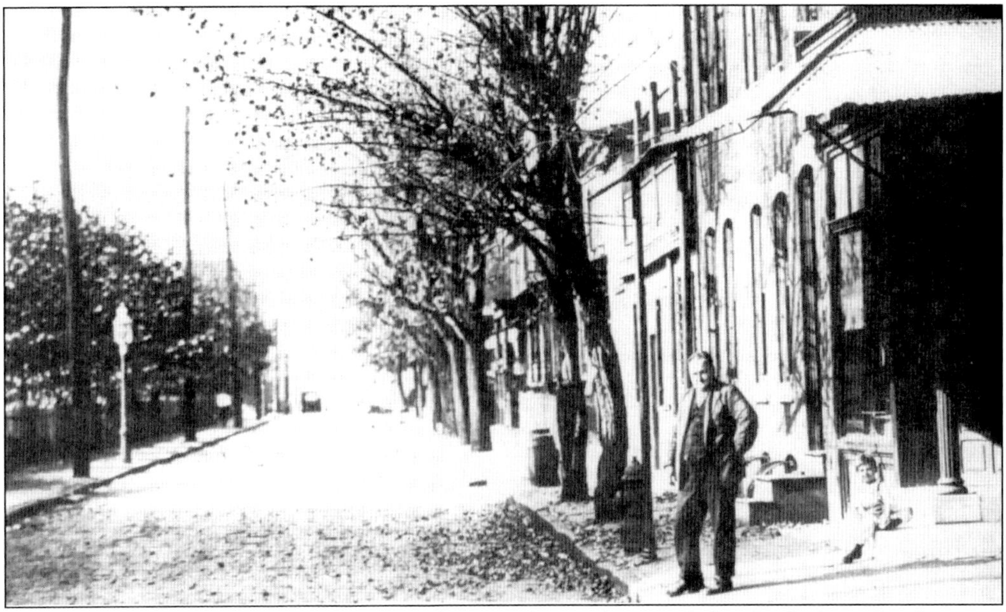

This view looks west on Pratt Street from Richmond toward the Bridesburg Presbyterian Church. The gentleman standing on the corner is Theodore Fuss, owner a hardware store that stood on the opposite side of Richmond Street. The boy on the steps is Charles Harris.

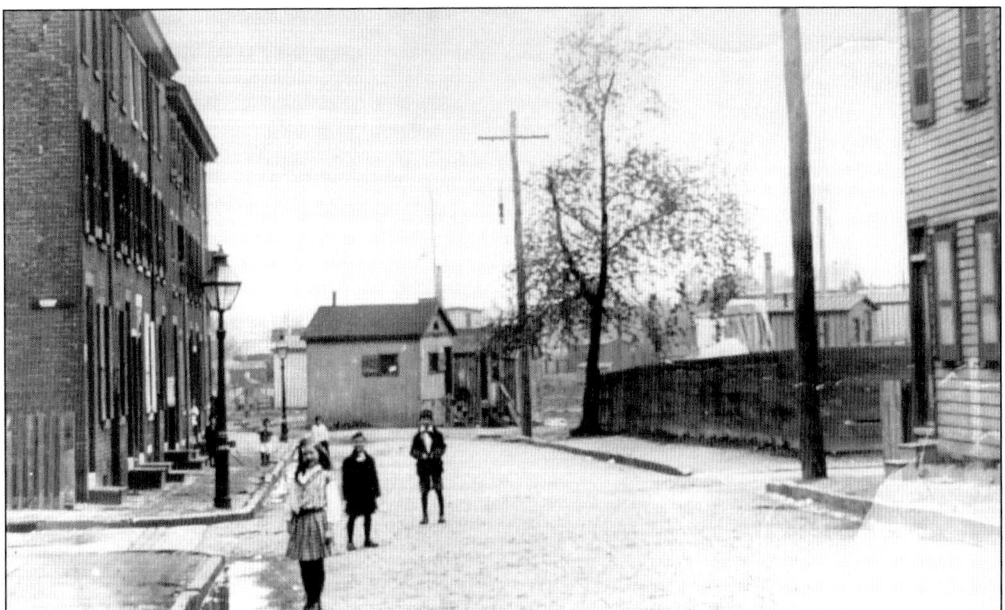

Here, children stop playing to watch William H. Sliker, Bridesburg's famed photographer, take a photograph of the western end of Church (now Pratt) Street, at the Frankford Creek. Buildings seen in the distance are those of the former H. C. Allen Lumber and Coal Yard.

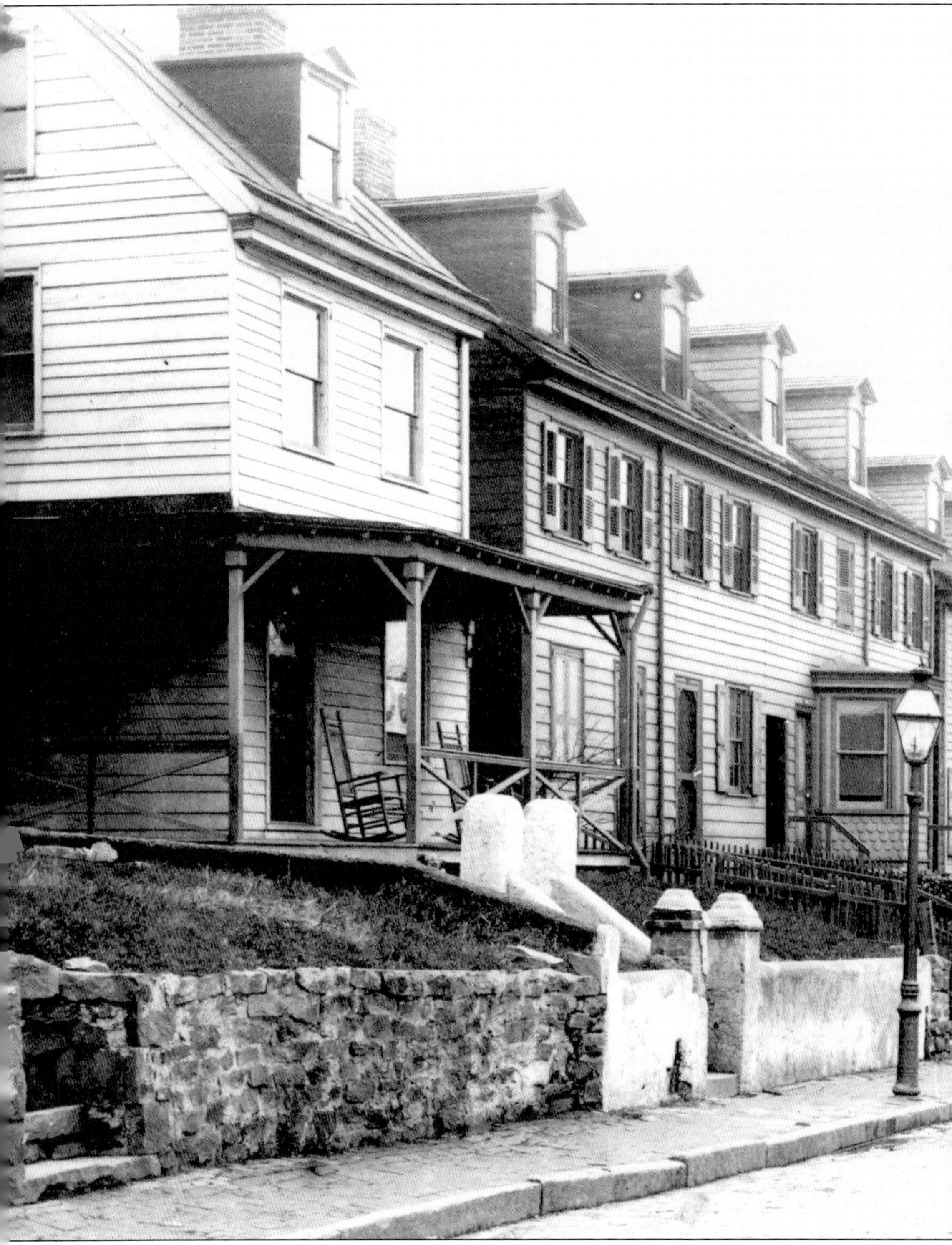

This scene of Church (now Pratt) Street dates from long before the advent of the automobile, as evidenced by the number of horse-drawn wagons in view. Taken just south of Edgemont

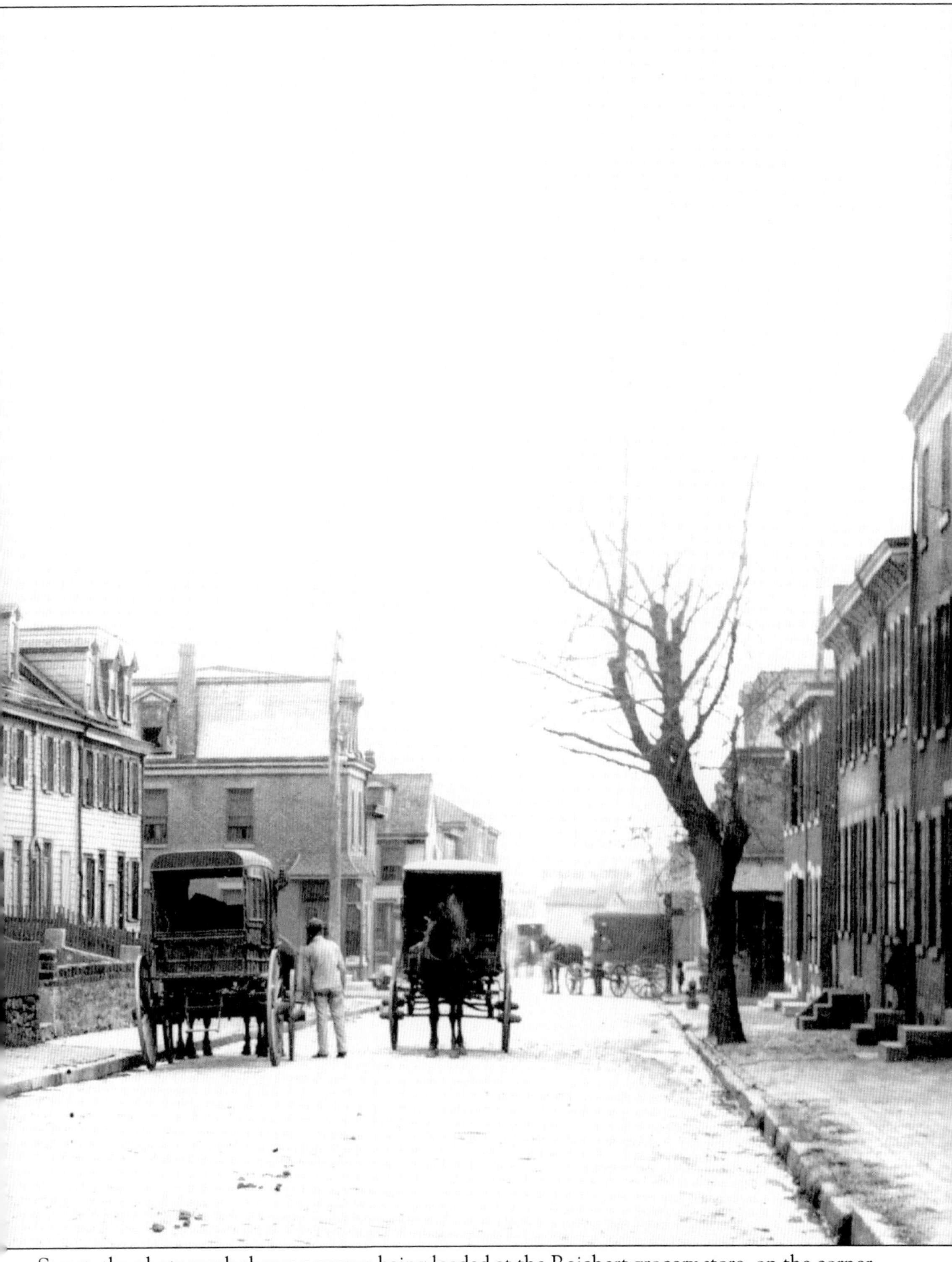

Street, the photograph shows a wagon being loaded at the Reichert grocery store, on the corner at Thompson Street.

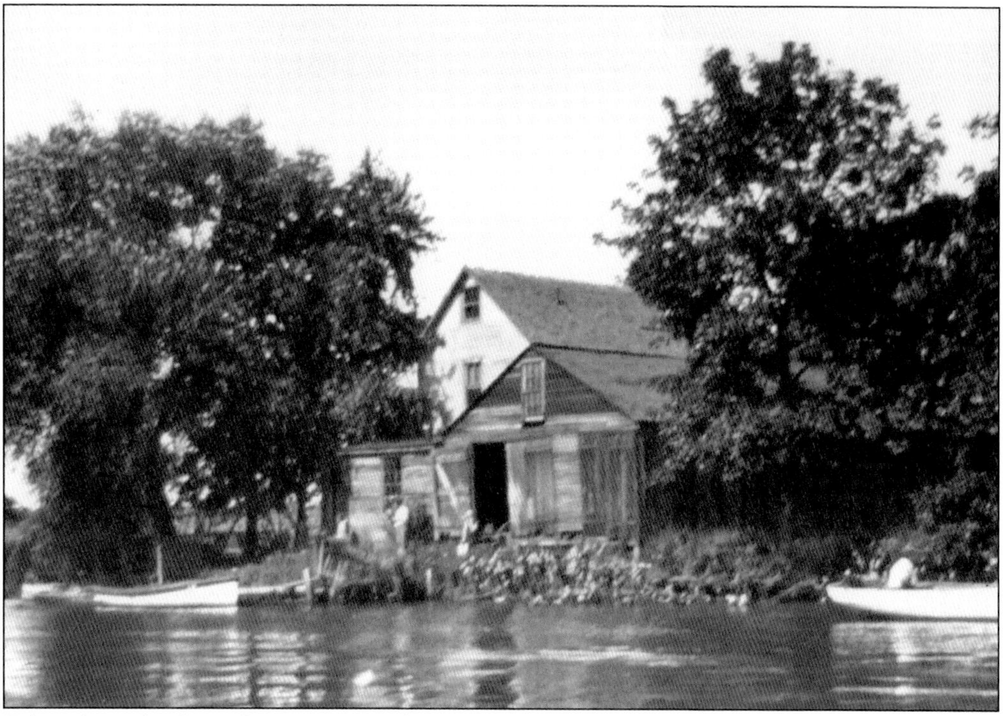

Taken from the foot of Pratt Street, this bucolic scene of the opposite bank of the Frankford Creek shows an old house and outbuilding, with fishing boats on the water. Over the years, the width of the creek was reduced in order to provide more building space at its banks.

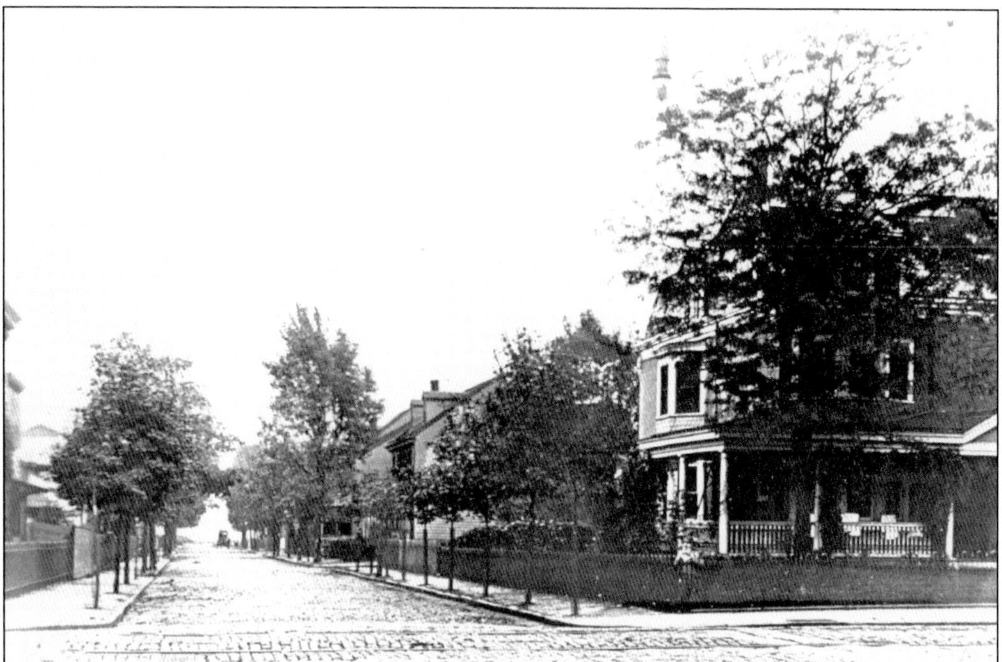

One of the finer homes in Bridesburg, shown on the right, still stands at the southeast corner of Richmond and Kirkbride Streets.

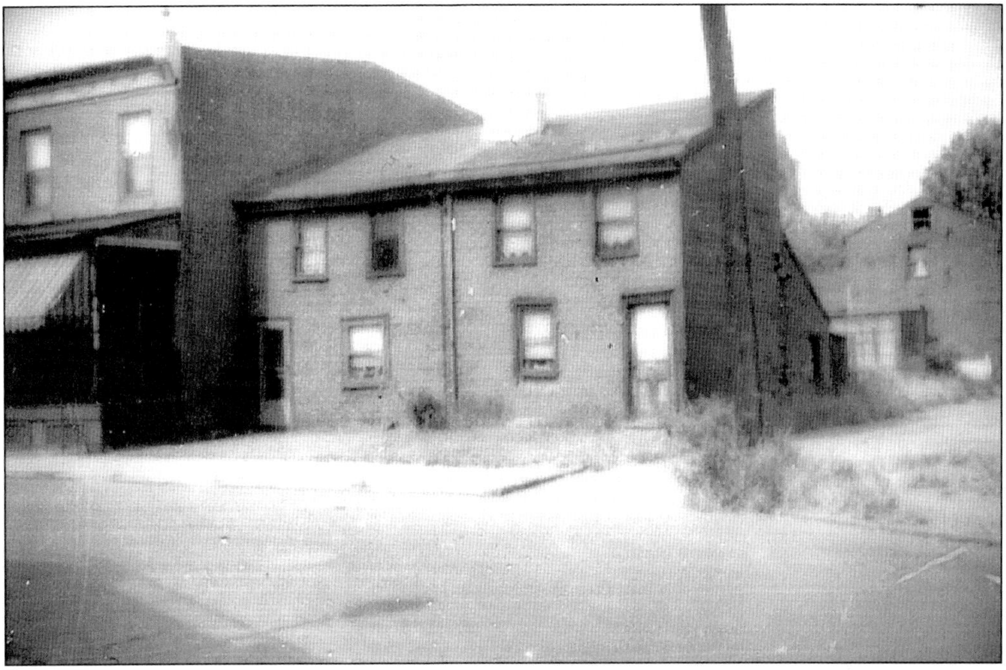

These Kirkbride Street houses were among the very first to be built in Bridesburg. They were typical of the small homes built to accommodate the new, smaller families moving into the community in the early 19th century. Once located at the back of the old police station, they no longer stand.

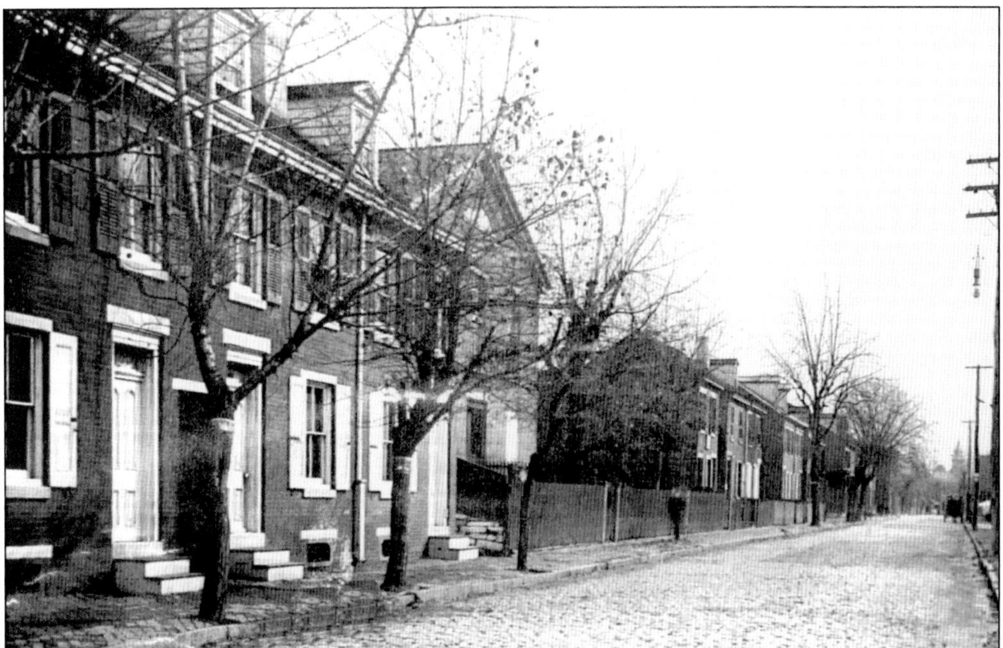

This view looks east on Kirkbride Street from Thompson. On the left is the original Bridesburg Methodist Church building. Kirkbride Street marked the southern boundary of the village, planned and developed by Joseph Kirkbride, founder of Bridesburg.

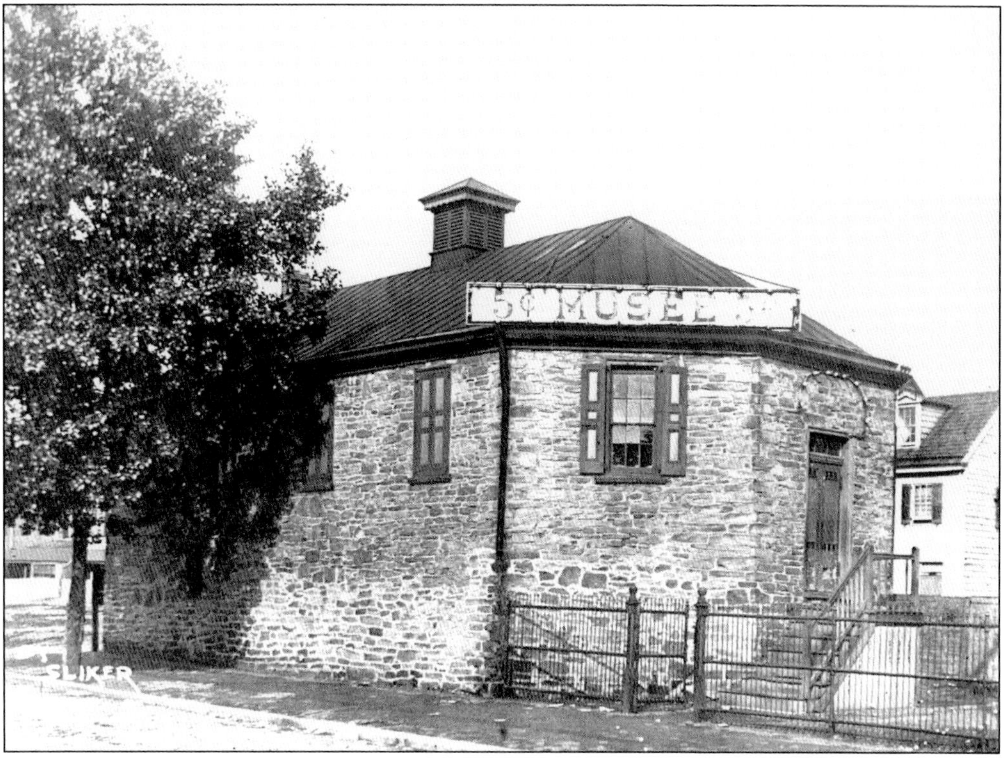

The old town hall was built on land donated by Joseph Kirkbride. It served many purposes over the years: town meeting place, school, church, police station, jail, and even a very early movie theater known as the Musee.

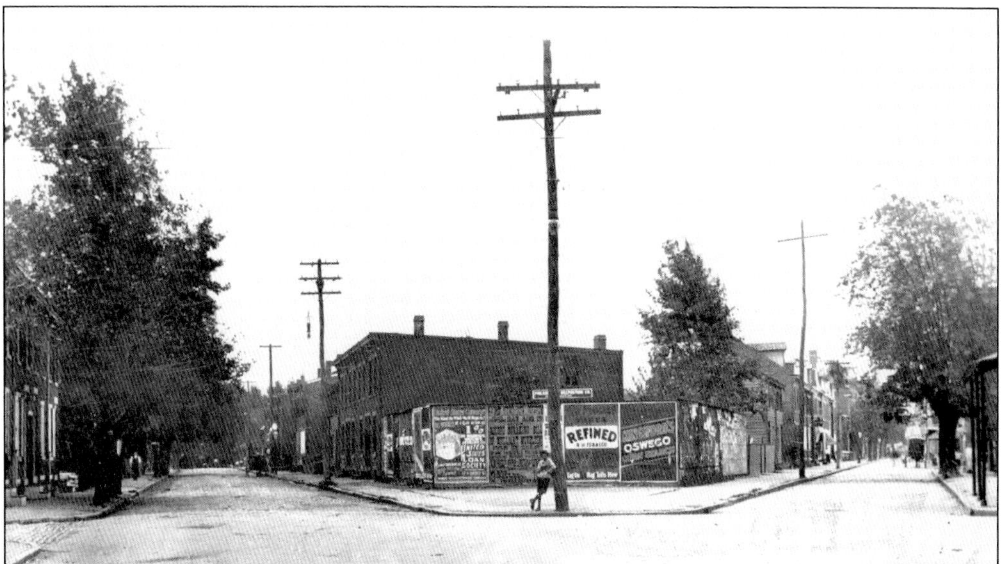

The intersection of Kirkbride, Ash, and Thompson Streets is the site of the present Citizens Bank, originally the Corn Exchange Bank, so marked at the time with a bronze plaque displaying ears of corn.

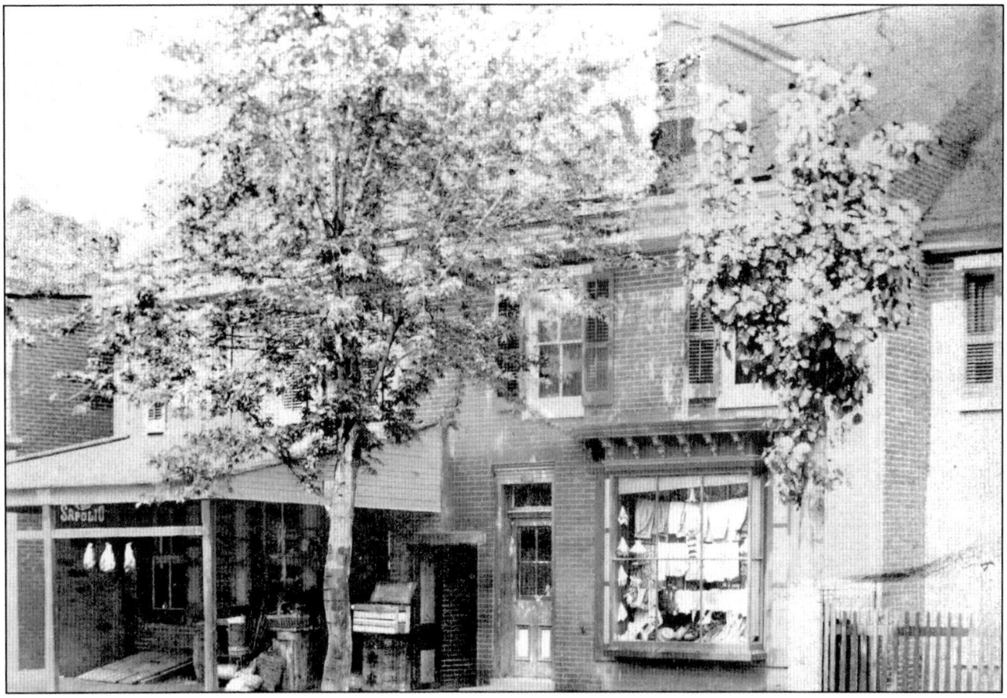

In the mid-1800s, a number of mom-and-pop stores were located throughout the community. Shown here on Ash Street near Salmon Street are two. On the left is a small grocery store, and on the right is a dry goods store. Note the three hams hanging from the railing in front of the grocery.

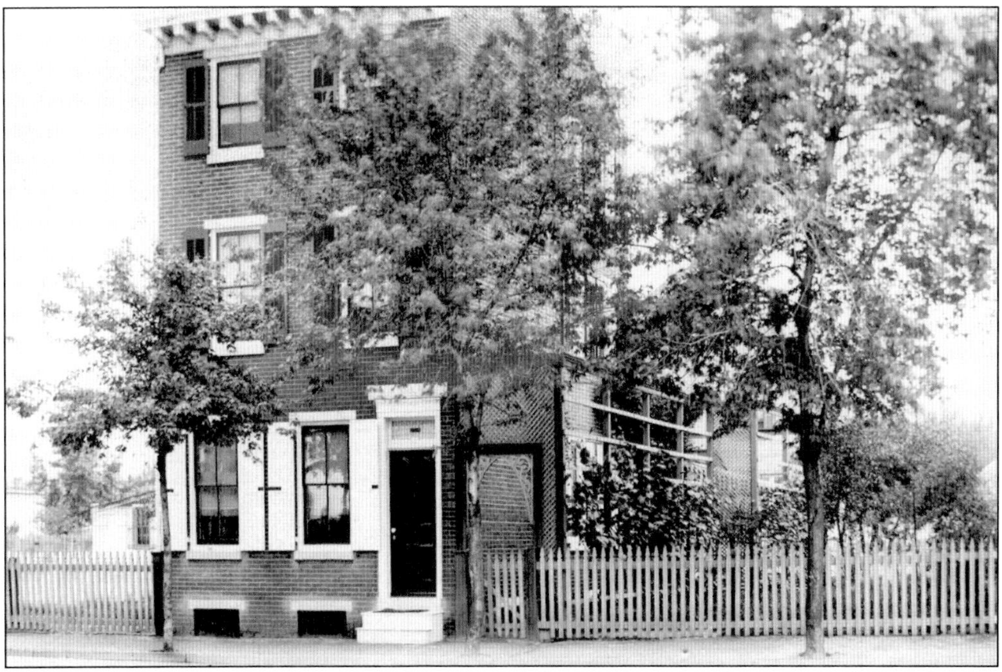

The prominent Stegman family owned this home when it was moved west on Ash to make way for Thompson Street.

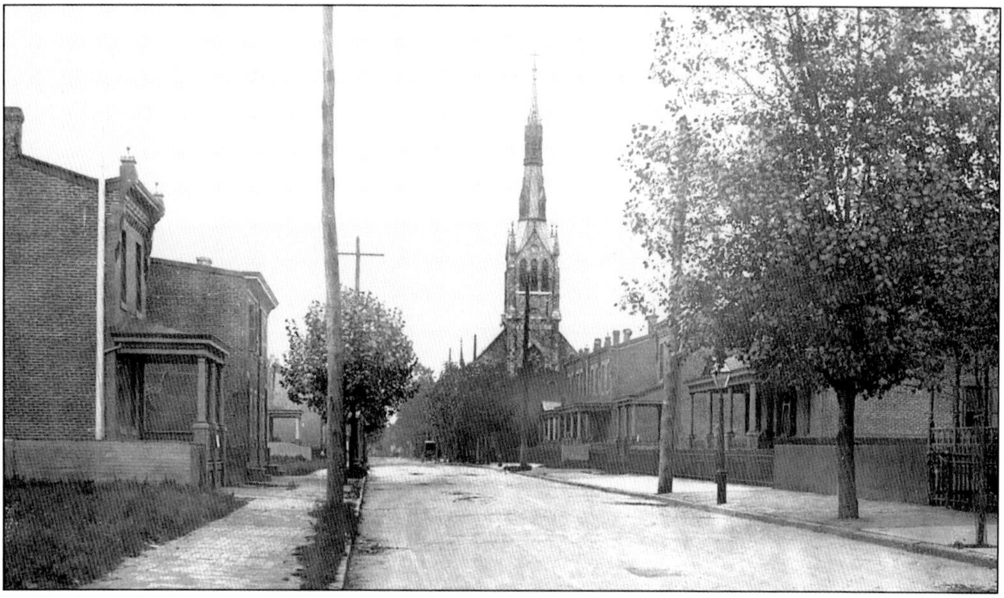

In the late 19th century, many of Bridesburg's streets were tree lined, as can be seen from this view of Thompson Street, looking north from Lefevre. In the distance is the tall steeple of All Saints Roman Catholic Church. In later years, the height of the steeple was lowered as a result of damage caused by a hurricane.

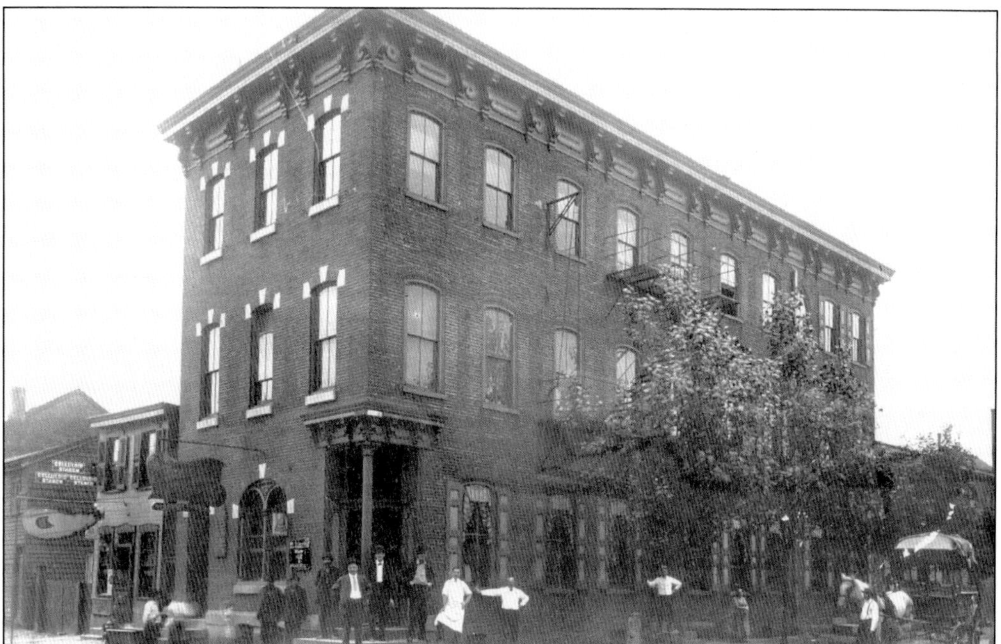

The Edgemont Hotel and Saloon, located at Ash and Edgemont Streets, stood on the site of the former Andreas Erdrick Bridesburg Brewery. Today, the building is an apartment complex.

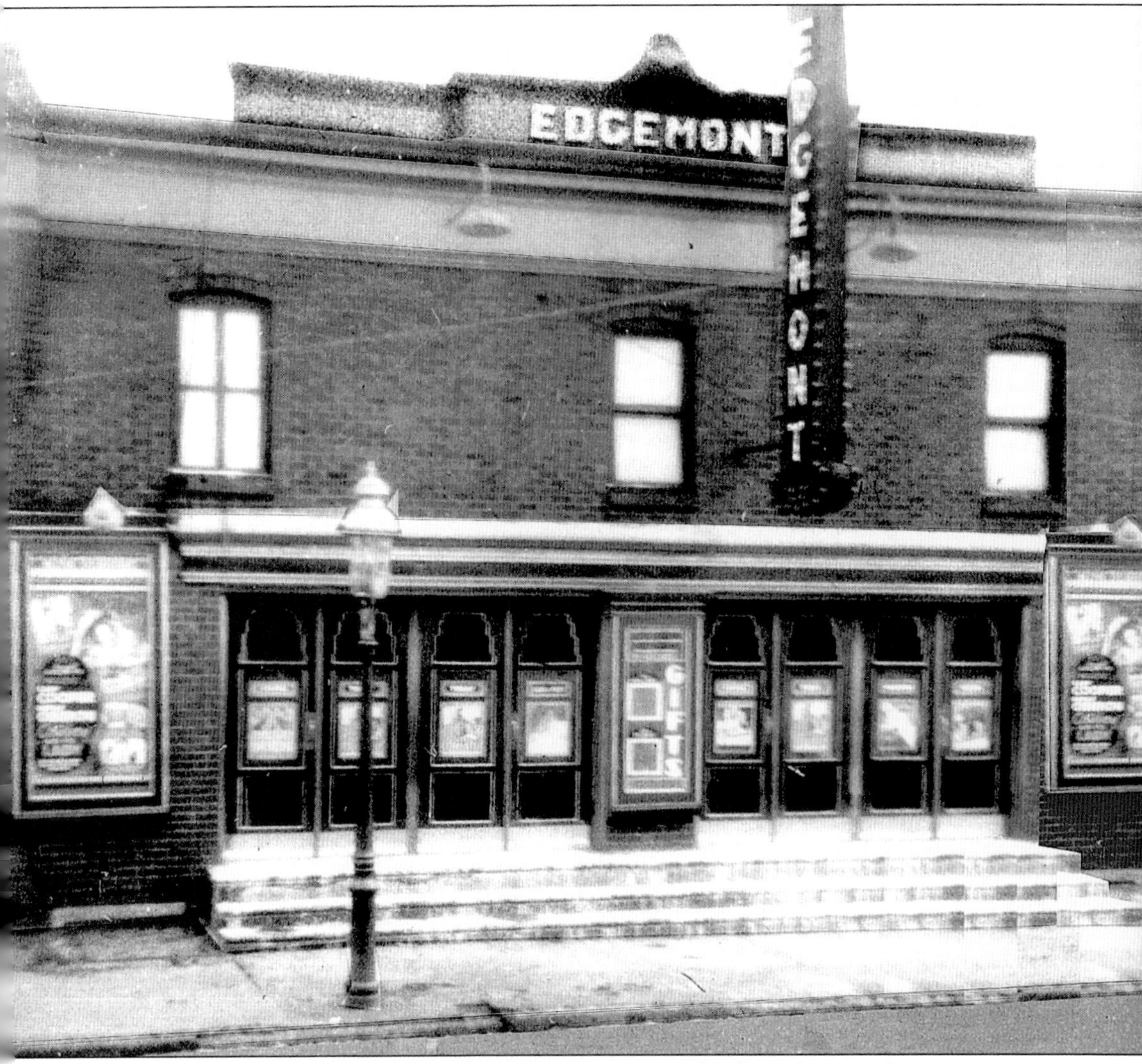

Although the original town hall on Thompson Street was the first place to show movies in Bridesburg, the Edgemont Theater, built *c.* 1920, was a mainstay for filmed entertainment until the early 1960s. It is now the home of the Edgemont Caterers.

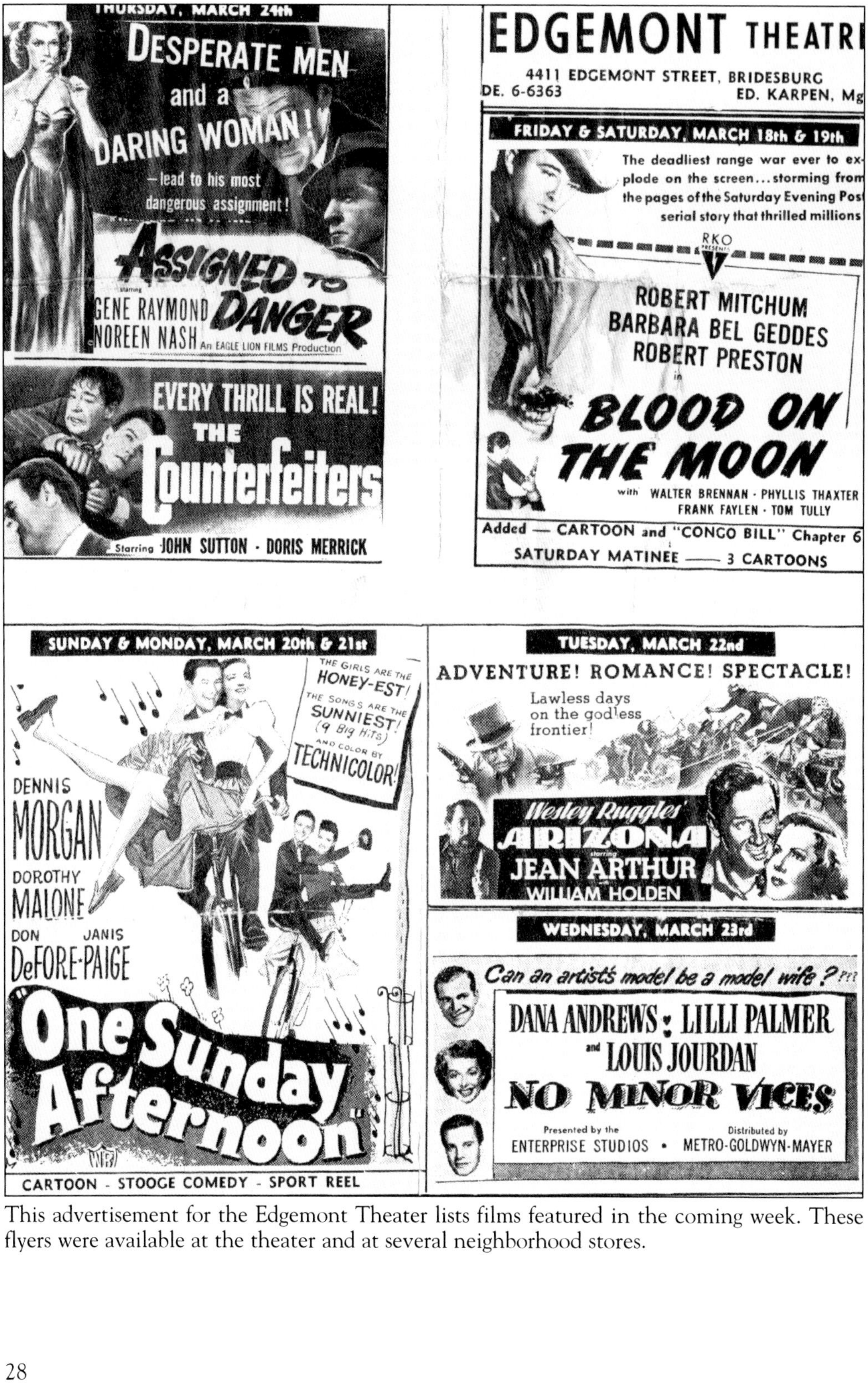

This advertisement for the Edgemont Theater lists films featured in the coming week. These flyers were available at the theater and at several neighborhood stores.

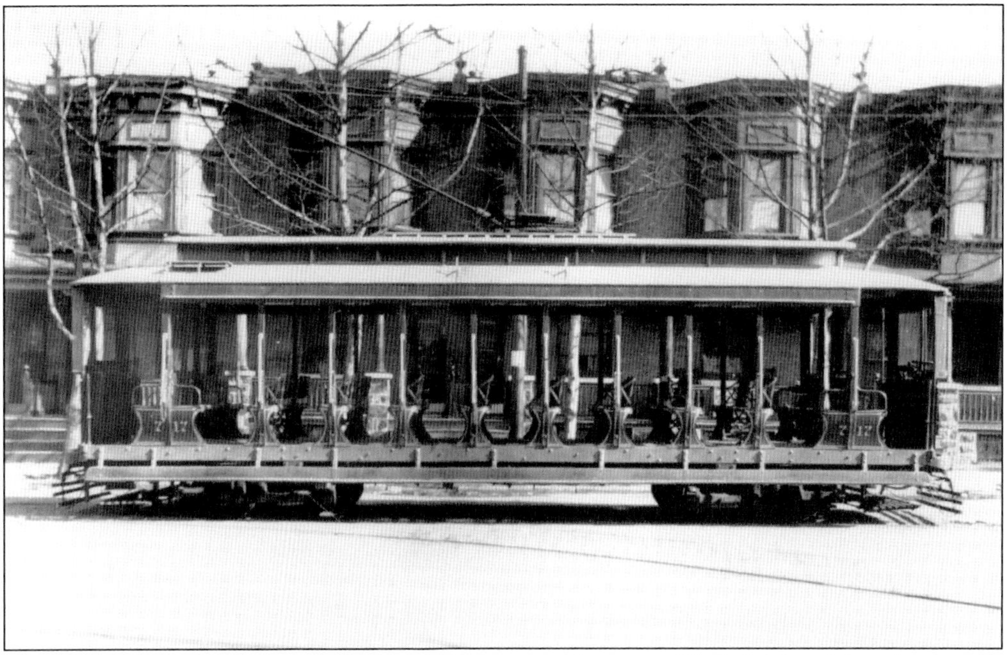

Open-air streetcars ran in Bridesburg and throughout the city of Philadelphia. This photograph was taken at the terminus, located on Orthodox Street just west of Richmond.

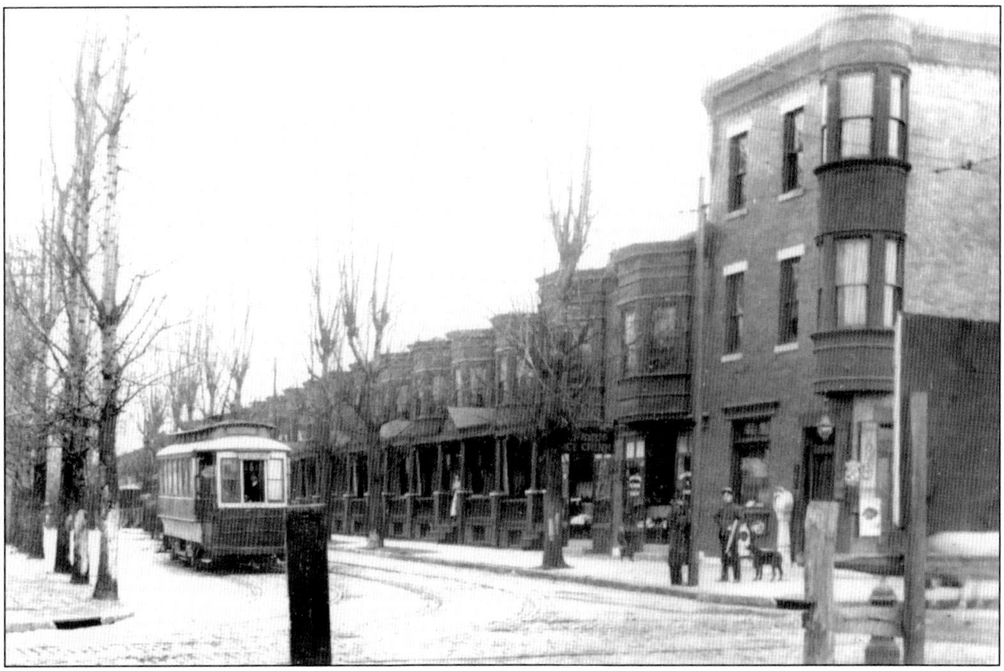

This trolley approaches the well-known intersection of Richmond and Orthodox Streets. Most of the fine, porch-fronted homes on Orthodox Street were converted to storefronts in the early 1900s.

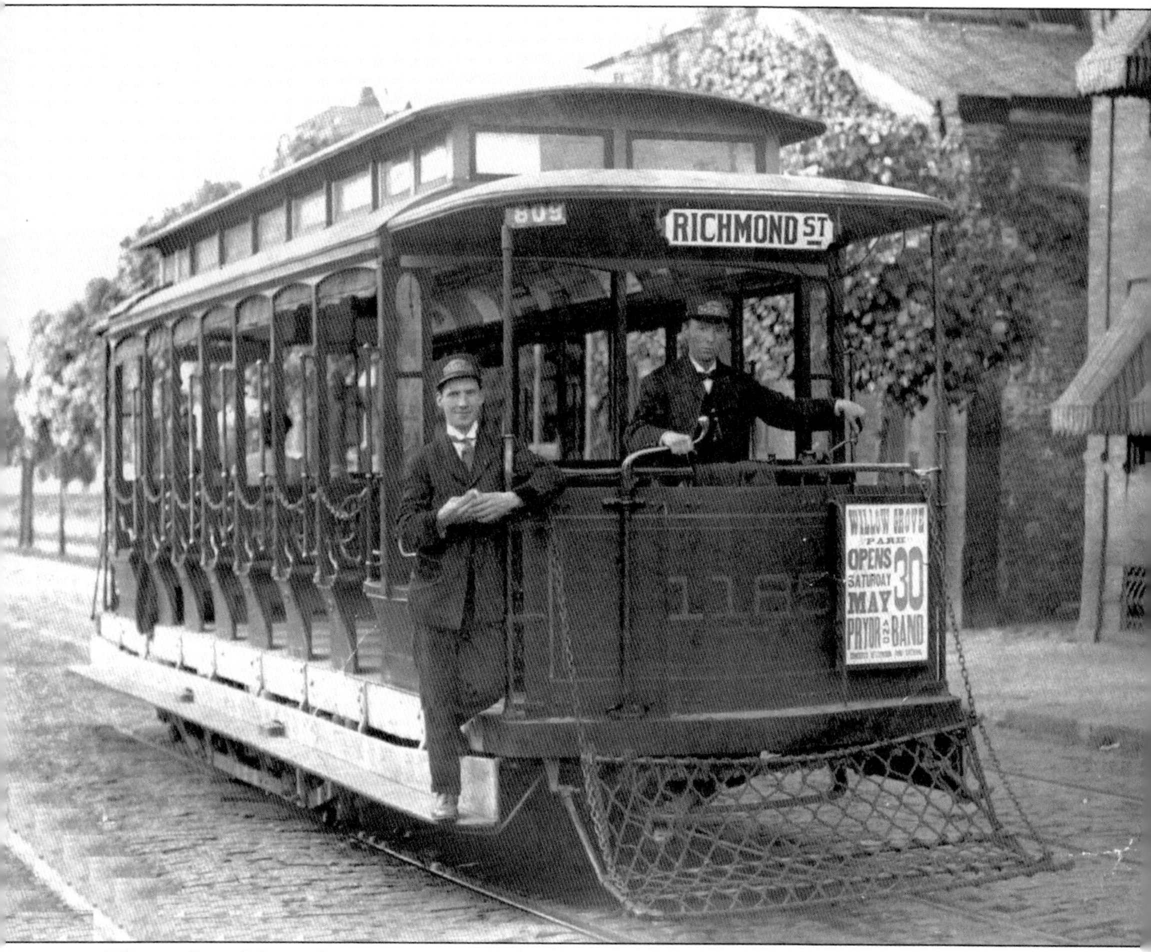

These cheerful conductors wait to welcome passengers from Richmond Street aboard their jolly trolley.

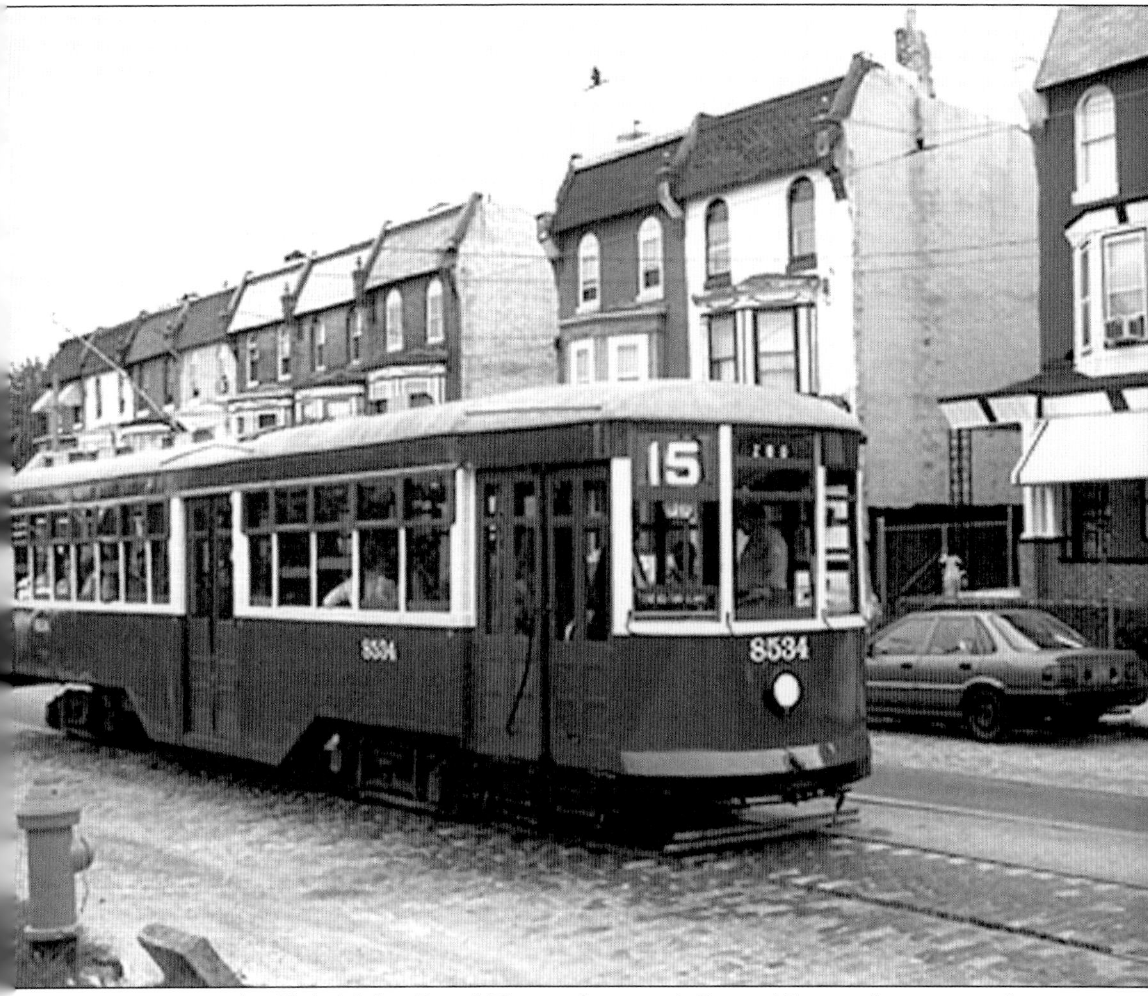

For many years, the Philadelphia Rapid Transit Company's Route 15 carried passengers from the Frankford Arsenal to 63rd Street and Girard Avenue.

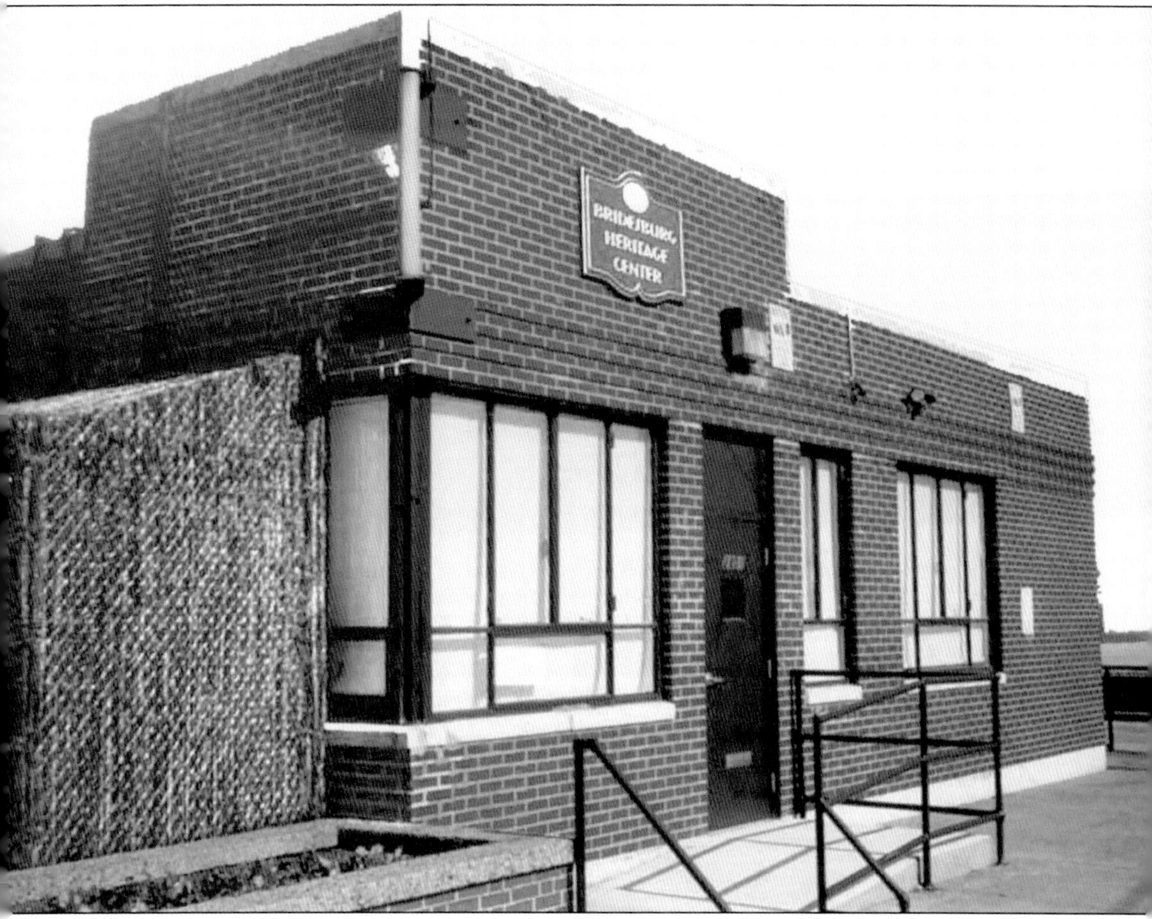

Through the generosity of Rohm and Haas, this building on Brill Street east of Richmond was remodeled for use by the Bridesburg Historical Society and is now known as the Bridesburg Heritage Center. Originally, it served as a gatehouse for the company employees' access to the plant.

Two

DISTINGUISHED HOMES

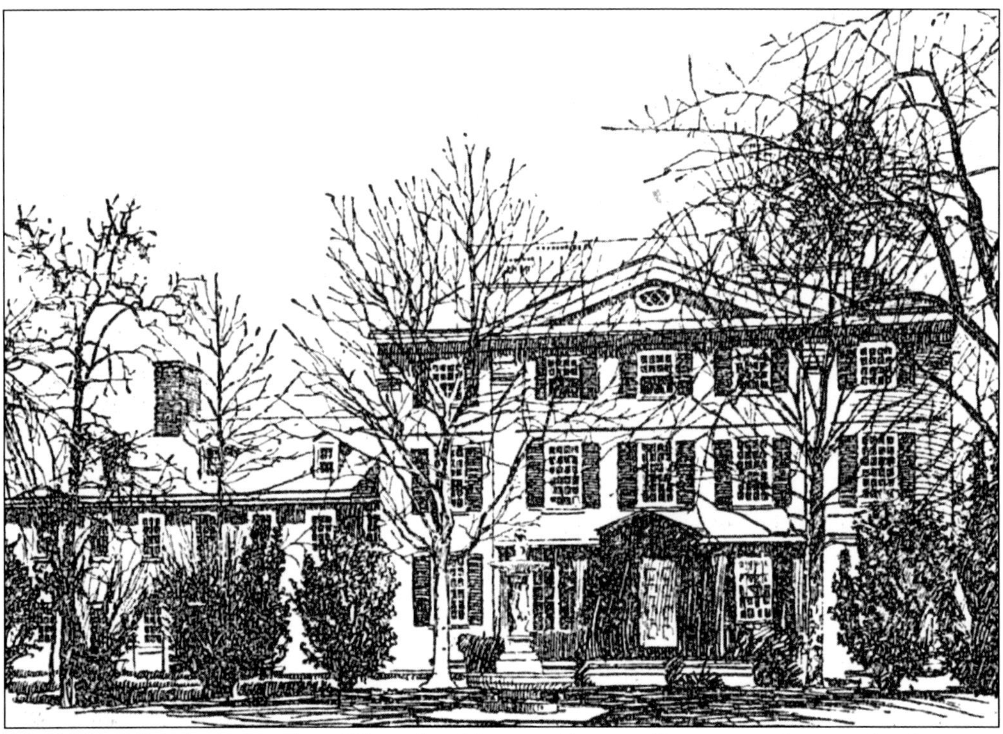

Chalkley Hall, which stood on Wheatsheaf Lane at Sepviva Street, was the grandest home in the area. Thomas Chalkley, a renowned Quaker and merchant ship owner, built the first part of this mansion in 1721. In the years that followed, his son-in-law Abel James expanded it to its full development. After many years of misuse and neglect, it was torn down in 1952.

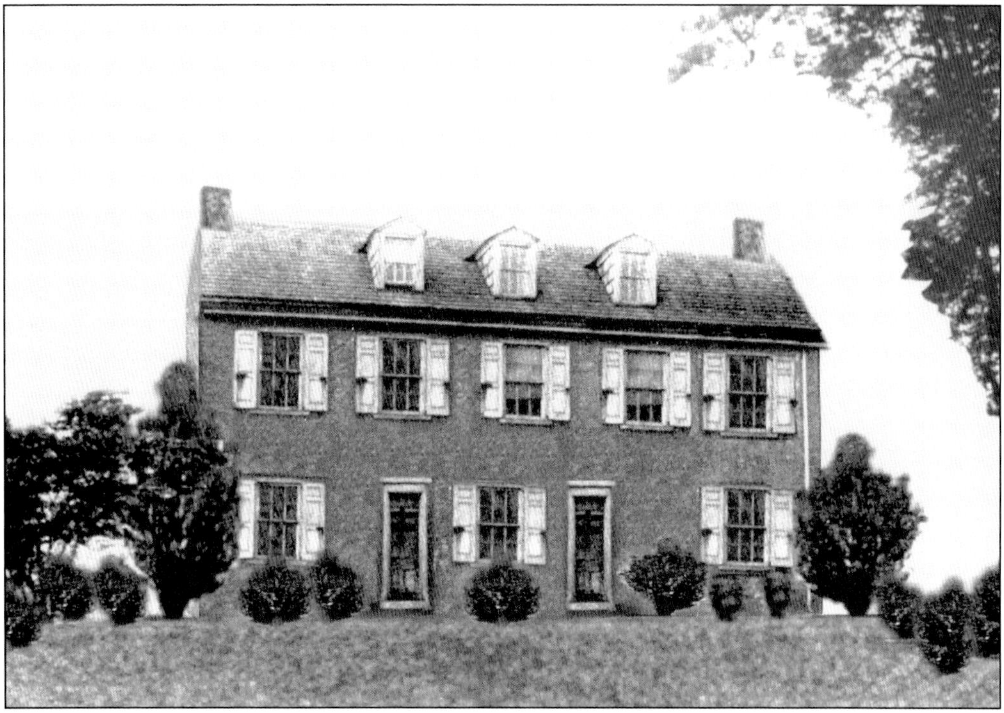

Giltback Mansion stood on the corner of Richmond and Buckius Streets. During Colonial days, it was the residence of Gen. Daniel Morgan, known as George Washington's Ranger of the Revolution, while he was a member of the Continental Congress. Later, in 1864, the building served as the Bridesburg Orphanage, a home for Civil War orphans. In 1867, the orphanage was moved to Womelsdorf, Pennsylvania, and renamed the Bethany Children's Home.

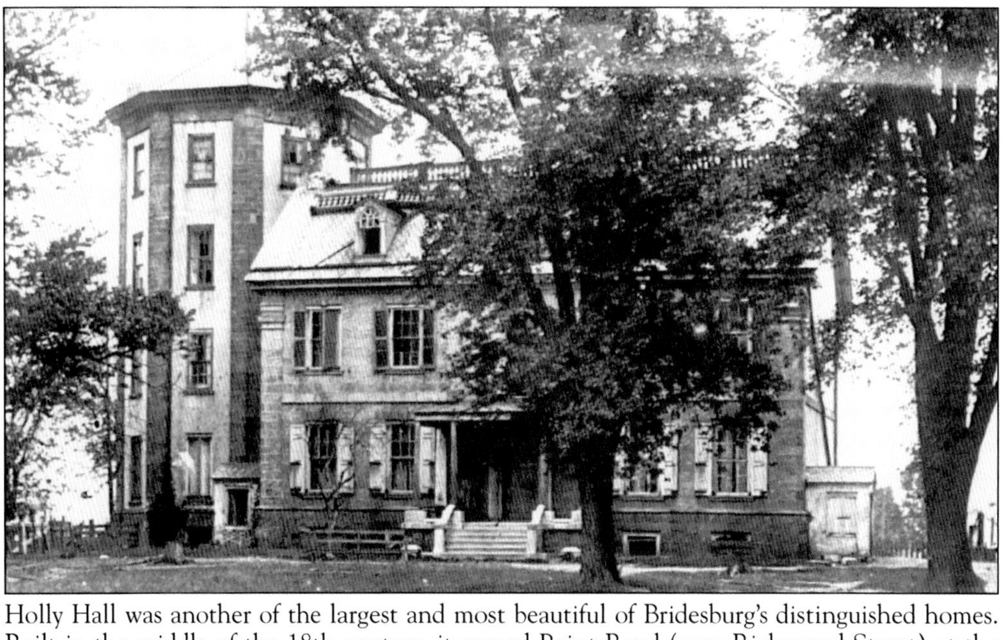

Holly Hall was another of the largest and most beautiful of Bridesburg's distinguished homes. Built in the middle of the 18th century, it graced Point Road (now Richmond Street) at the southwest corner of Orthodox Street.

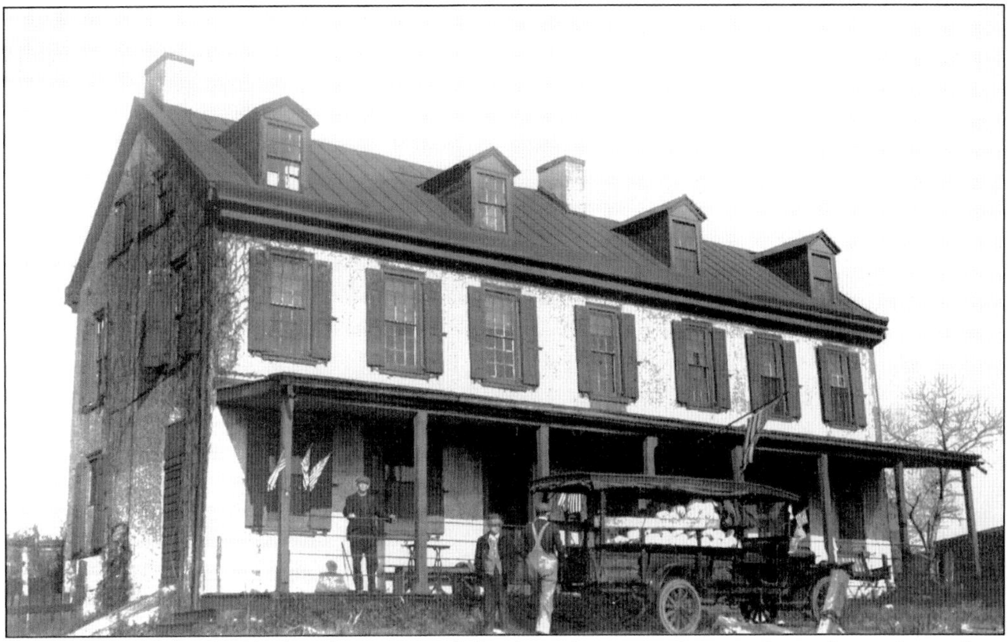

Ira Jenks, brother of Alfred Jenks, occupied this large home on the riverfront. It was located on Cedar Walk, so named for the spread of cedar trees in the area.

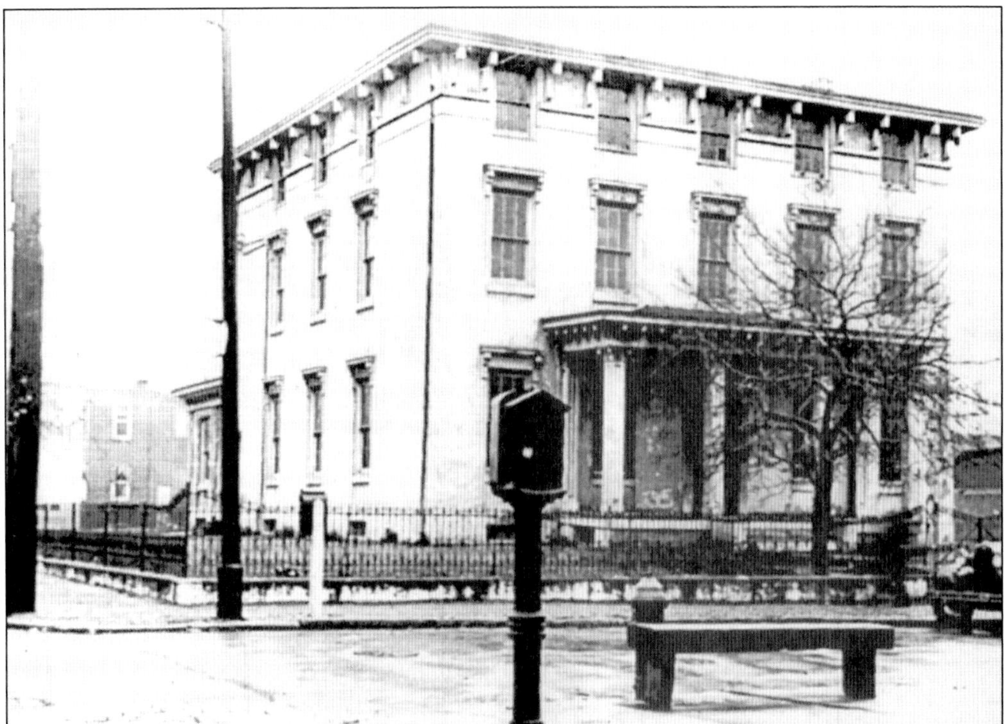

The John Lennig Mansion was located on the corner of Richmond and Bridge Streets. John was the son of Frederick Lennig, who founded the Tacony Chemical Works at the mouth of the Frankford Creek and the Delaware River.

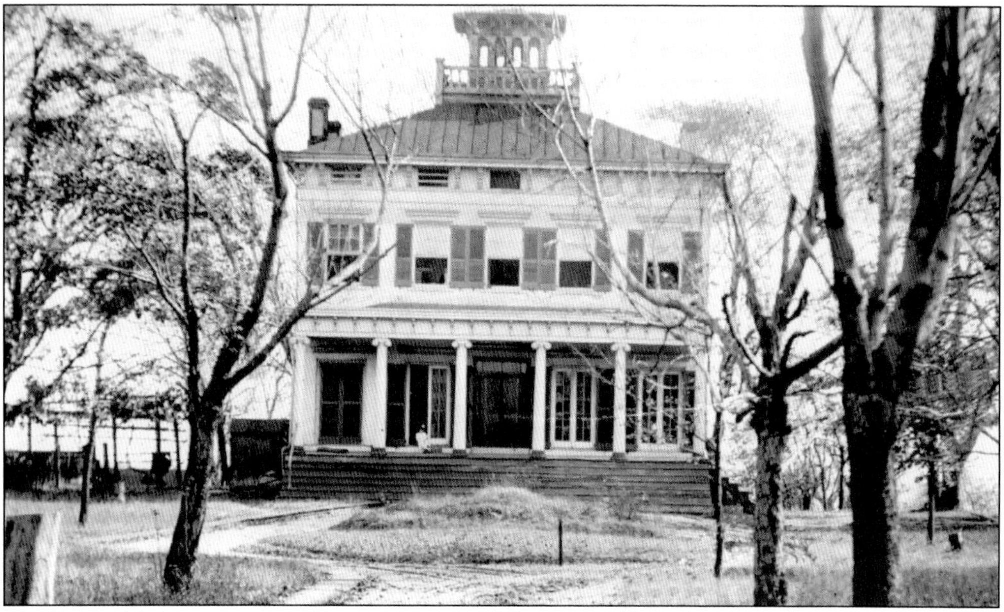

The Reynolds Mansion was the centerpiece of the Reynolds farm, located on the east side of Richmond Street between Buckius and Ash Streets. Herbert Reynolds, a wealthy farmer and town benefactor, built the home. Because of his generosity and good works for the community, Bridesburg's Reynolds Street was named on his behalf. The site eventually became the Bridesburg Community Park.

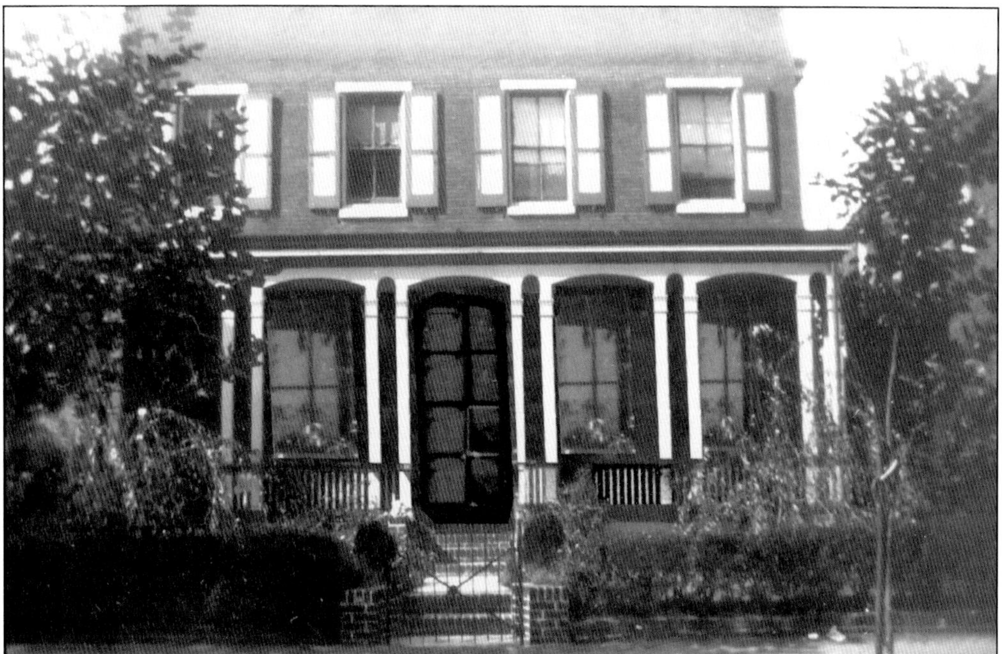

This 1992 photograph displays the Van Dusen Mansion, which is likely the oldest building in present-day Bridesburg. Behind the squared-off top of the front façade is a peaked roofline. It is believed that the first part of the home was built c. 1750 and was owned by the Massey family during Colonial days.

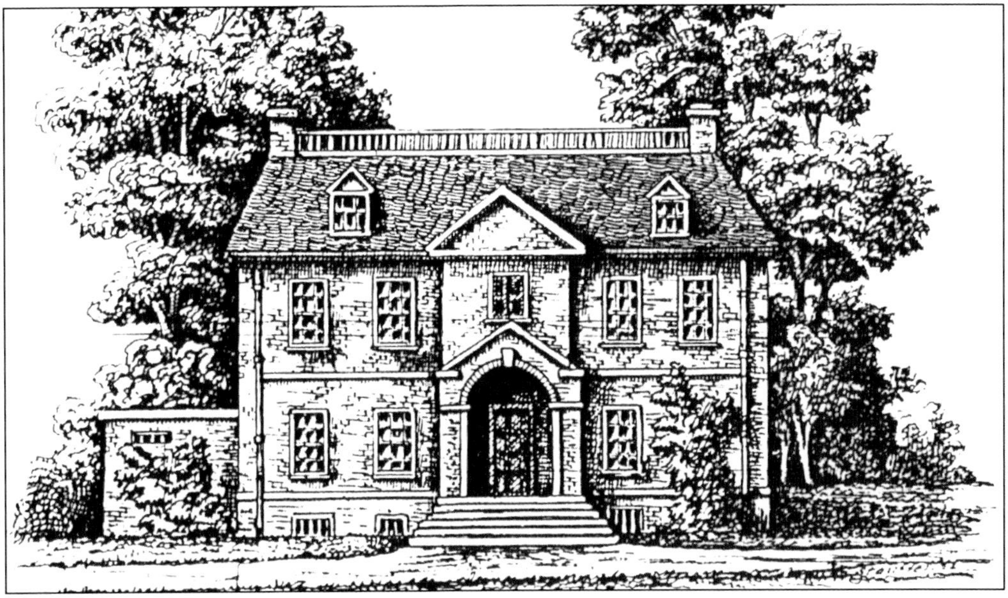

This woodcut depicts the Pine Grove Mansion, which once stood back from Point Road (now Richmond Street), near present-day Lefevre Street. Hugh Roberts, a close friend and working associate of Benjamin Franklin, built the mansion in 1767. Along with Franklin, Hugh Roberts was cofounder of the Library Company of Philadelphia, Franklin's Junto, and the Pennsylvania Hospital, where he also served as treasurer.

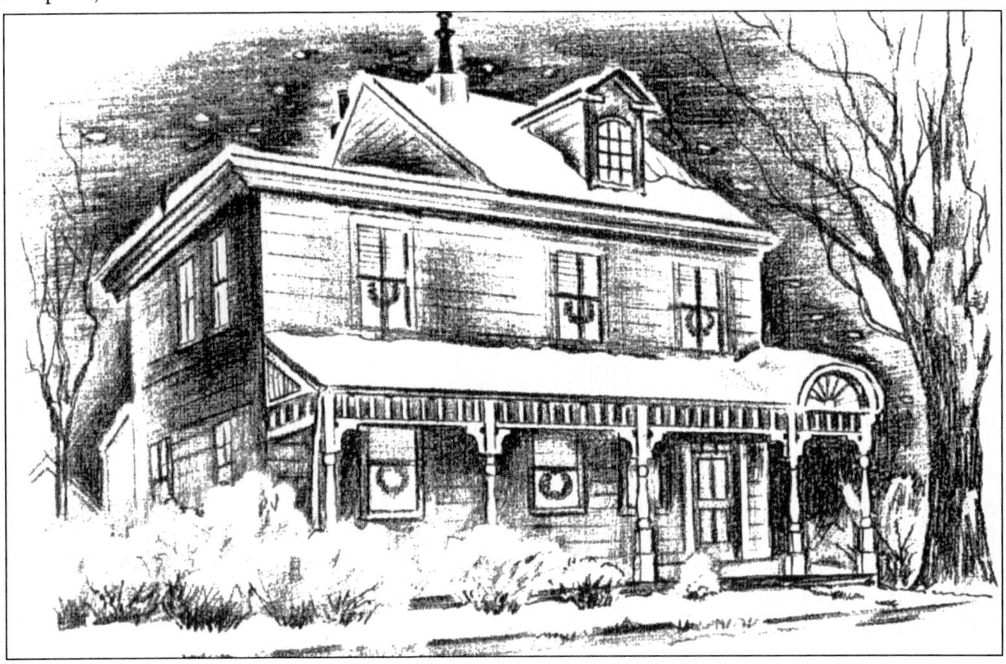

One of the best-known and most beloved, this homestead was built on Garden Street, just north of Reynolds, in 1847. Originally occupied by the Brownell family, it was most closely associated with its second owner, William Heydrick. Three generations of the Heydrick family lived here, and the house was expanded at some unknown time. The home was owned by several others and, much to the dismay of the community, was torn down in 2003.

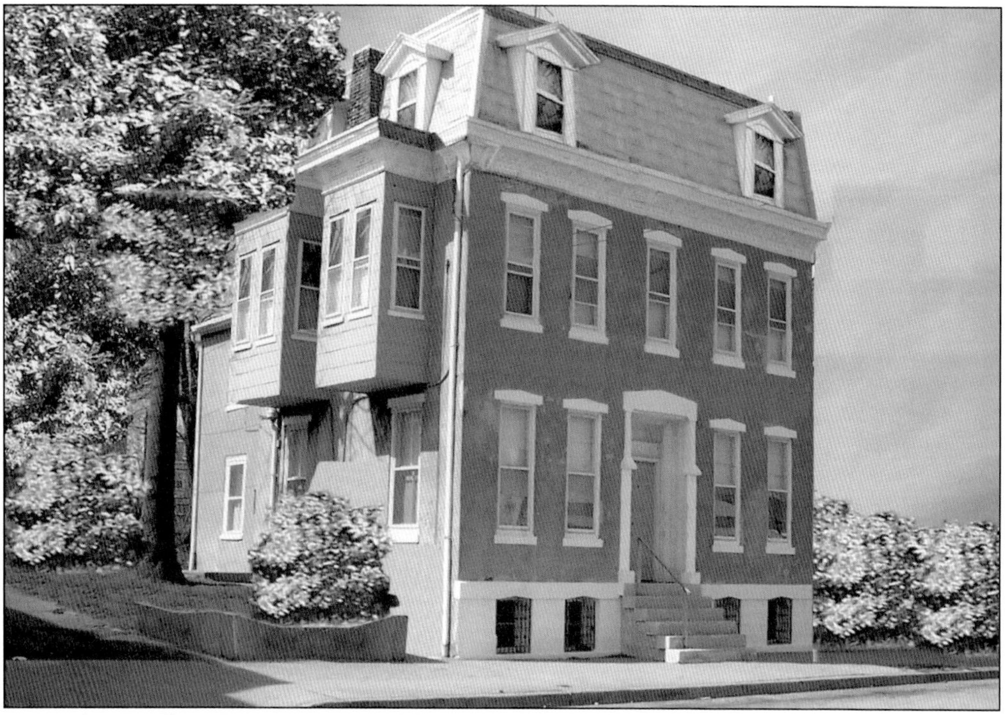

Leonard McMillan's home was one of the largest on Bridge Street, and Isabel McMillan spent all of her life there. It has since been converted into an apartment building.

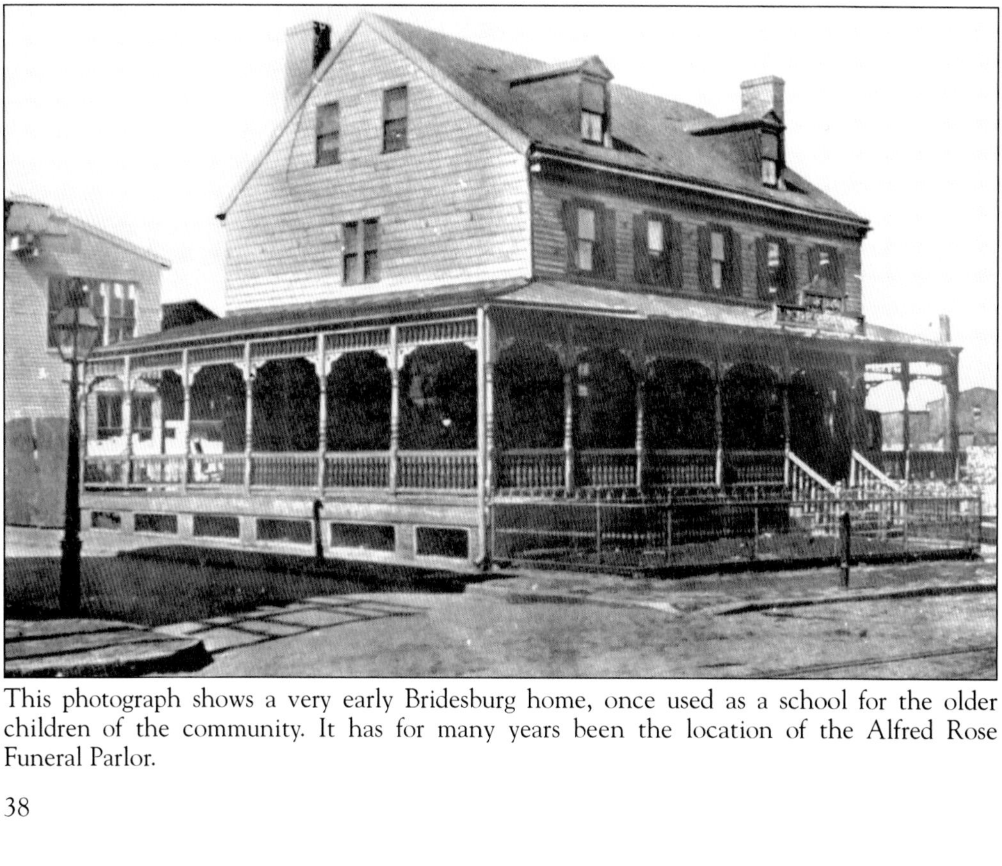

This photograph shows a very early Bridesburg home, once used as a school for the older children of the community. It has for many years been the location of the Alfred Rose Funeral Parlor.

Three

PEOPLE

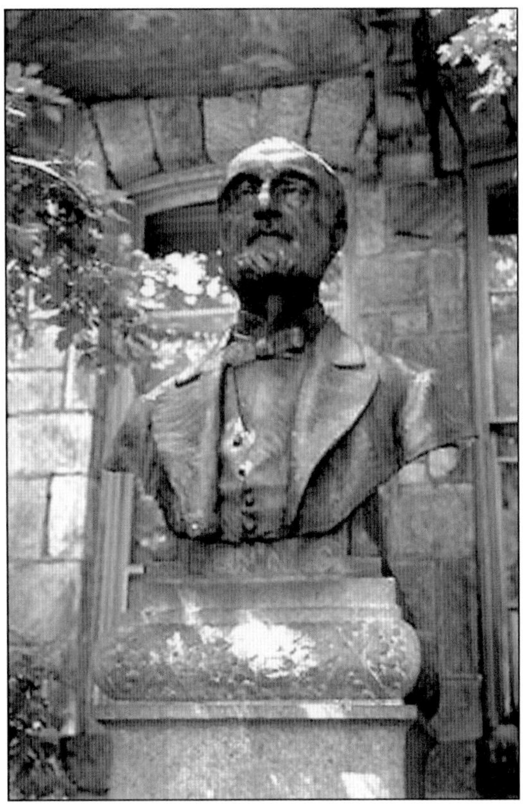

Charles Lennig was one of the owners of the Tacony Chemical Works (later the Charles Lennig Chemical Company). He was a major contributor to the University of Pennsylvania, and in recognition of that, this bronze bust is prominently displayed outside College Hall.

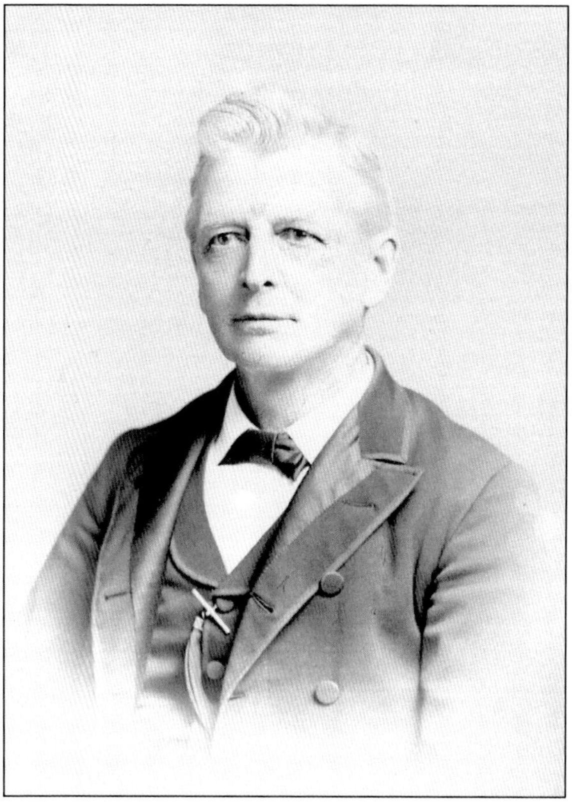

William Heydrick Sr. moved to Bridesburg in the mid-1800s and purchased the Brownell home, located on Garden Street near Reynolds. Despite being considered one of the treasures of the community, the home has since been demolished.

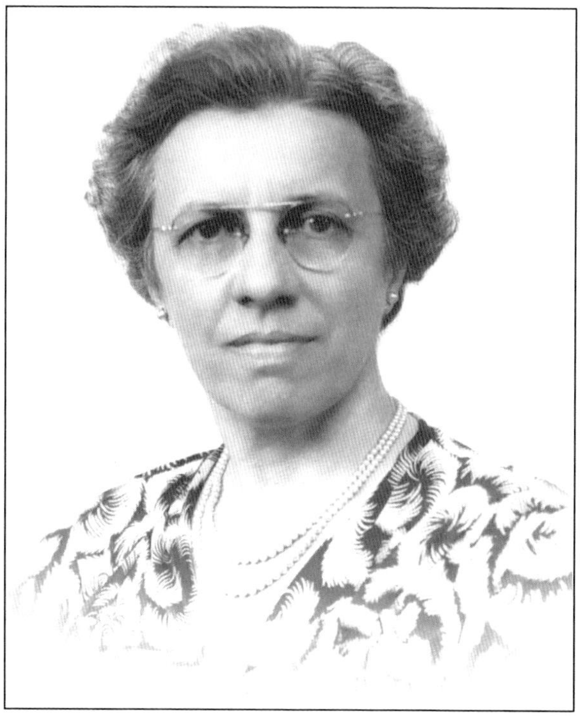

Helen Heydrick was one of the best-known leading ladies in Bridesburg. Very early, it became clear that Helen was a woman determined to get the most out of life. Her philosophy was to love family, church, and community. The only female member of the original Philadelphia Charter Committee, she also served as president of the Soroptimist Club of Philadelphia and as a member of the Sentry Club and the Business and Professional Women's Club. To crown off her life as a career woman, mother, and grandmother, she was chosen as Pennsylvania Mother of the Year in 1954.

Lydia Ann Kirkbride Shipley, granddaughter of Joseph Kirkbride, founder of Bridesburg, appears here with her granddaughter.

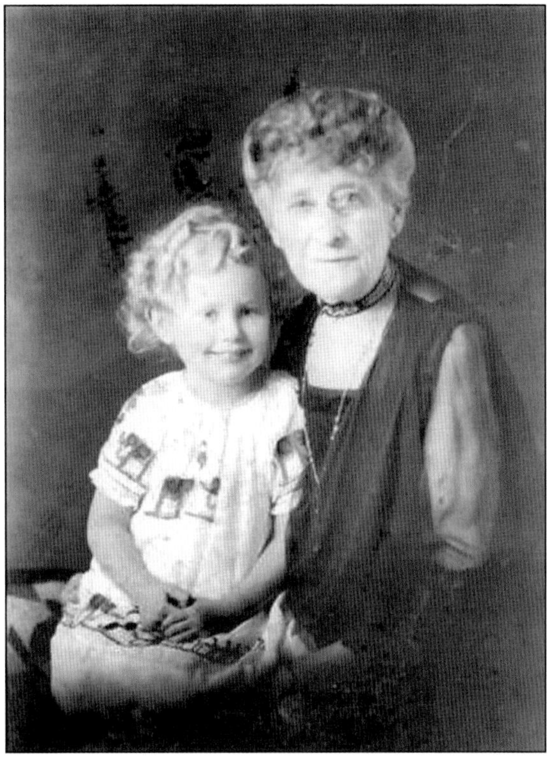

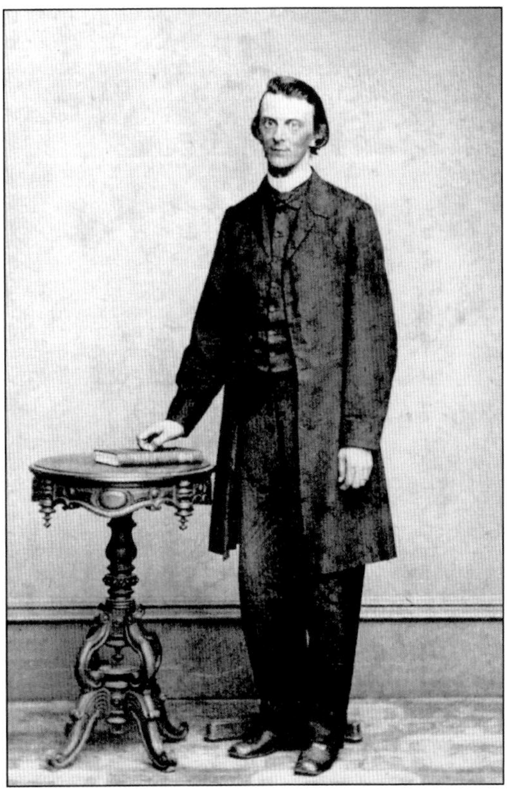

David Heydrick was the first member of the Bridesburg Presbyterian Church to enter into the ministry.

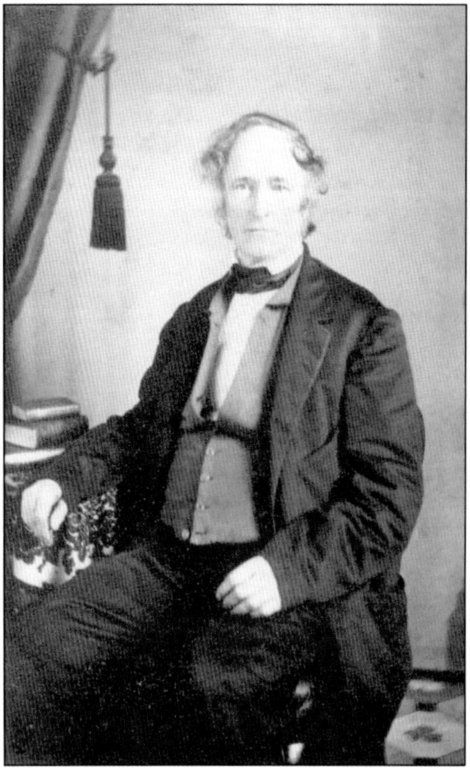

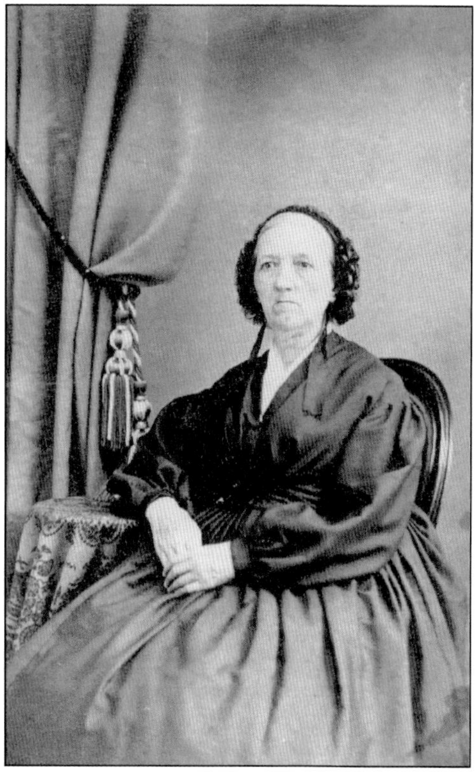

When Alfred Jenks moved his weaving-machine factory to Bridesburg, he brought several siblings to work with him. Pictured here are his brother Ira and his wife, Hannah. Ira was also one of the founding members of the Bridesburg Presbyterian Church.

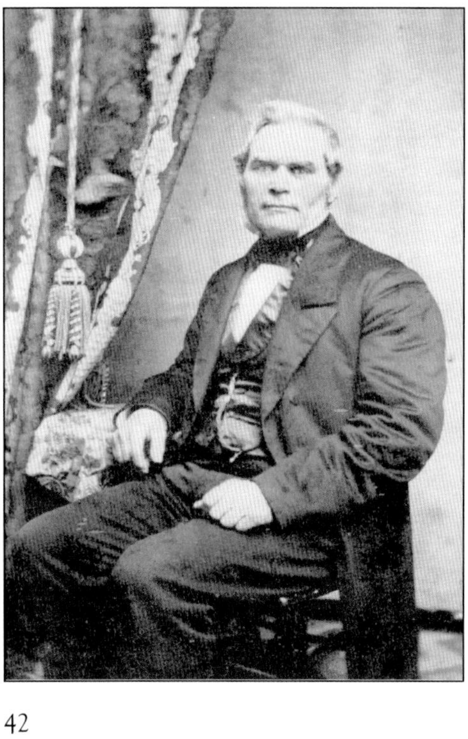

Charles Ramsey was an outstanding member of the community during the mid-1800s and was a founding member of the Bridesburg Presbyterian Church.

Perhaps the best-known resident during the mid- to late 1800s was Herbert Reynolds. A farmer and large landowner, he was the builder of the Reynolds Mansion, on Richmond Street. He was a benefactor to both the Bridesburg United Church of Christ and the Bridesburg Methodist Church, having sold them property for token amounts of money.

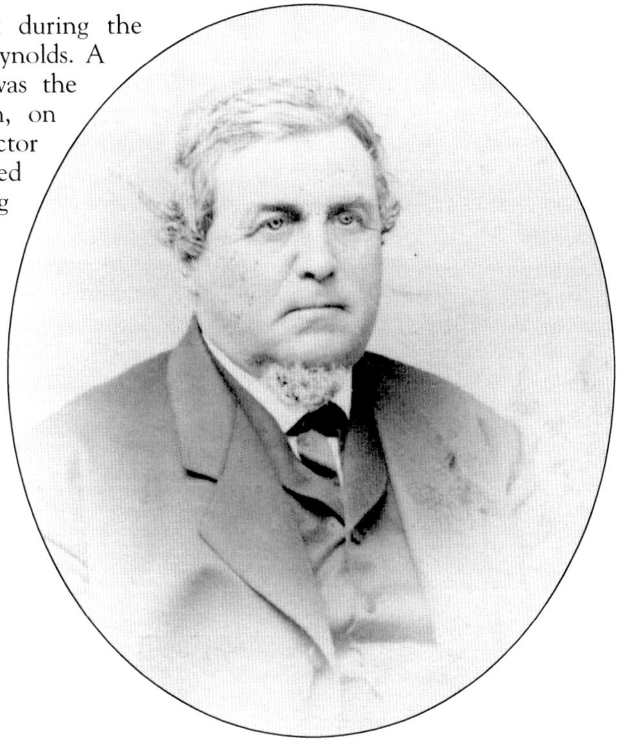

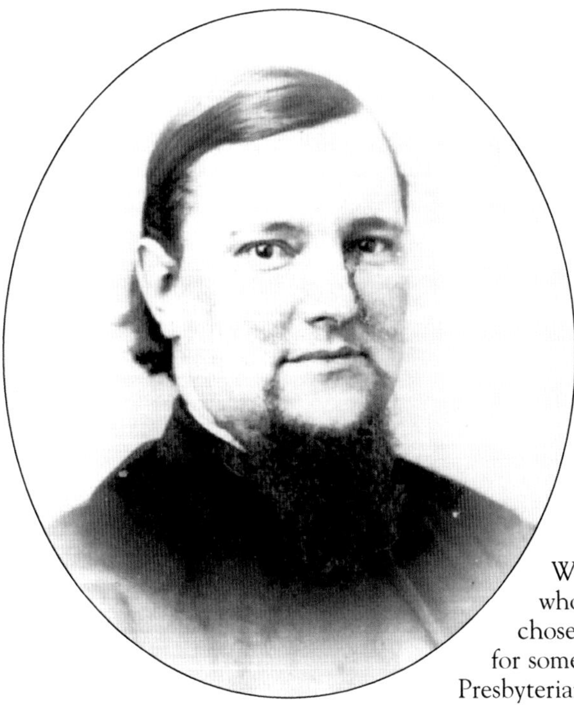

William Jenks was one of the few Jenkses who did not go into the family business. He chose instead to enter the religious life and for some time served as pastor of the Bridesburg Presbyterian Church.

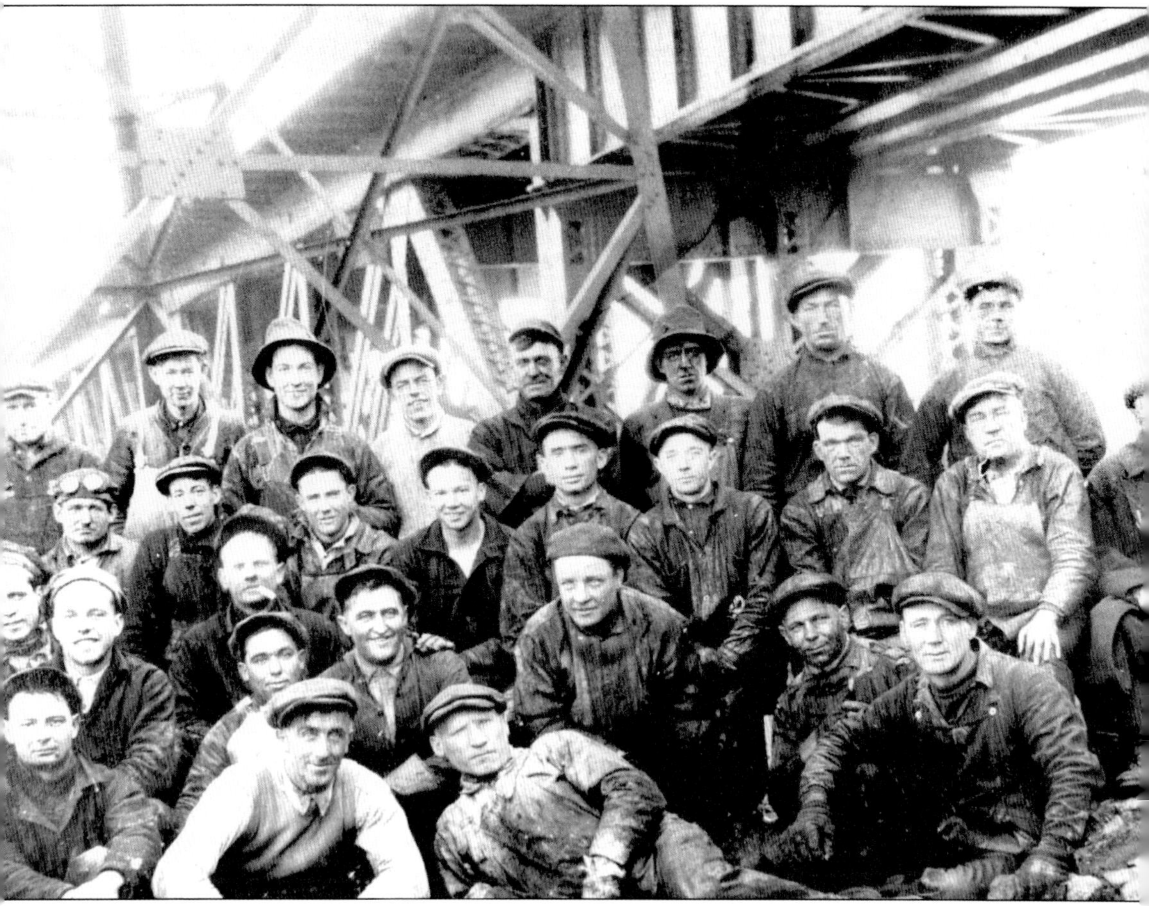

These immigrants, hired to paint the Delair Railroad Bridge, are pictured at their work site. Commonly known as the Black Bridge, it crosses the Delaware River from Bridesburg at Lewis Street. Among the workers is Charles Rosenberg (first row, center), father of Bridesburg historian Donald Rosenberg.

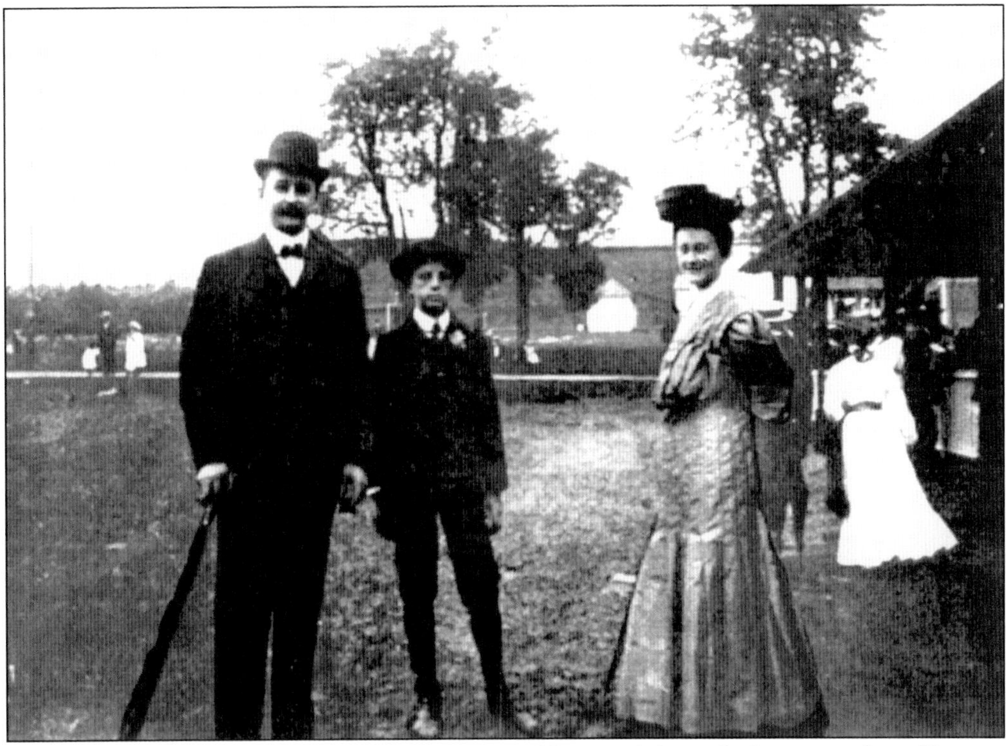

Herman Heim, owner of a grocery store, is pictured here with his wife, Louisa, and son Herman Heim Jr. on one of the festive days at the park grounds.

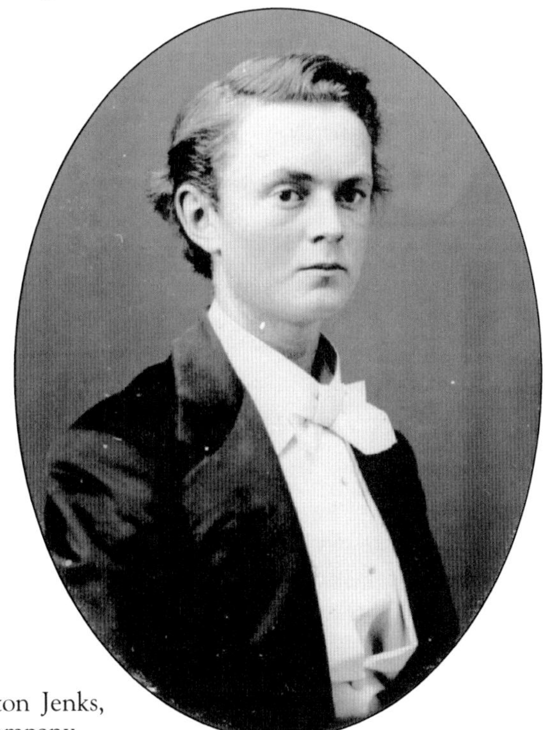

Walter Barton Jenks was the son of Barton Jenks, owner of the Bridesburg Manufacturing Company.

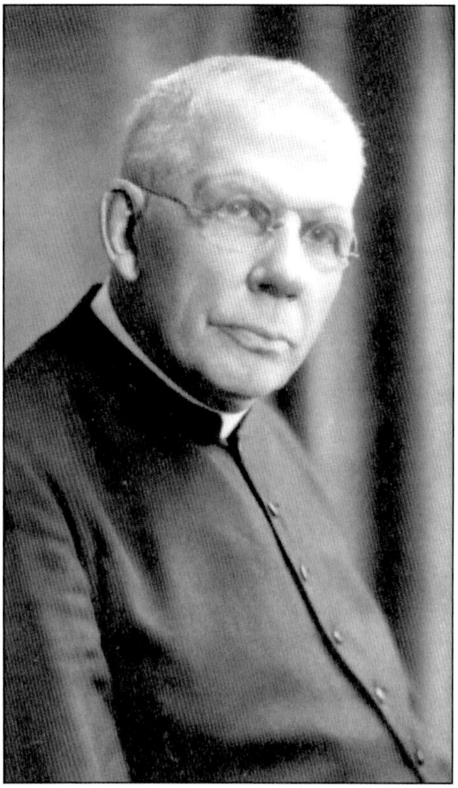

Rev. Ernest Deham was pastor of All Saints Roman Catholic Church from 1886 until his death in 1934.

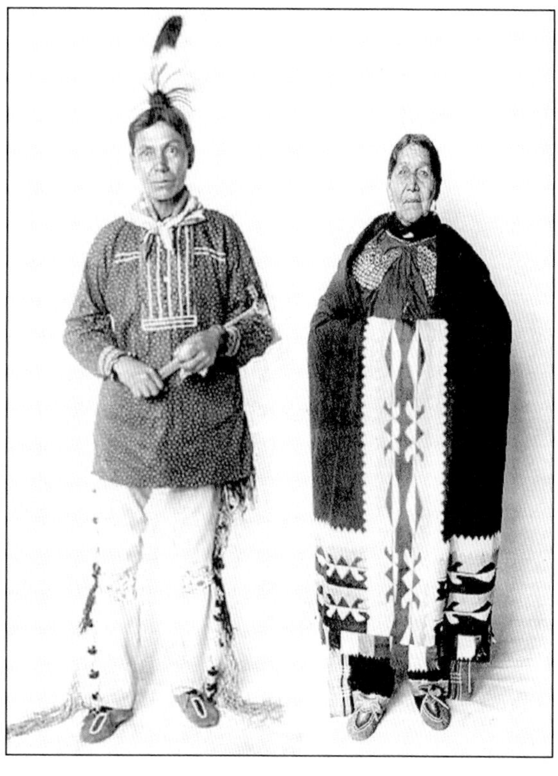

The Asoedek Indians, part of the Lenni Lenape tribe, once lived in the area now known as Bridesburg. This photograph shows the type of dress they might have worn.

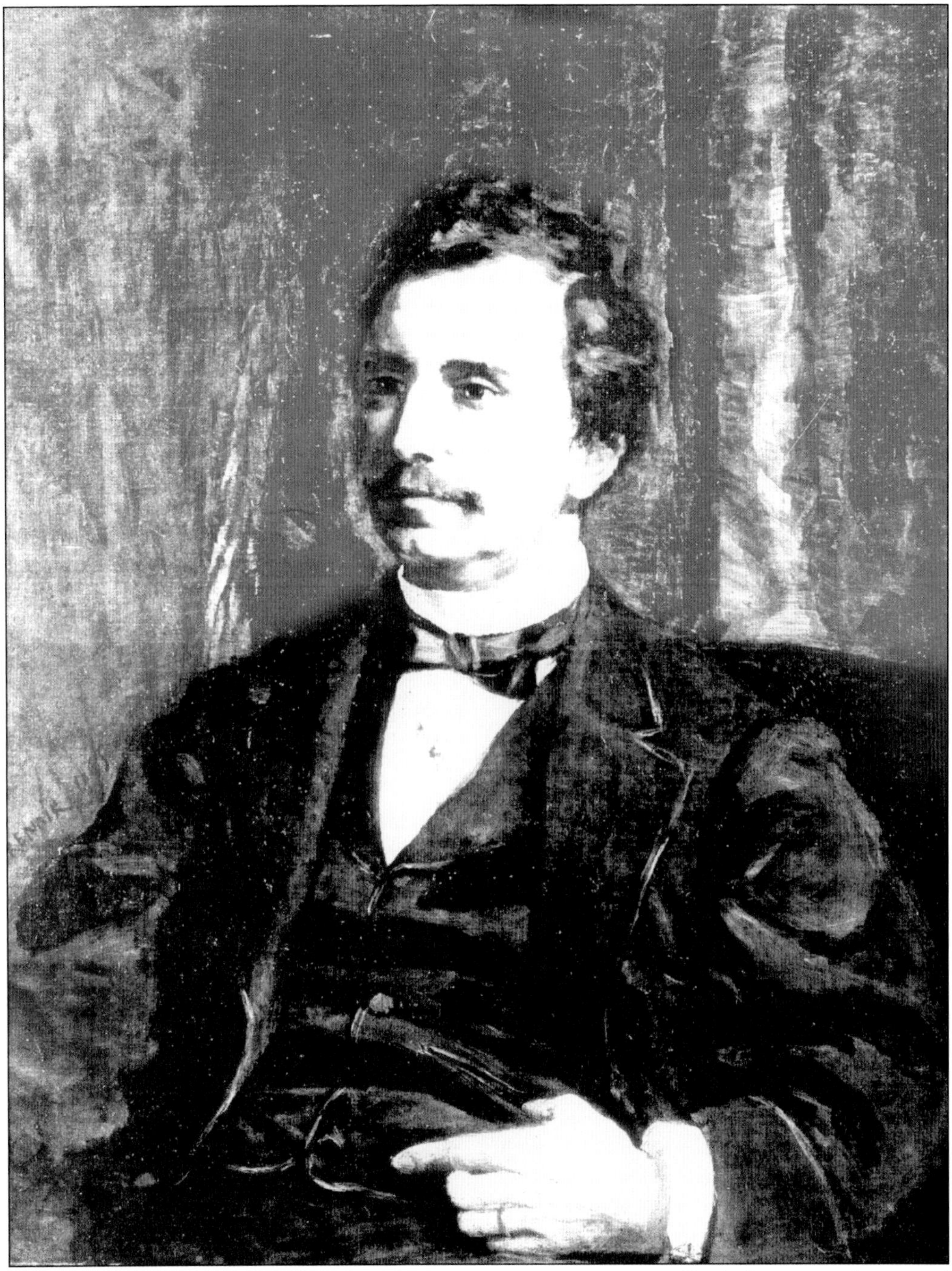

Barton Jenks, likely the wealthiest and most prominent citizen in Bridesburg, was the son of Alfred Jenks. This portrait of Barton was painted at the Renoir Studio in Paris.

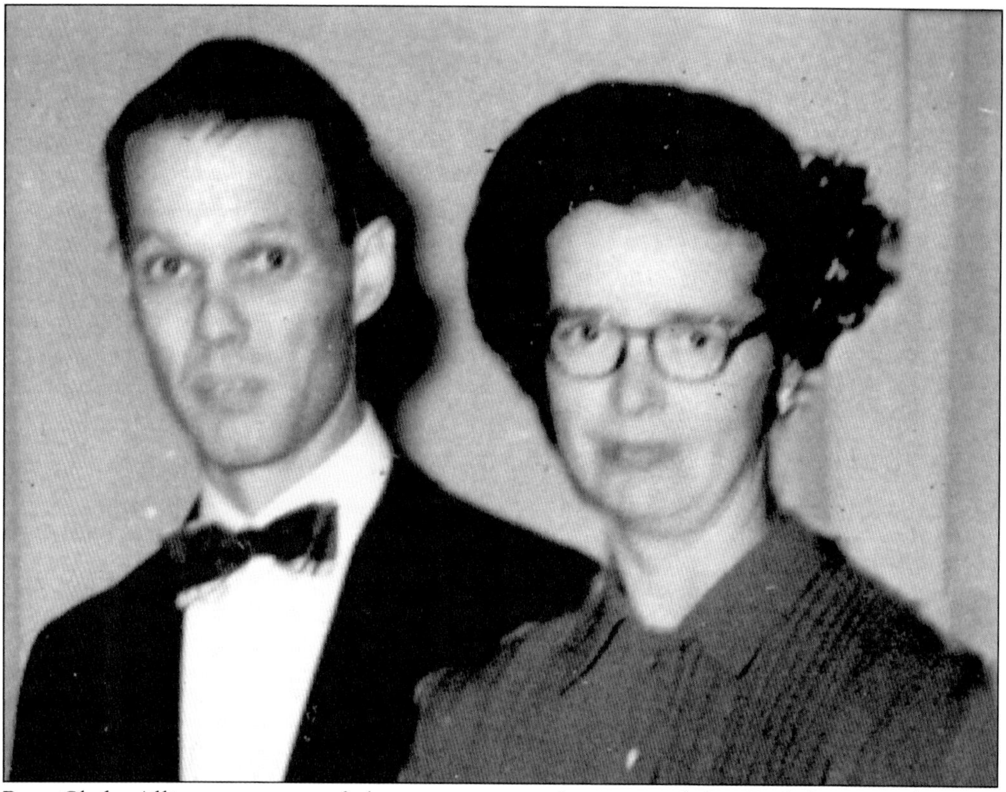

Rev. Clyde Allison was one of the most respected pastors of the Bridesburg Presbyterian Church. In 1950, he and his wife, Mary Emma, created the idea of Trick or Treat for UNICEF. The first year, the Philadelphia collection amounted to $17. It has since grown into a multimillion-dollar program.

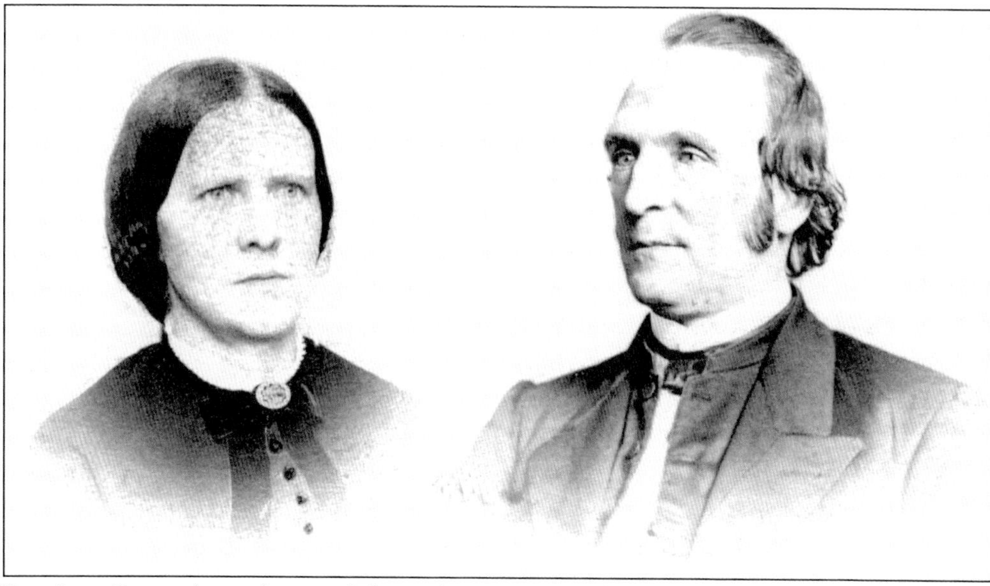

Rev. Jesse Davis, shown here with his wife, was pastor of the Bridesburg Presbyterian Church from 1862 until 1869.

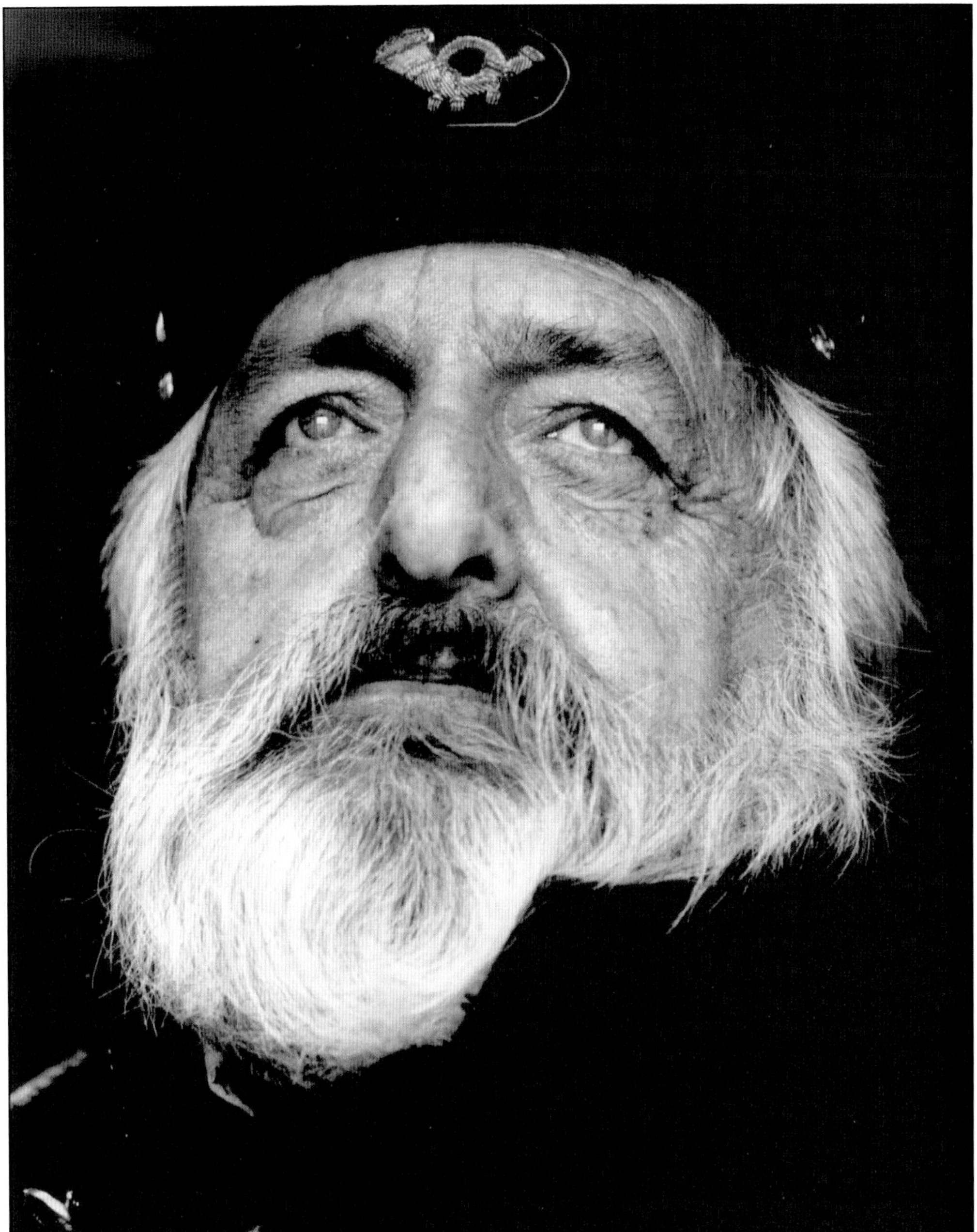

Pictured here is Don Rosenberg, a founder of the Bridesburg Historical Society. As an avid Civil War buff, he extended that interest into the gathering of historical information about the community in which he lived.

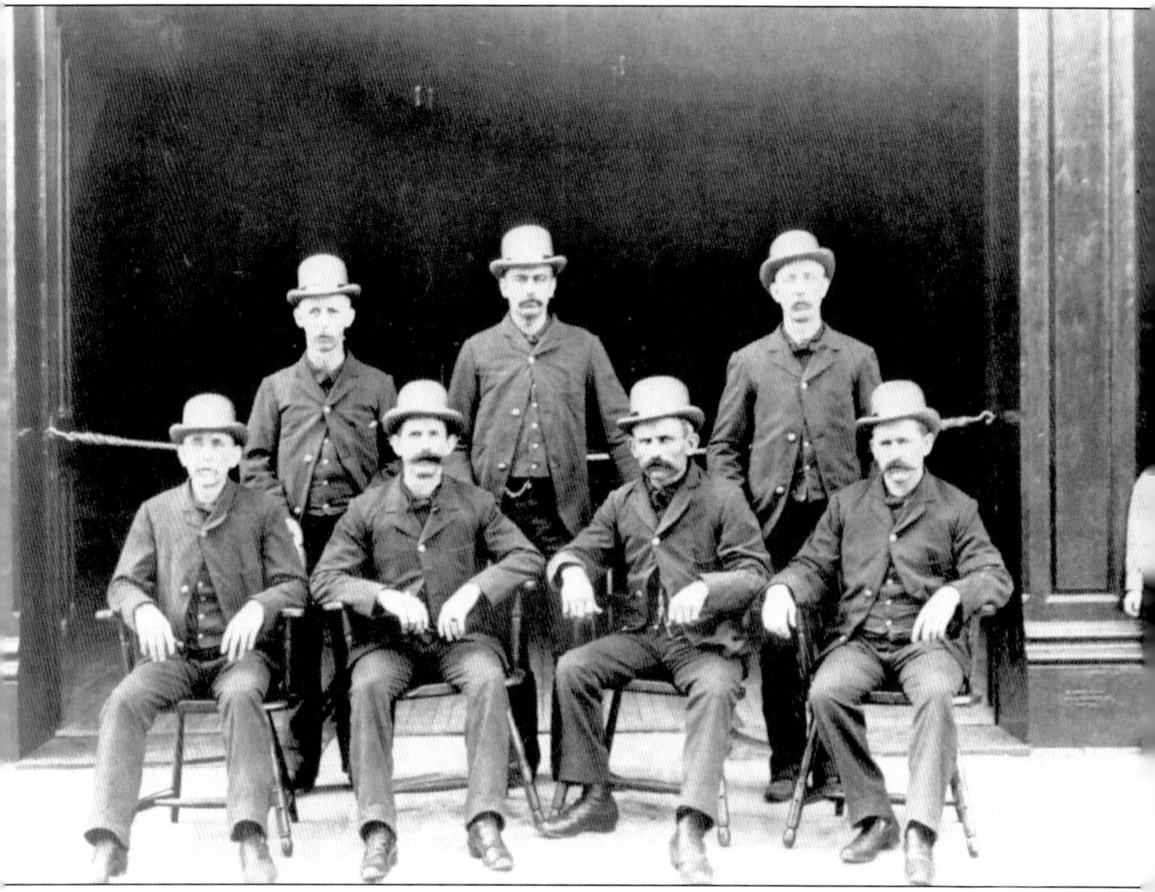

A group of firemen poses in front of the old Engine Company No. 33 on Richmond Street.

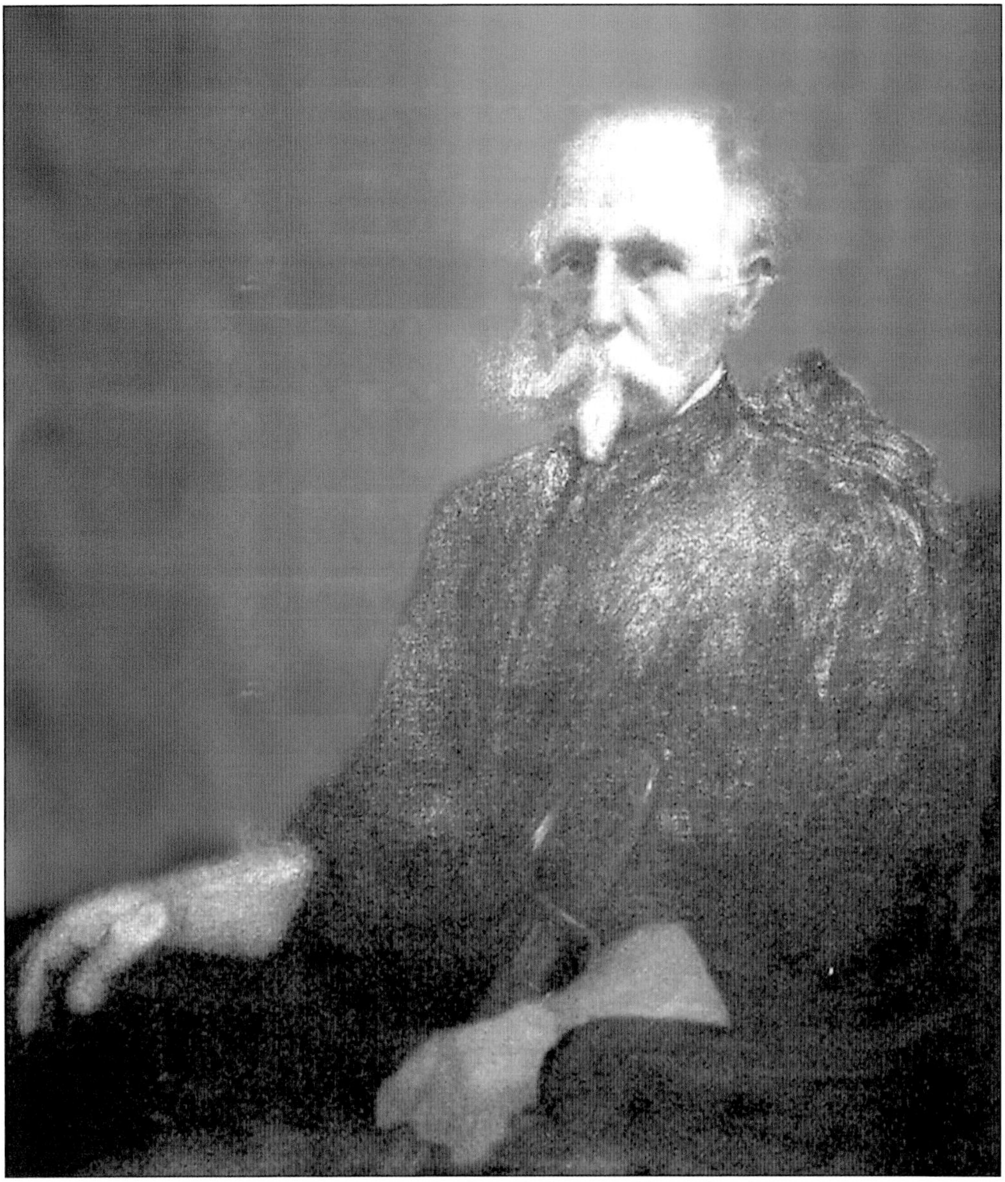

T. Worchester Worrell was the principal of Bridesburg Public School from 1889 until 1915. Born in 1842 to a prominent Frankford family, he married Nina Turner, a direct descendant of Betsy Ross. He is credited with teaching local children this verse explaining Point No Point: "Point Look out, Point Look in, Point No Point, Point Again."

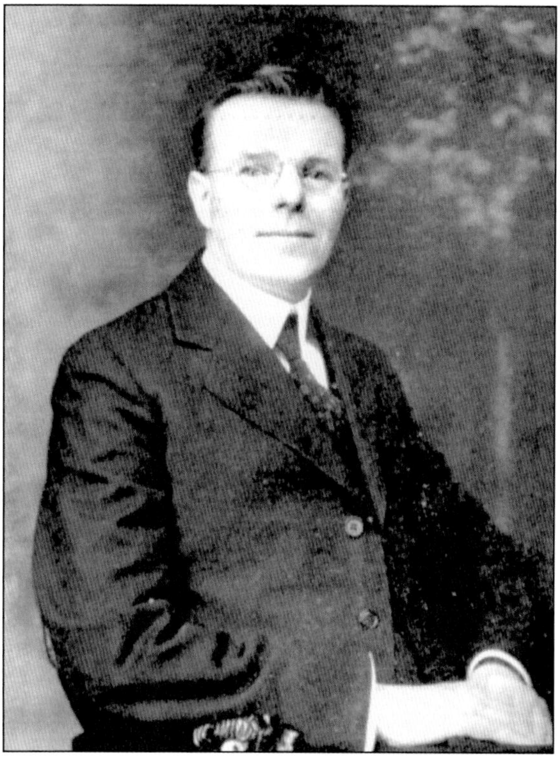

Rev. Harry P. Boughey was pastor of the Bridesburg Methodist Church from 1924 to 1929.

William Sliker and his wife, Anna, immigrated to the United States in the late 1890s and settled in Bridesburg. William then opened the Sliker Art Store, located on the corner of Pratt and Mercer Streets. Over the years, the Sliker Studio developed thousands upon thousands of rolls of film taken by the citizens of Bridesburg. Besides that, the business developed a reputation for its own formal photographs of graduations, weddings, communions, and other important events. These photographs, of which there are hundreds, document the visual history of Bridesburg from the turn of the century.

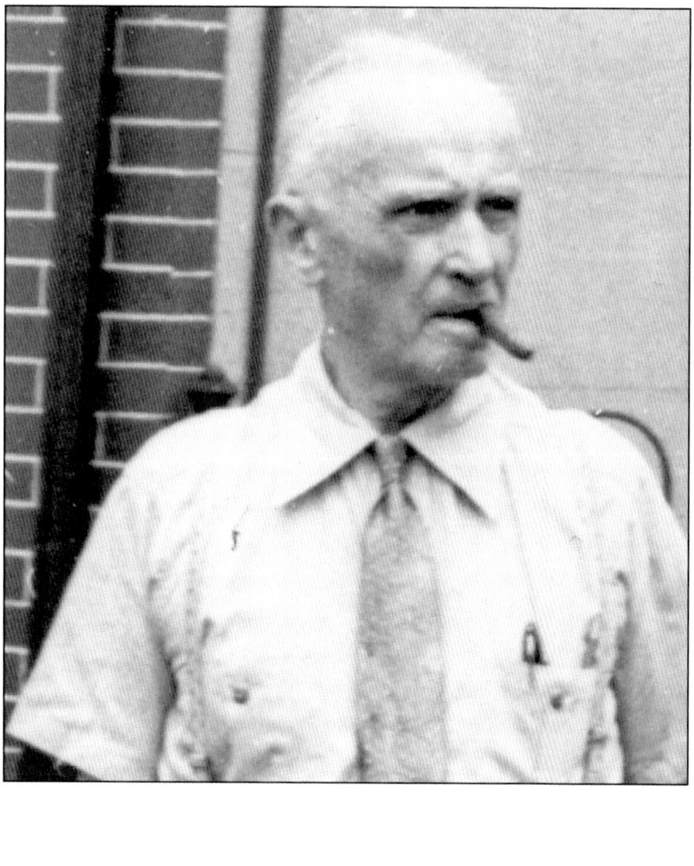

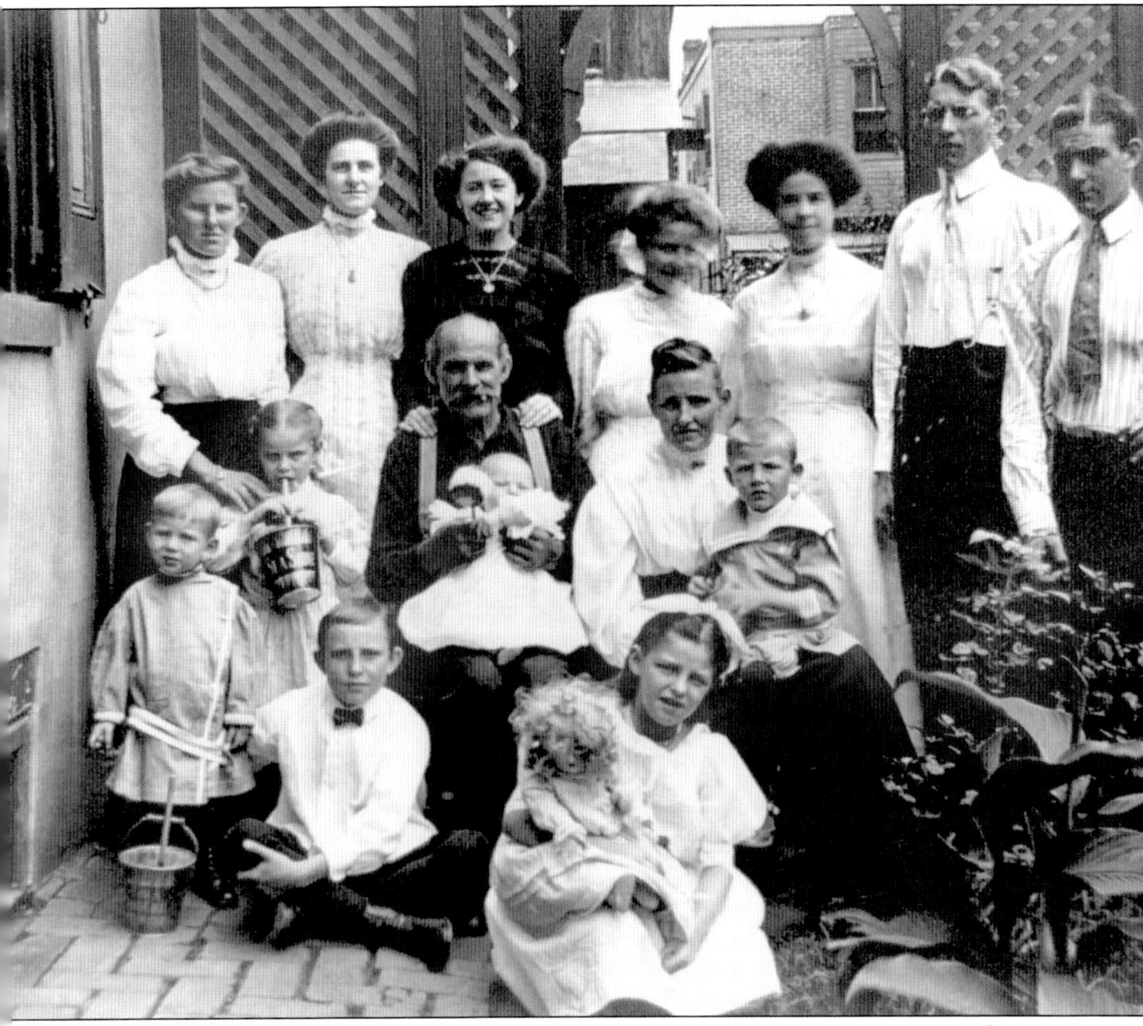

John and Mary Josephine Burger (middle row, seated), of 4704 Richmond Street, are shown here with their children, grandchildren, and their cousins, who were visiting from Baltimore.

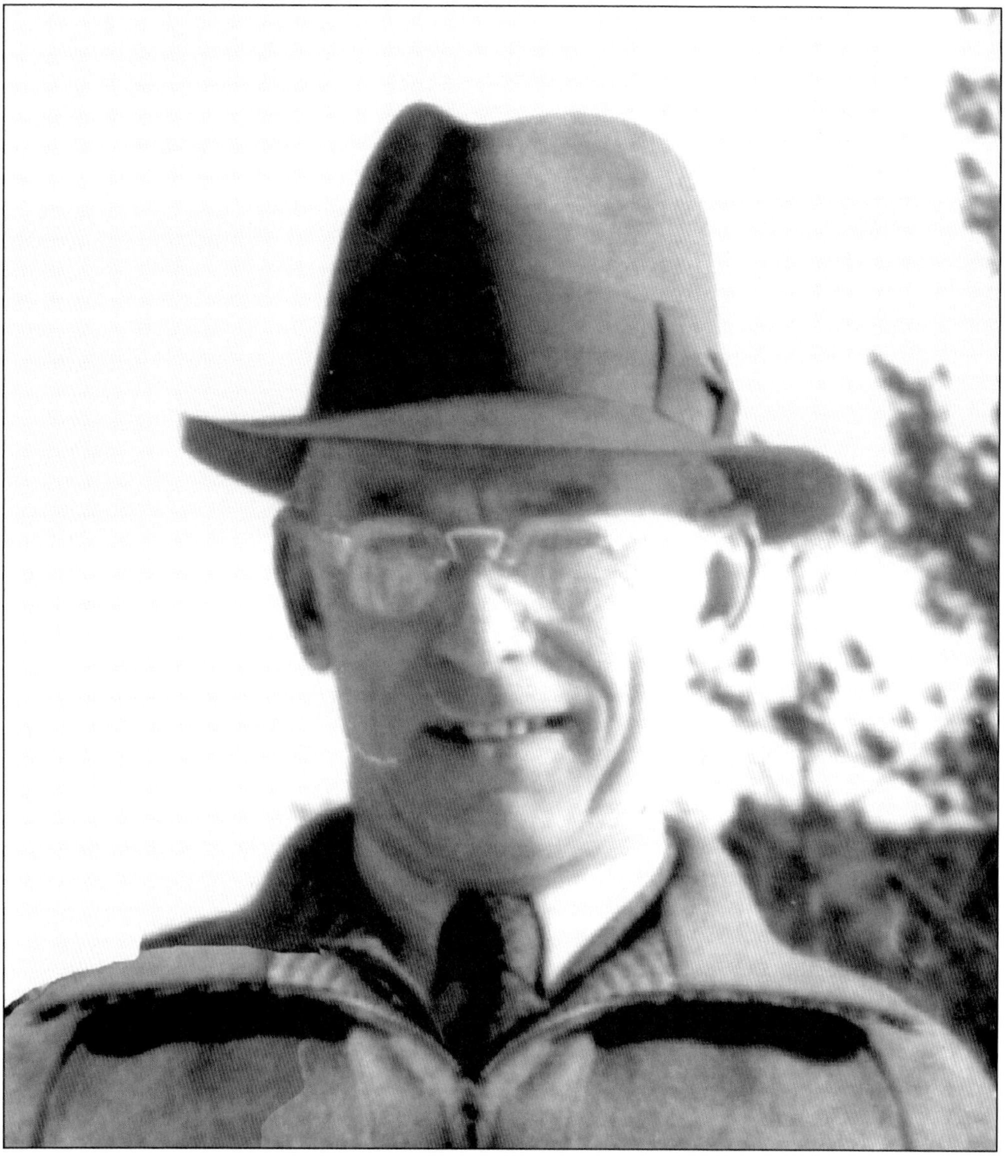

The Slikers were innovative in the field of photographic services. As a service, they allowed people to leave their box-camera films at local drugstores throughout the region. Charles Sliker, pictured here, rode horseback to the various stores to pick up the film for developing. The finished photographs would be delivered the next week.

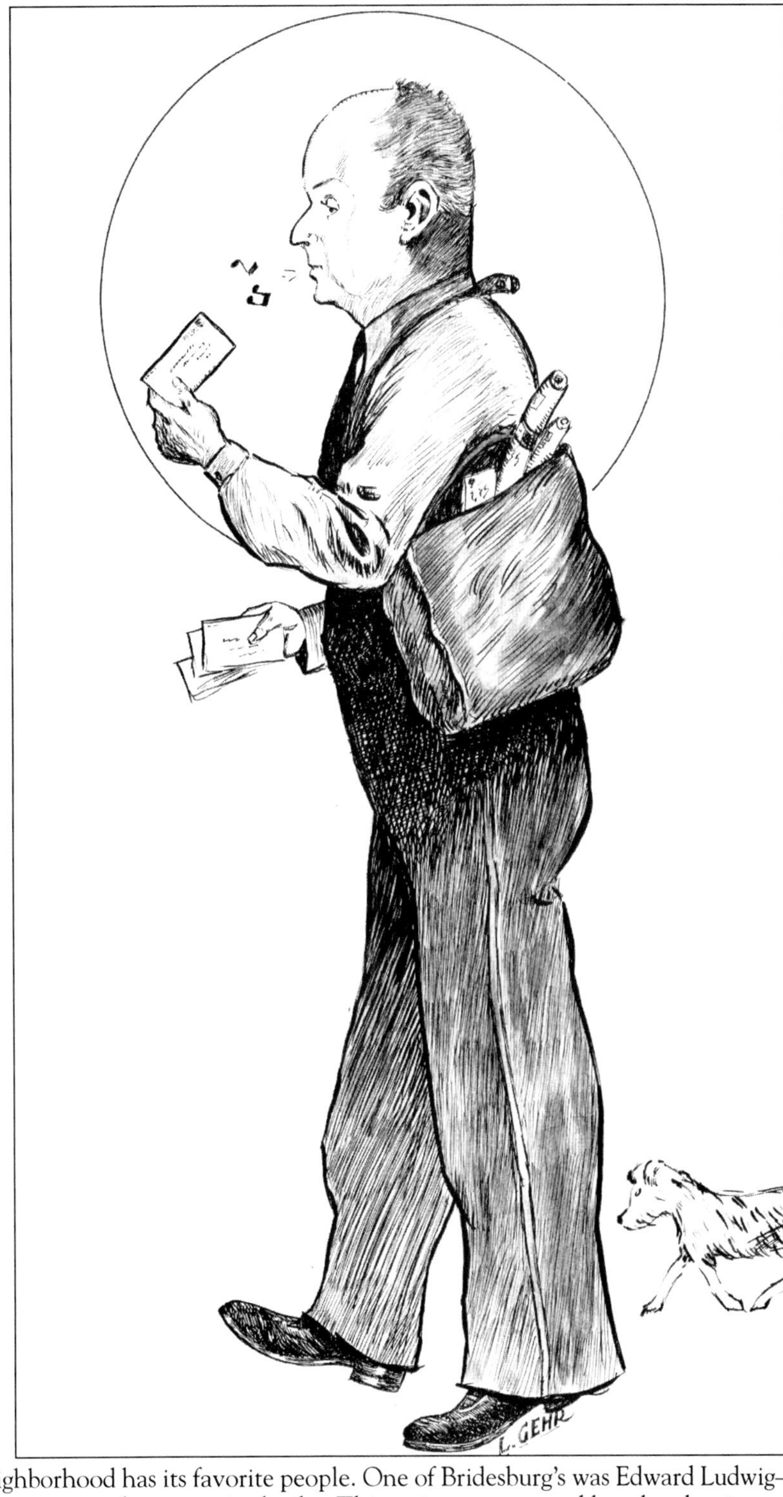

Every neighborhood has its favorite people. One of Bridesburg's was Edward Ludwig—mailman, town poet, artist, and community leader. This caricature, created by a local artist, truly projects his nature and the respect others had for him.

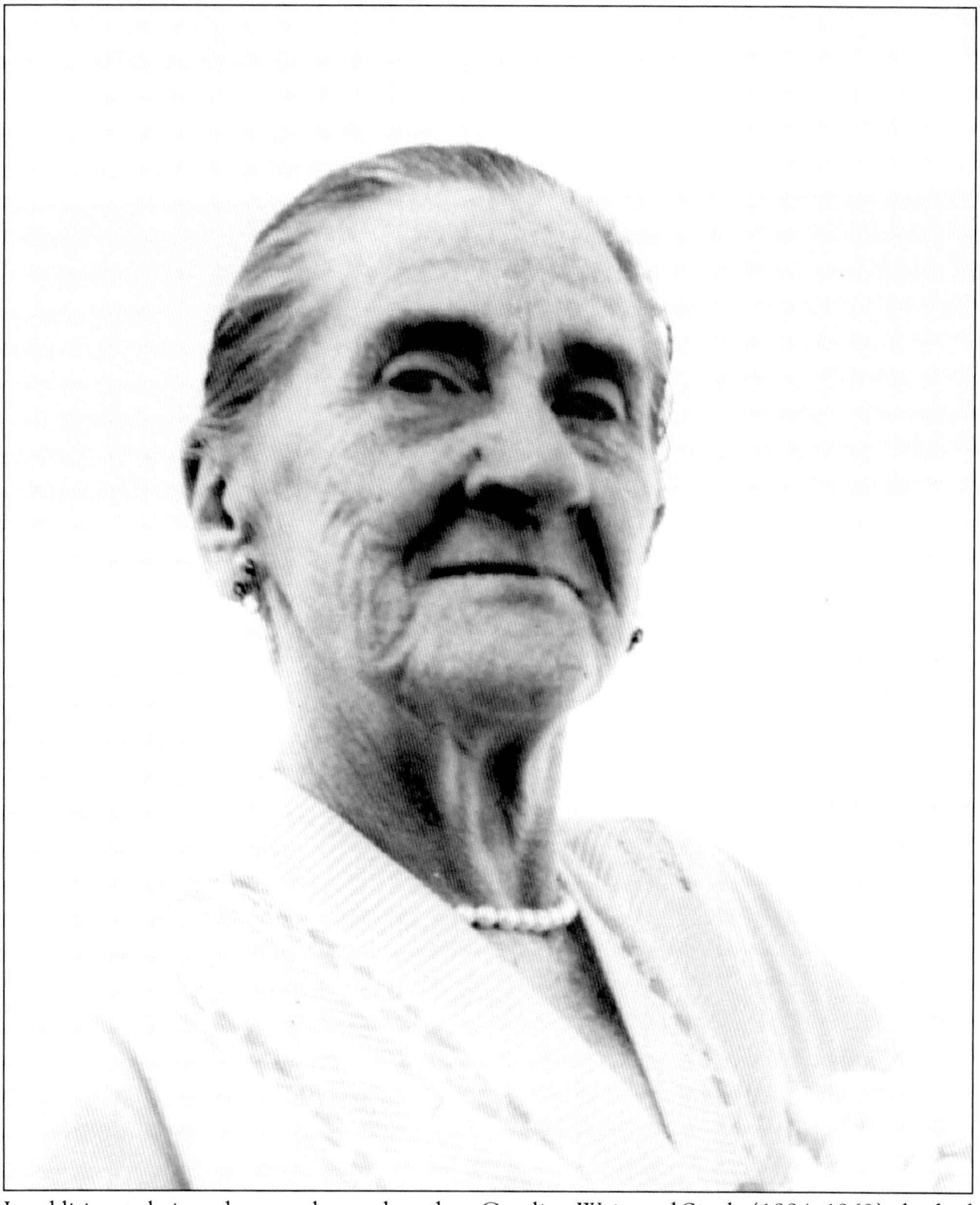

In addition to being a homemaker and mother, Caroline Weingard Siegle (1884–1969) also had a career as a midwife and baby nurse. She participated in a significant number of births, assisting several doctors in making deliveries and, in some cases, making the deliveries herself. In the 33 years from 1924 to 1957, she helped bring into the world at least 127 babies.

Four

LOCAL BUSINESSES

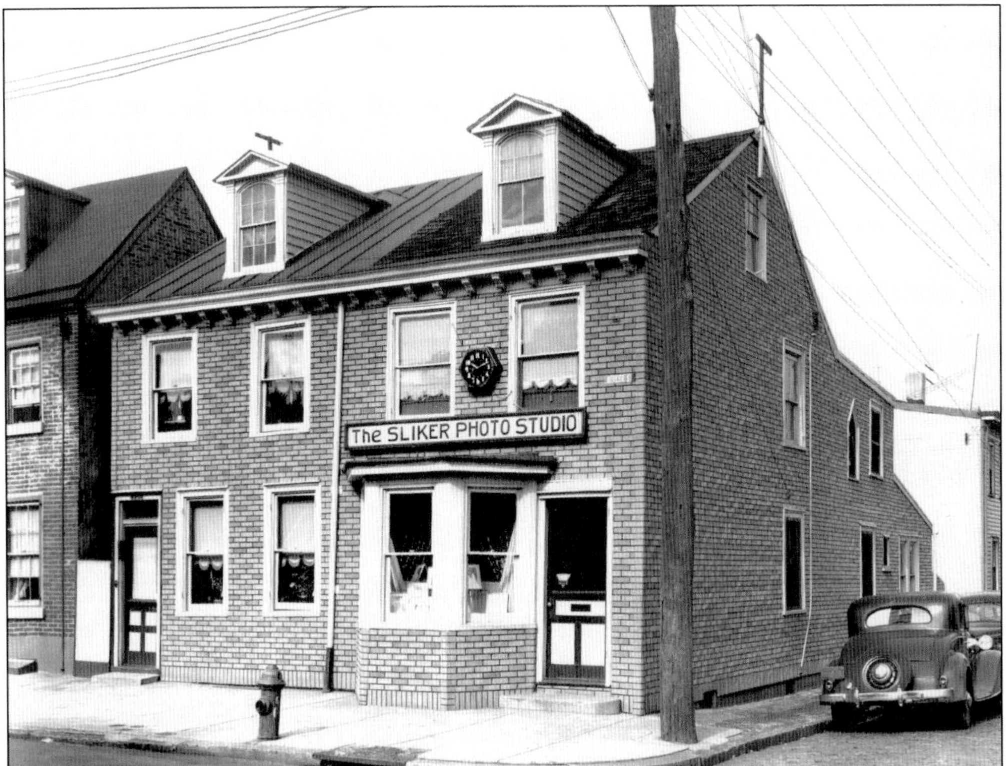

Likely the best-known store in Bridesburg, Slikers is where the enormous library of photographs of old Bridesburg was born. William Sliker and his son Charles were avid photographers. Virtually all of the street-scene images in the collection of the Bridesburg Historical Society were produced here. In addition, almost every graduation, communion, church, and sports photograph was likewise created here.

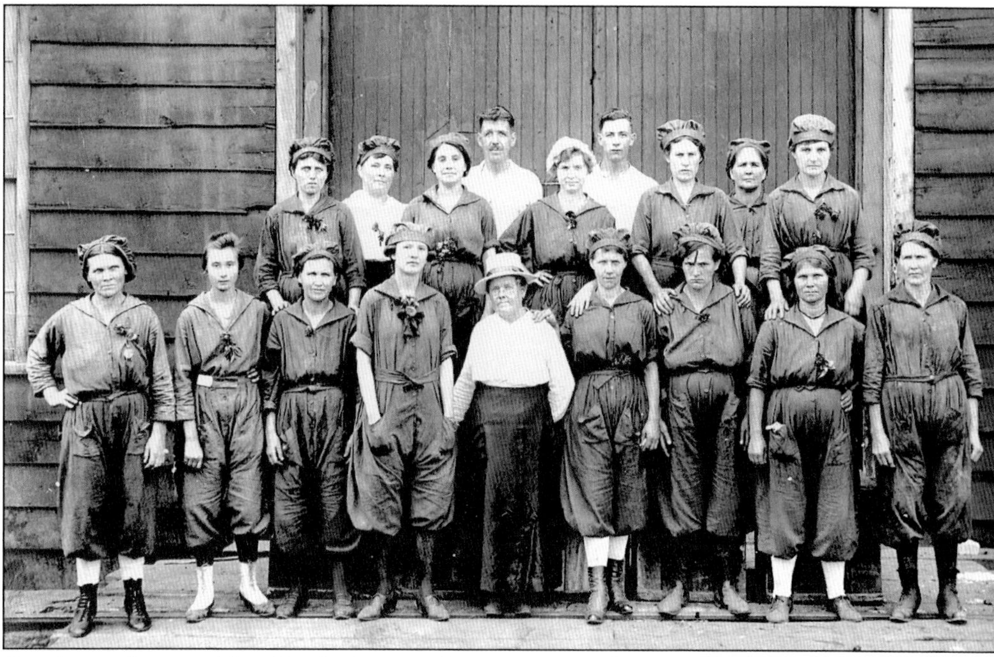

Female employees of the Charles Lennig Company, in a photograph dated 1915–1917, pose in their work uniforms.

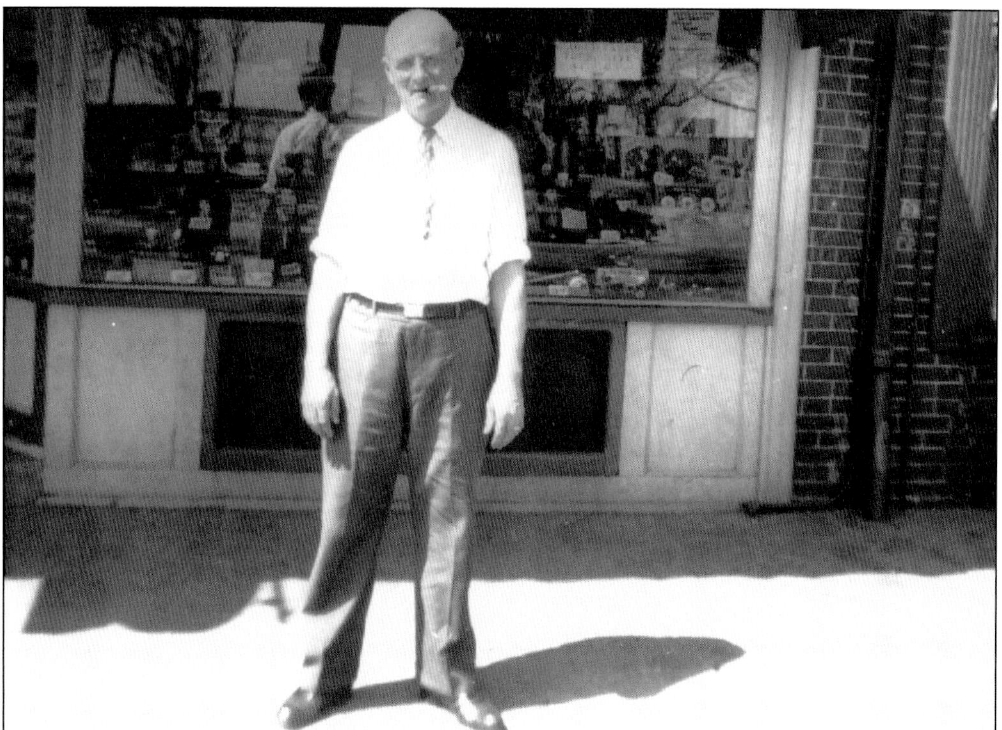

George Bloomquest stands before his candy shop on Richmond Street. A favorite spot of children of all ages, it was noted for its penny candies and hand-dipped Breyers ice cream.

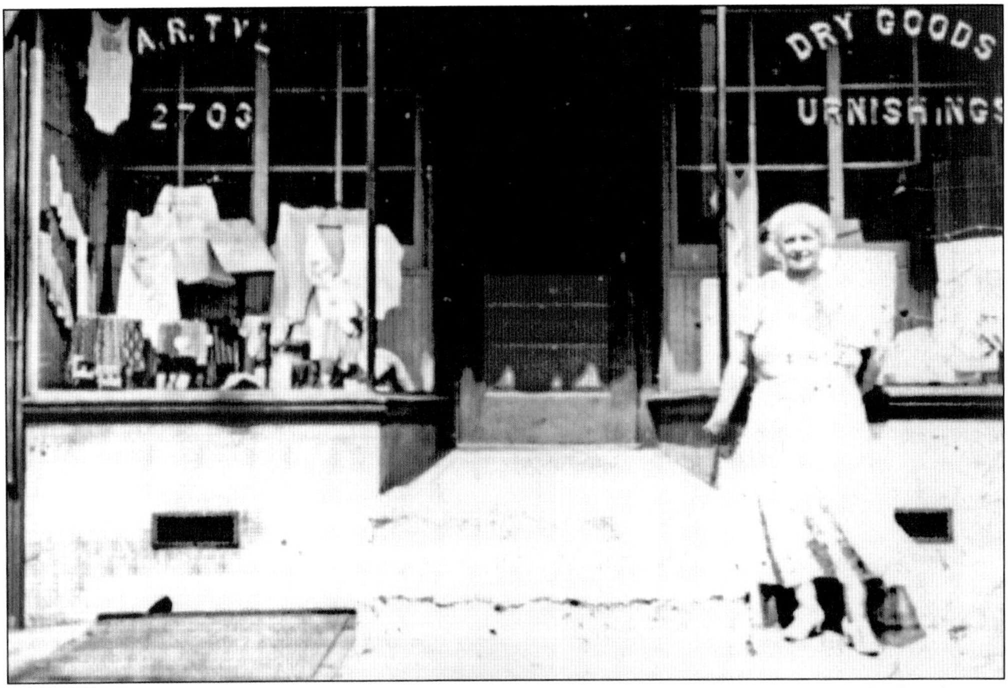

Rose Tyl appears in front of her dry goods store at 2703 Orthodox Street. With the demise of small mom-and-pop concerns, this storefront, like many others, has been converted to a standard home.

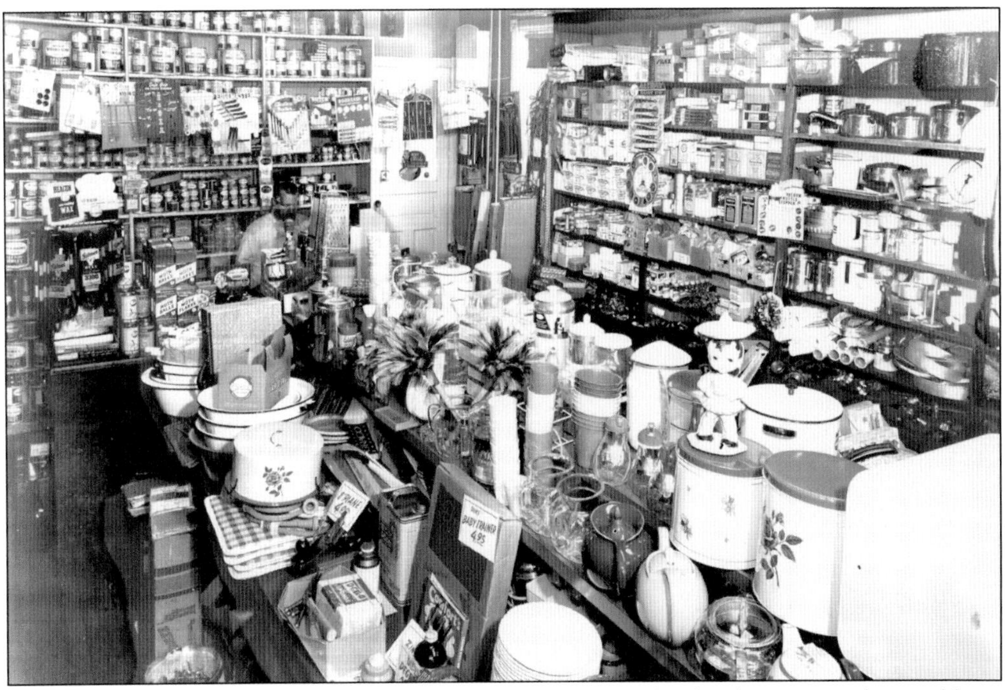

If a customer could not find what he wanted at E. J. Furmanski's hardware store, he would not find it anywhere else in Bridesburg. Conveniently located in the heart of town, on Lefevre Street near Thompson, it was one of four other hardware stores in the community.

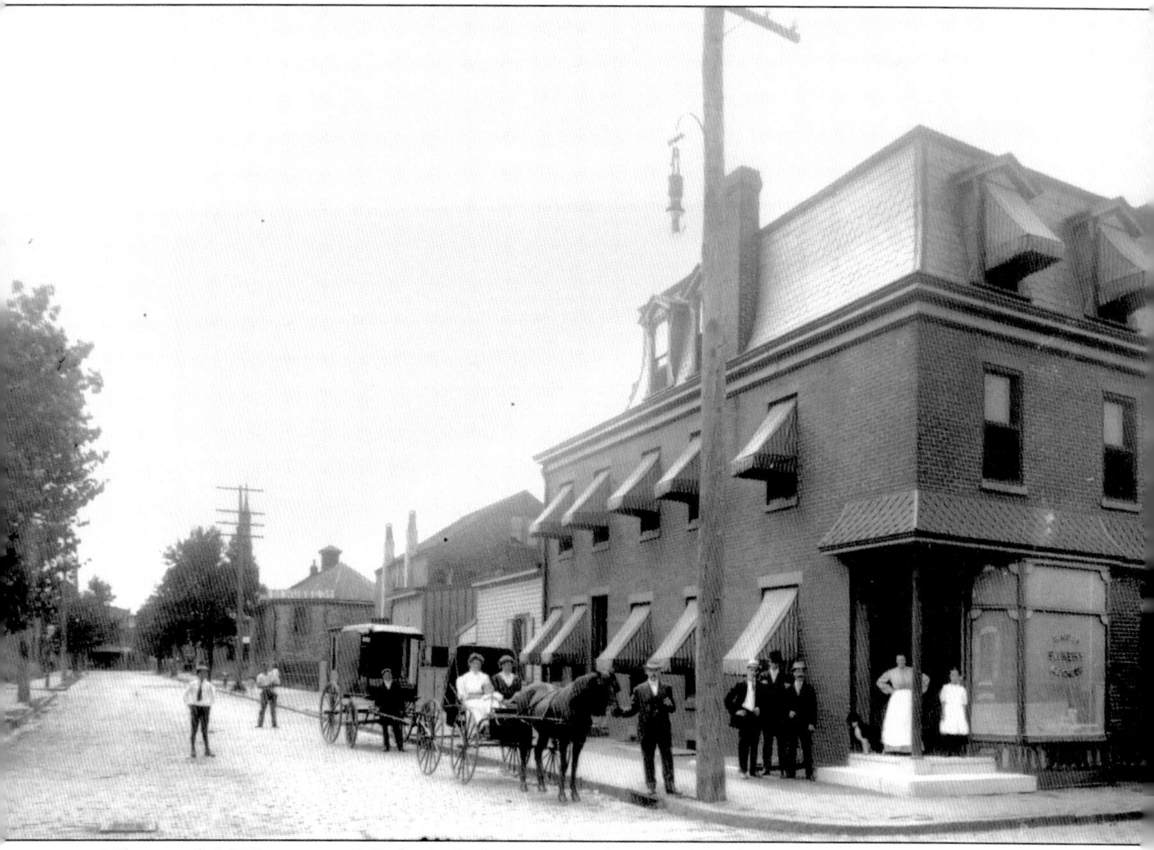

This mid-1800s view of Kuhn's Bakery was taken on Washington (now Thompson) Street, looking south from Church (now Pratt) Street. In the distance, the steeple of All Saints Roman Catholic Church can be seen, and just in front of that, the original town hall.

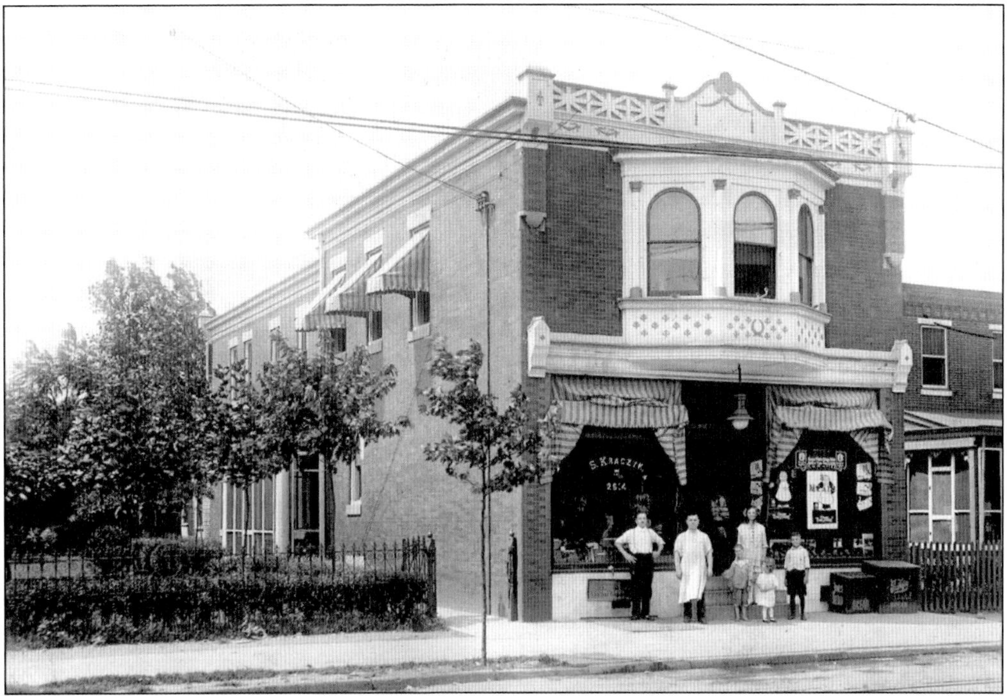

This fine establishment is the S. Kraczik grocery store, located on the south side of Orthodox Street. In later years, this building would be remodeled into the Slablinski Funeral Parlor.

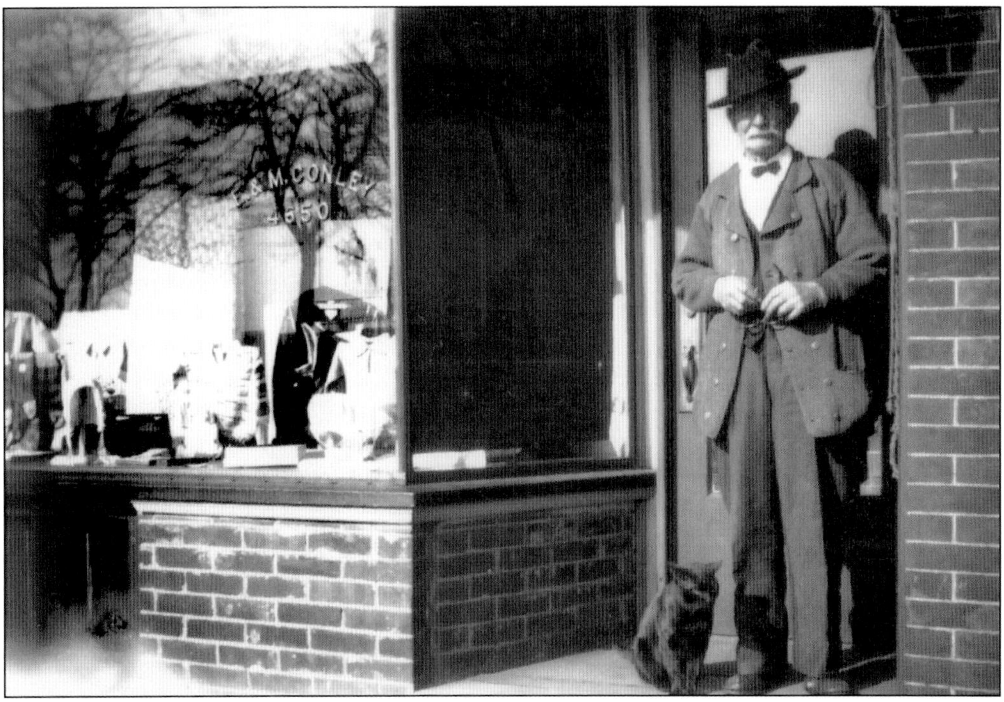

The Conley family was prominent in the community, owning and operating several businesses. In this photograph, the family patriarch stands at the entrance of the Conley dry goods store, on Richmond Street opposite the Bridesburg Park.

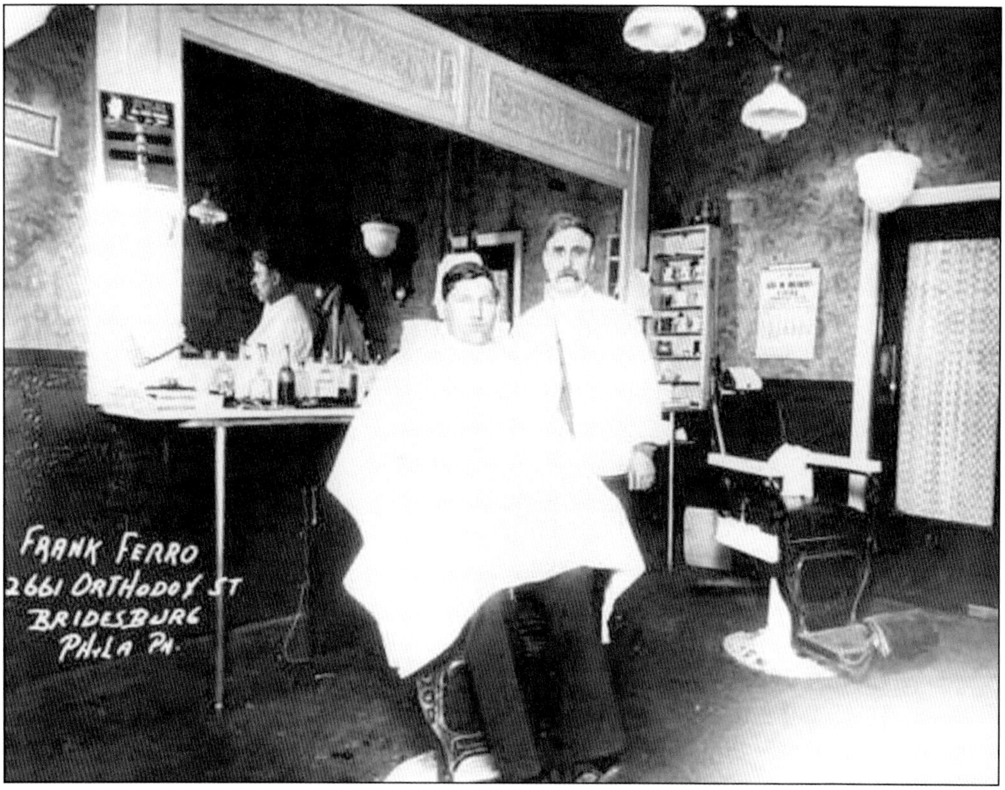

Lorenzo Ferro opened his barbershop on Orthodox Street in 1909. His son August helped out in the 1930s and eventually opened his own shop, which is now operated by his son Kenneth at the same location.

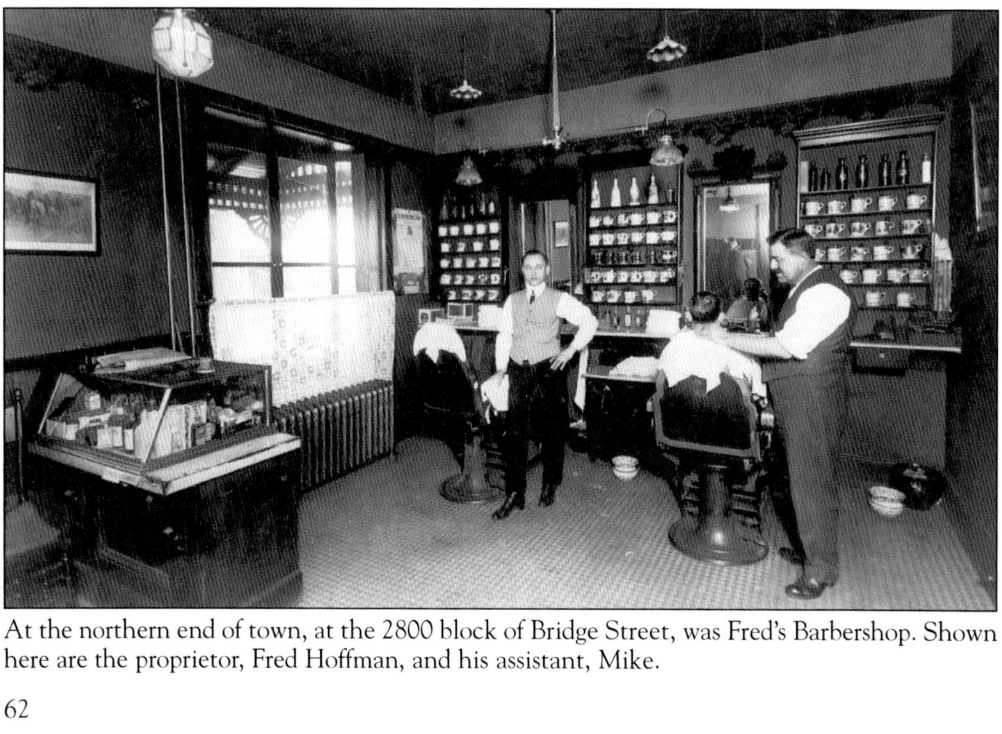

At the northern end of town, at the 2800 block of Bridge Street, was Fred's Barbershop. Shown here are the proprietor, Fred Hoffman, and his assistant, Mike.

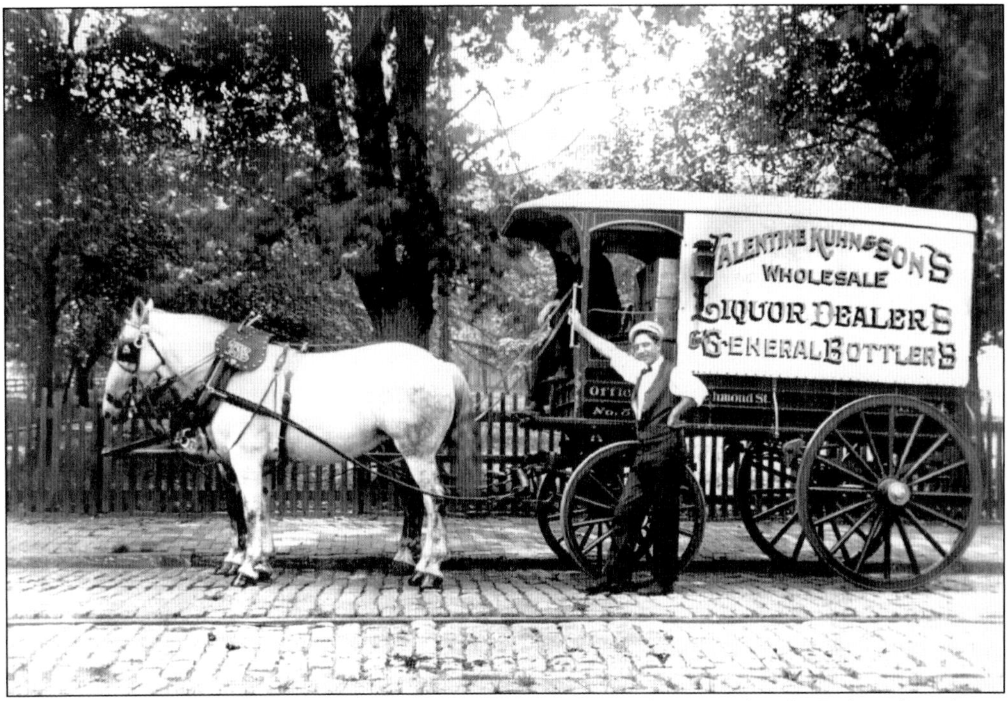

In the early days of Bridesburg, the Kuhns were a prominent business family. Before the advent of state liquor stores, alcoholic beverages were sold at neighborhood concerns. Valentine Kuhn started the business on Bridge Street. In later years, his sons Valentine and John produced soft drinks from their bottling plant on Mercer Street.

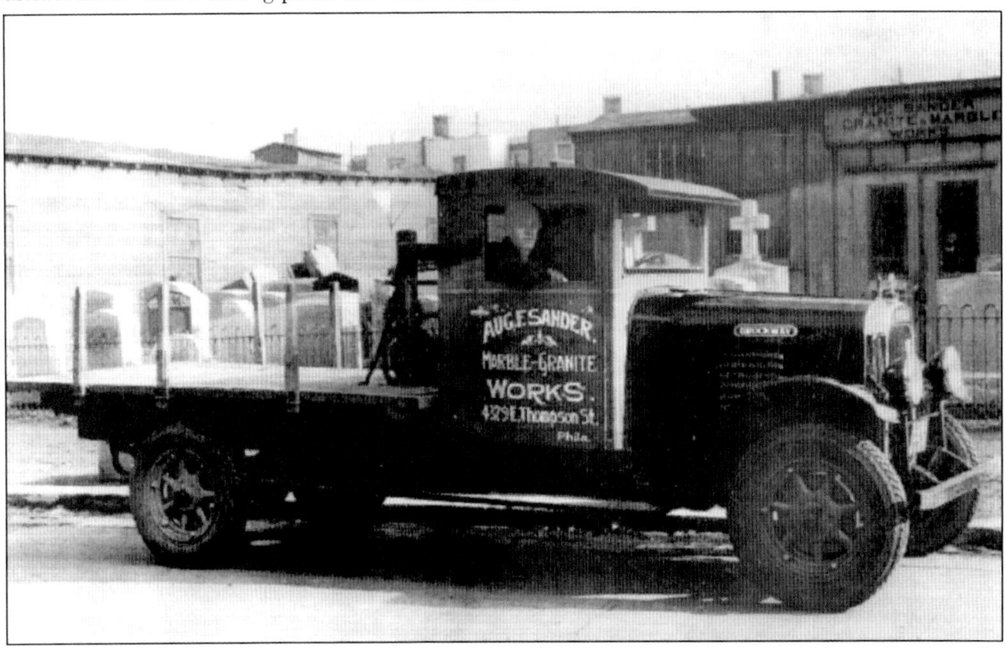

August Sander established his cemetery memorials business in 1907. His son August Sander Jr. worked there as young man and carried on the business. In this 1925 photograph, the younger August sits in the company truck in front of the display yard on Thompson Street.

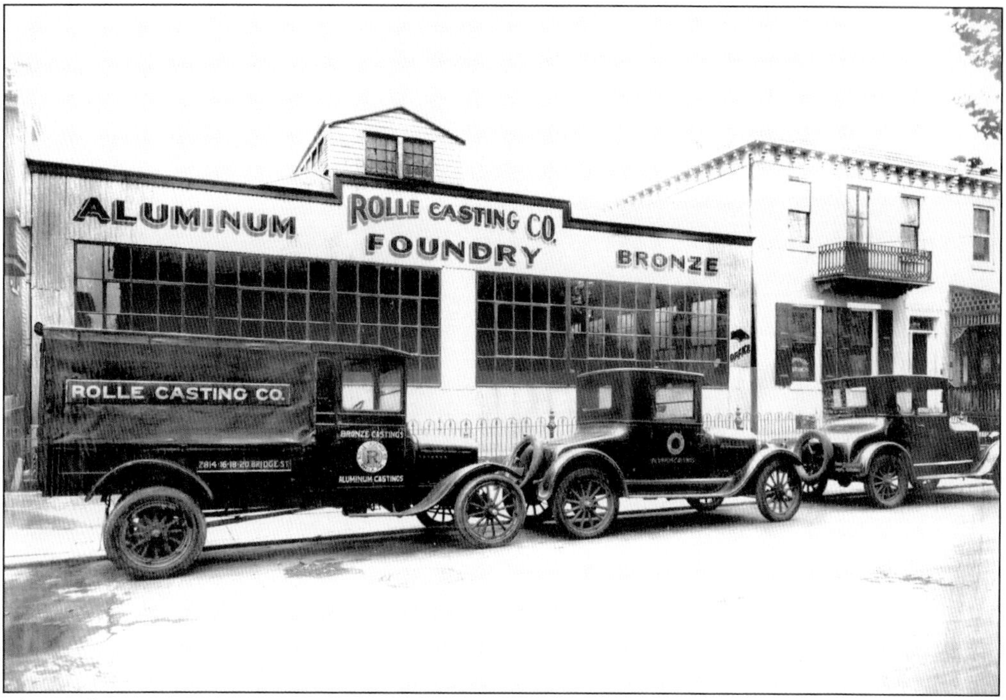

The Rolle Casting Company was located on Bridge Street just east of Richmond. Although the company cast both bronze and aluminum, it was most noted for its aluminum products. The company was called upon to create special lightweight aluminum grease fittings for Charles Lindberg's *Spirit of St. Louis*.

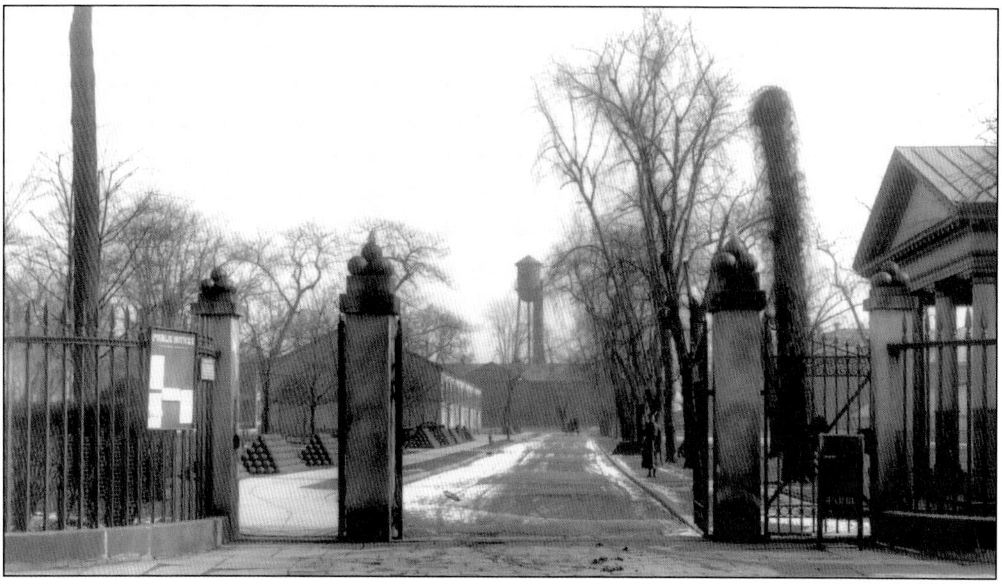

Bridesburg's economy was built on a large number of neighborhood stores and a few sizable industries. This photograph displays the main gate of the United States Arsenal on Frankford Creek, the largest employer for Bridesburg and surrounding communities. Established in 1816, it served through the nation's many conflicts until the government closed the facility. At its peak in World War II, it employed a staff of nearly 25,000 workers.

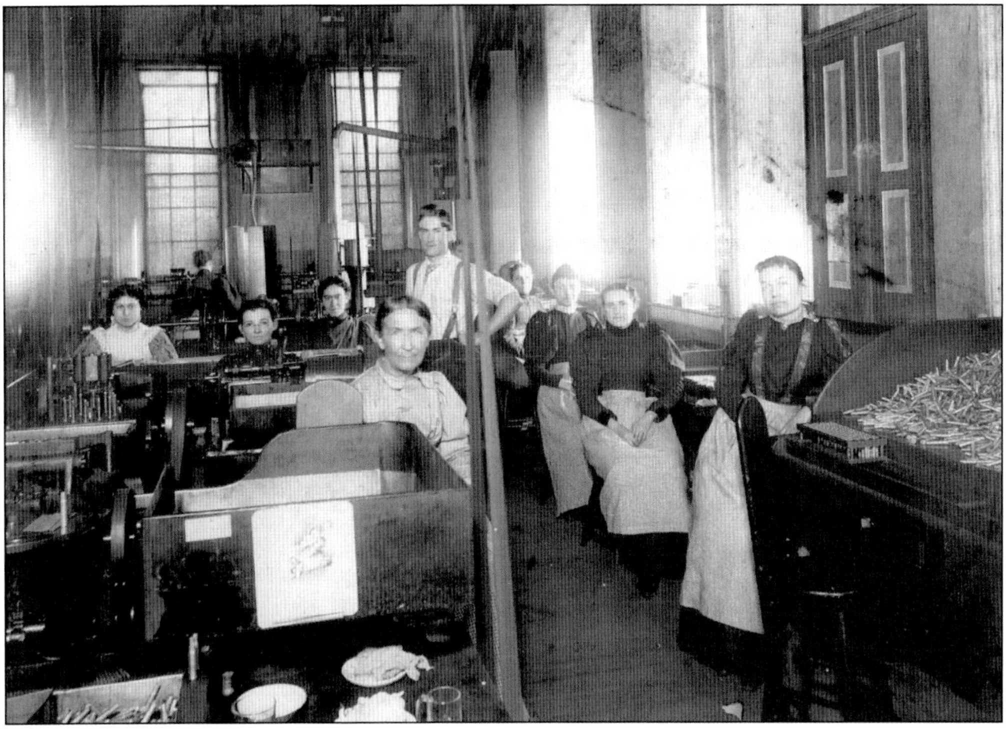

This recently uncovered photograph was taken in a bullet assembly shop at the Frankford Arsenal. Though not accurately dated, it appears to have been taken in the mid- to late 1800s.

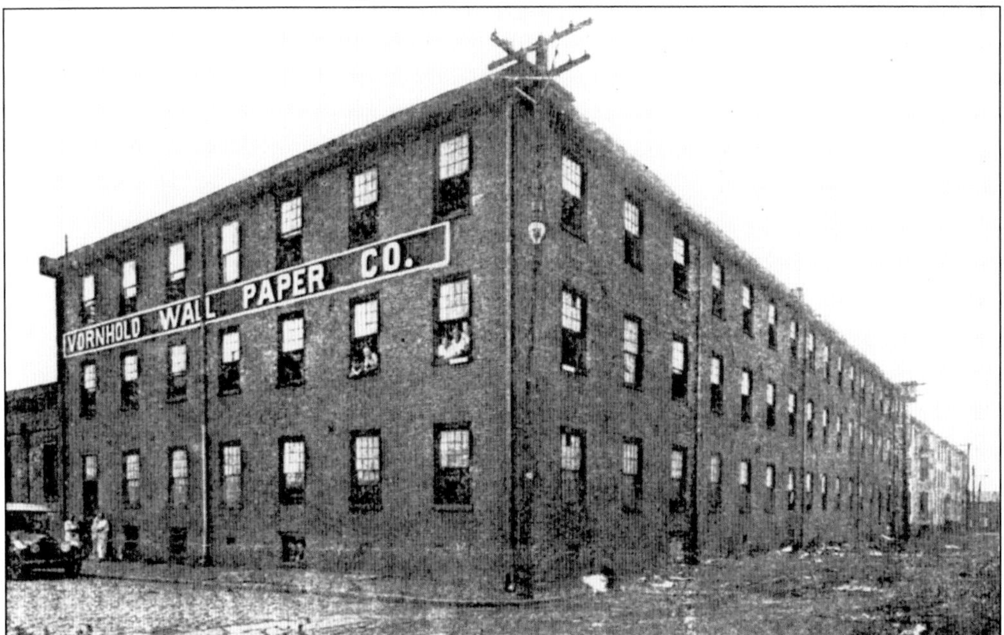

William Vornhold founded the Vornhold Paper Company in 1895. The company was incorporated in 1907 and, at that time, was one of the largest manufacturers of commercial wallpaper, shipping eight carloads a week.

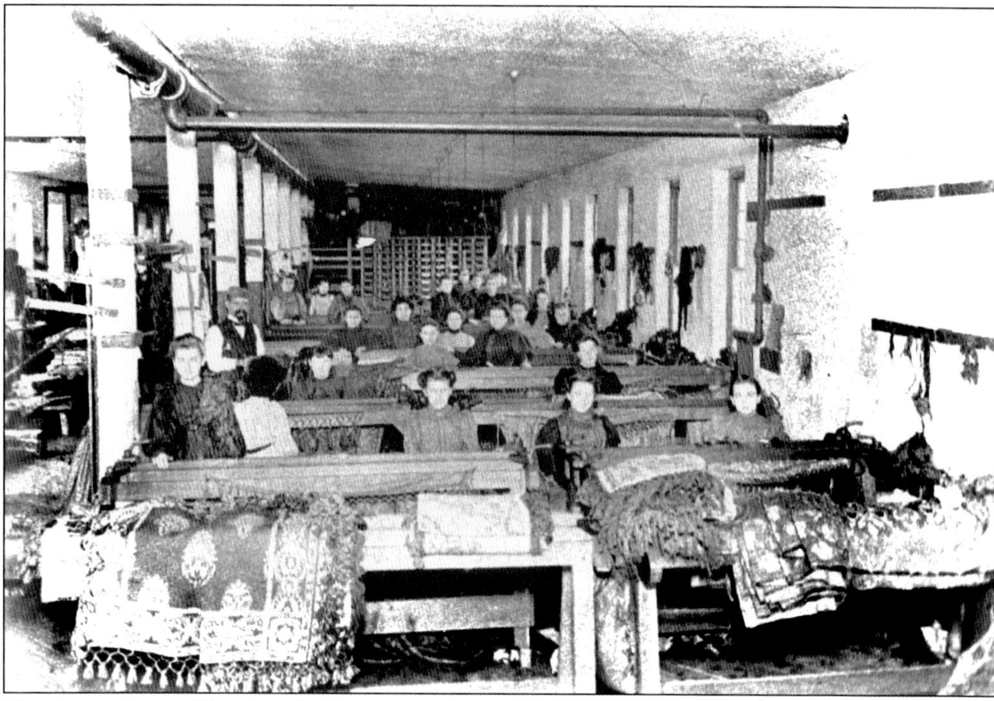

The Louis Muir Weaving Mills occupied space vacated by the Bridesburg Manufacturing Company at the end of the Civil War. This photograph, taken c. 1885, shows the women who worked in the final finishing area of the mill.

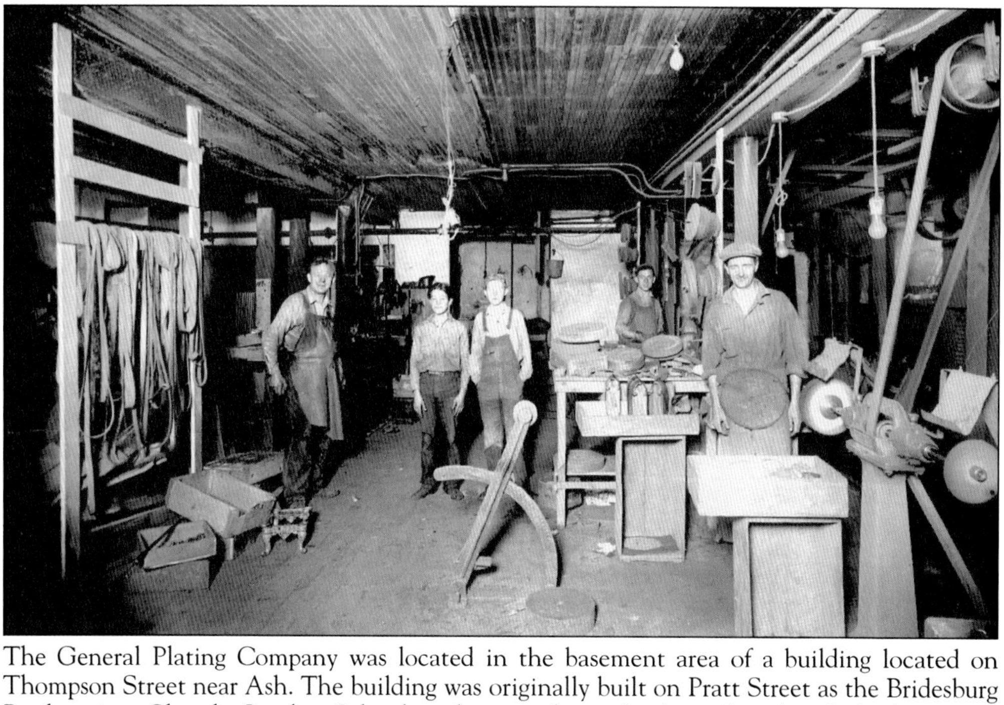

The General Plating Company was located in the basement area of a building located on Thompson Street near Ash. The building was originally built on Pratt Street as the Bridesburg Presbyterian Church Sunday School and was relocated when the church built a new, larger building.

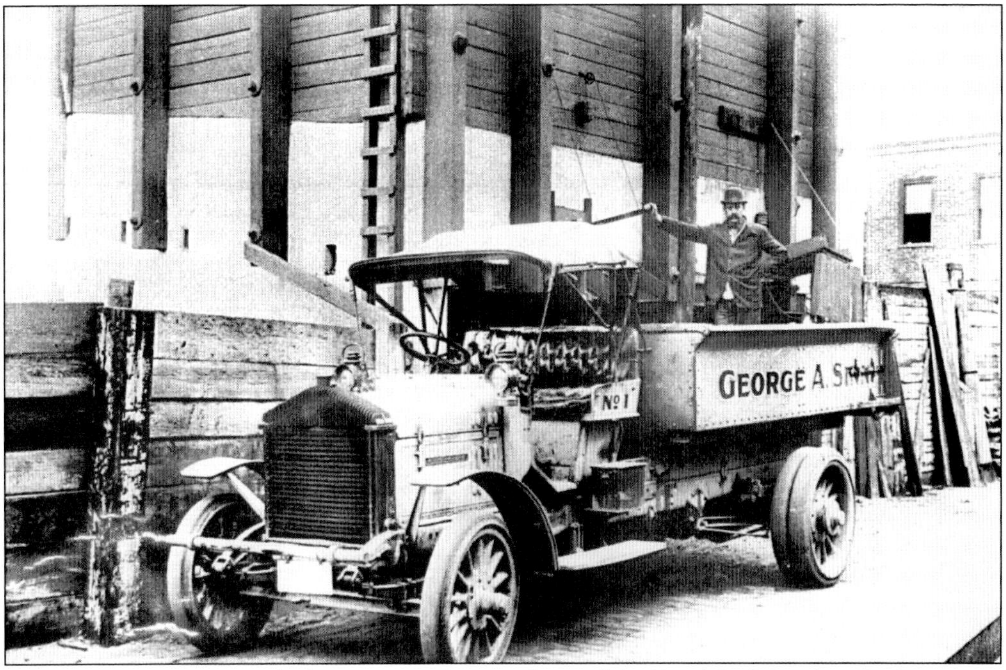

George A. Shinn operated a business on the east shore of the Frankford Creek at Bridge Street. He was primarily a purveyor of building materials but also sold various coal products.

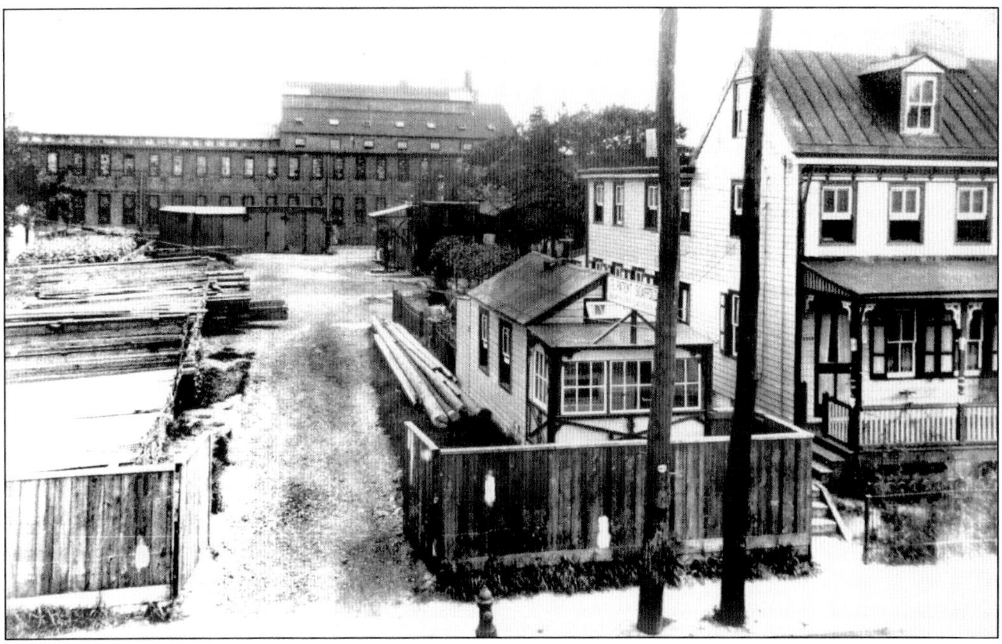
Patent Scaffolding occupied this location on Bridge Street for many years. Later, the property was sold, and the company relocated to Port Richmond. The site is now occupied by a large building, home of the Ellis Coffee Company.

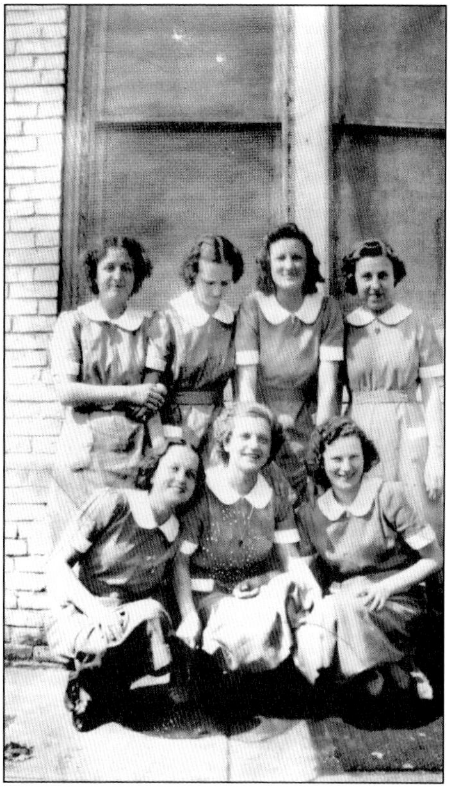

Commonly known as the "Spooney" due to its manufacture of disposable paper spoons, knives, and forks, the Sanitary Products Company was located on Lefevre Street. Here, some of the young female employees take time out for a group photograph.

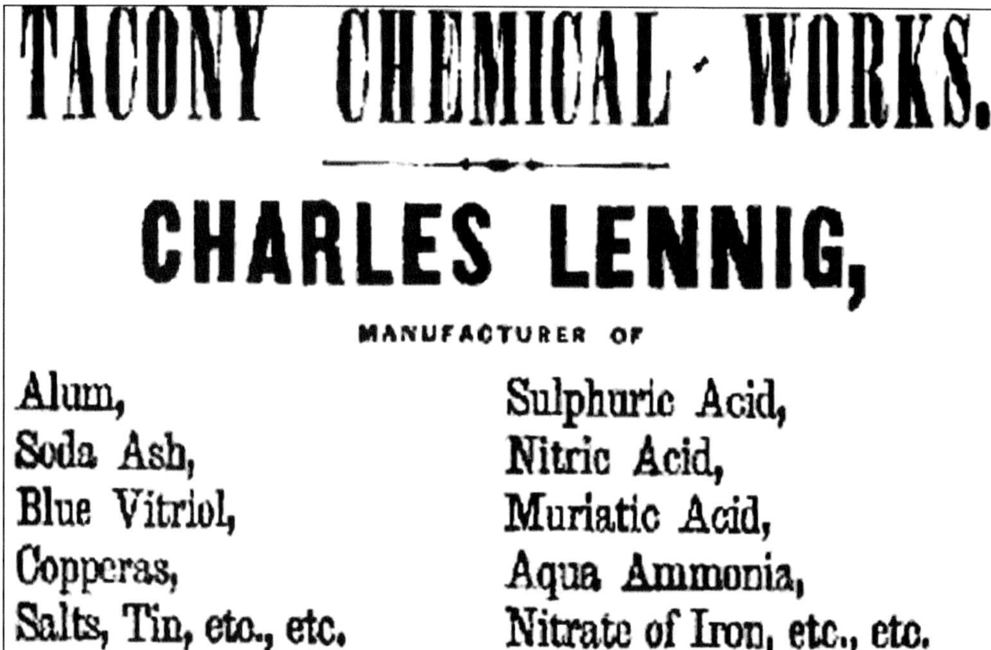

In the early 1800s, Frederick Lennig established his Tacony Chemical Works at the mouth of the Frankford Creek and the Delaware River. The name of the business later changed to the Charles Lennig Chemical Company, operating until it was sold to Rohm and Haas in 1921.

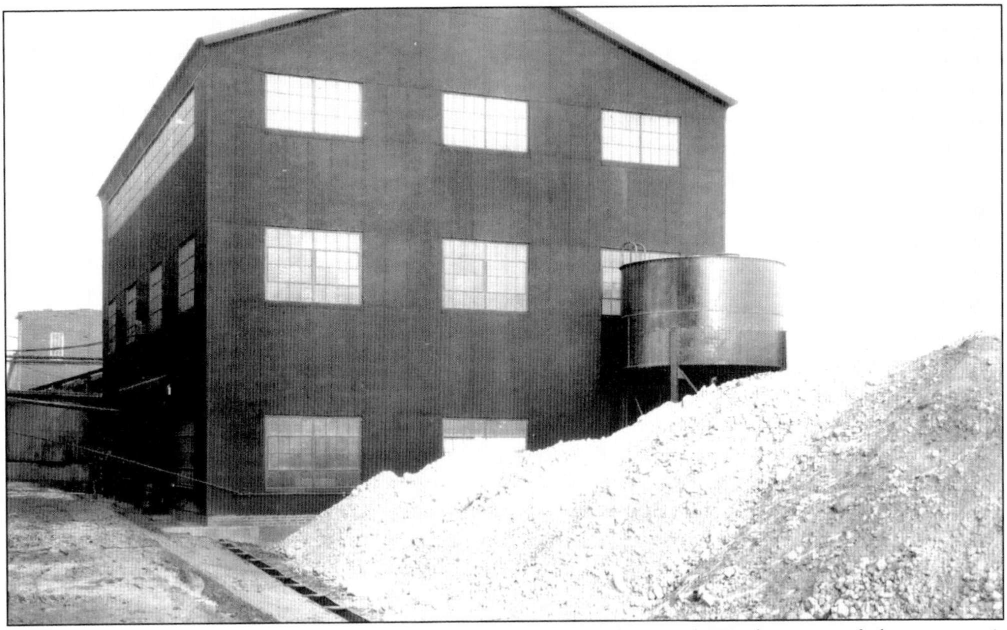

The first major industry in Bridesburg was the Tacony Chemical Works, one of the country's largest producers of sulfuric acid. This 1927 photograph shows the large mounds of brilliant-yellow sulfur, stored along the riverfront prior to being used in the manufacture of sulfuric acid.

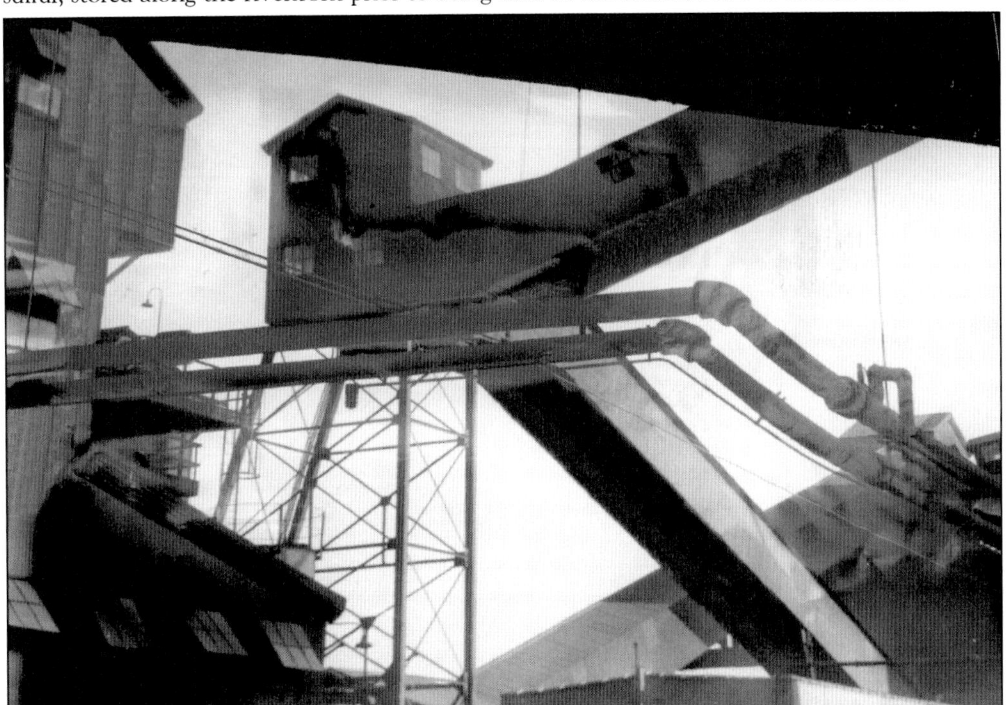

Another of the larger industrial firms to support Bridesburg's economy was the Philadelphia Coke Company, located between Richmond Street and the Delaware River. Bituminous coal was shipped into the plant on large ships where it was converted to coke, cooking gas, and other chemical byproducts.

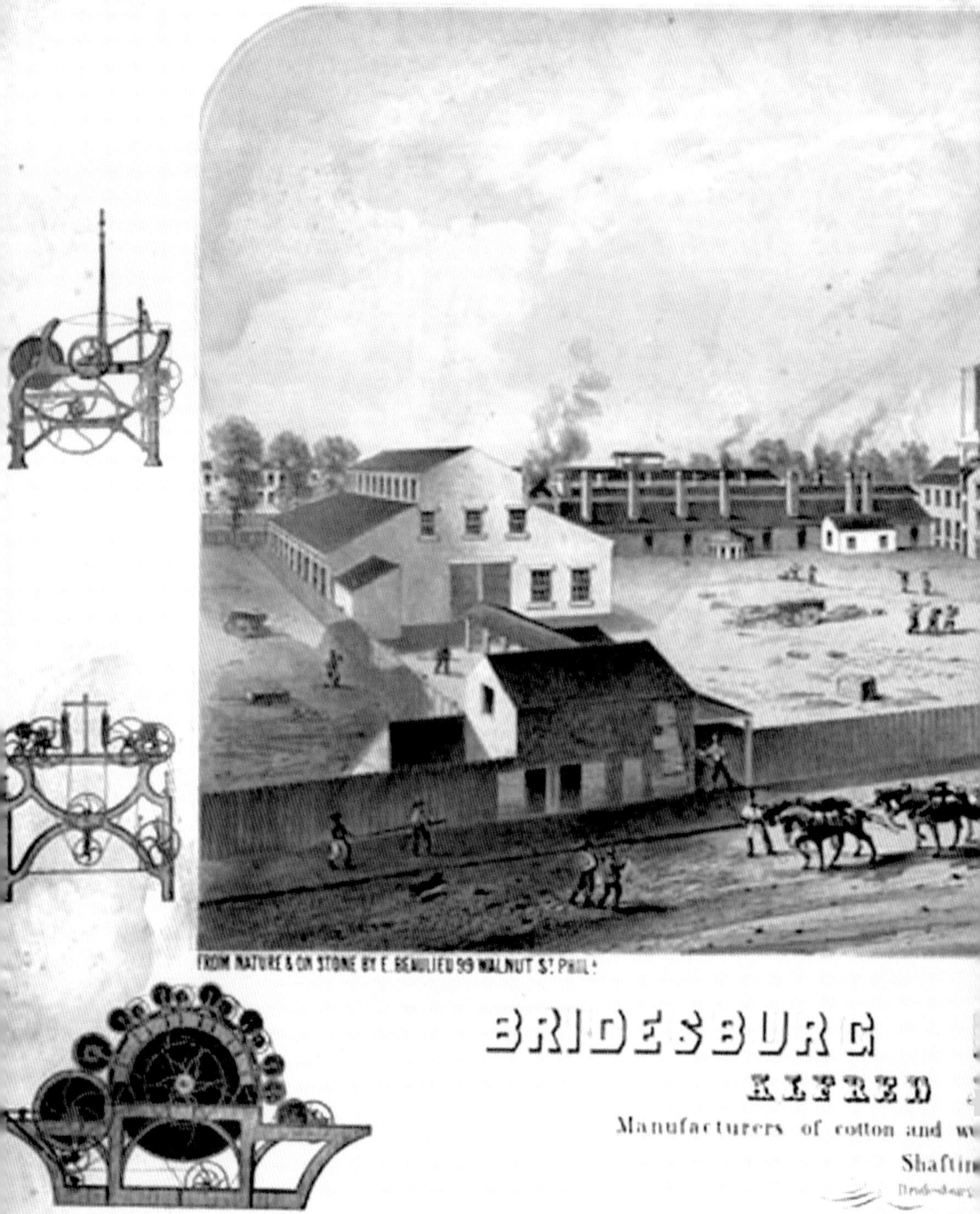

This 1873 poster advertises the Bridesburg Manufacturing Company, once located between Richmond Street and the Delaware River, one block north of Bridge Street. Known earlier as

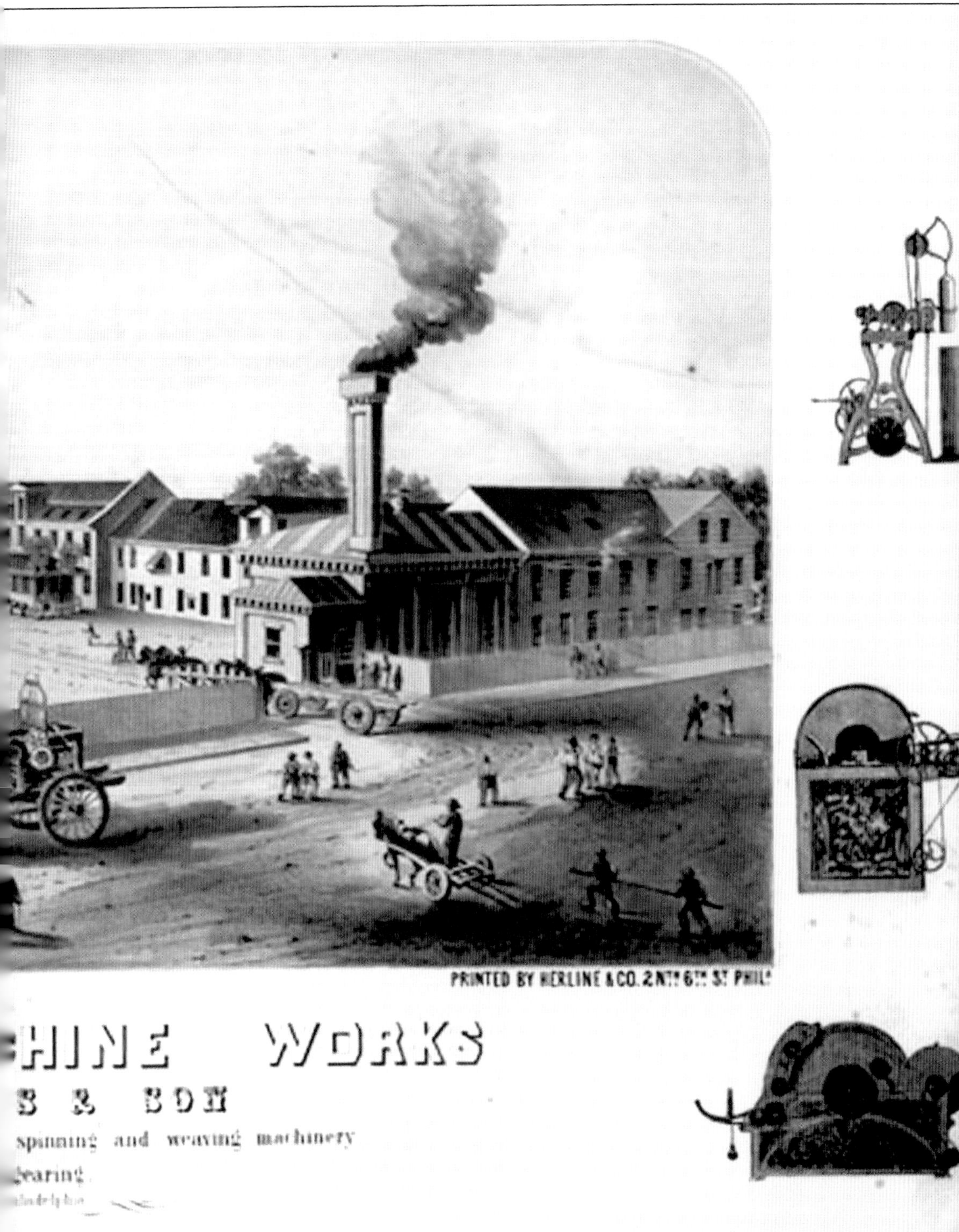

Alfred Jenks and Sons, the company designed and manufactured knitting machinery. In 1863, it produced muskets for the Union army.

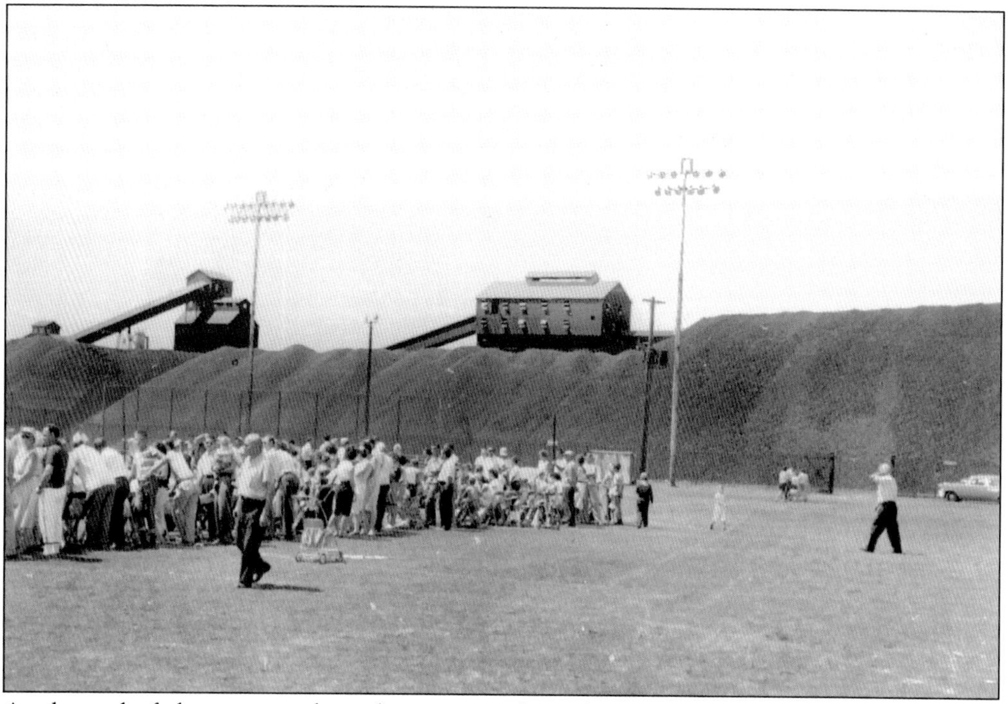

At the end of the process, the coke was stored on the property of the Philadelphia Coke Company in several very large mounds. The mounds were often 50 to 60 feet high and were sometimes two city squares long.

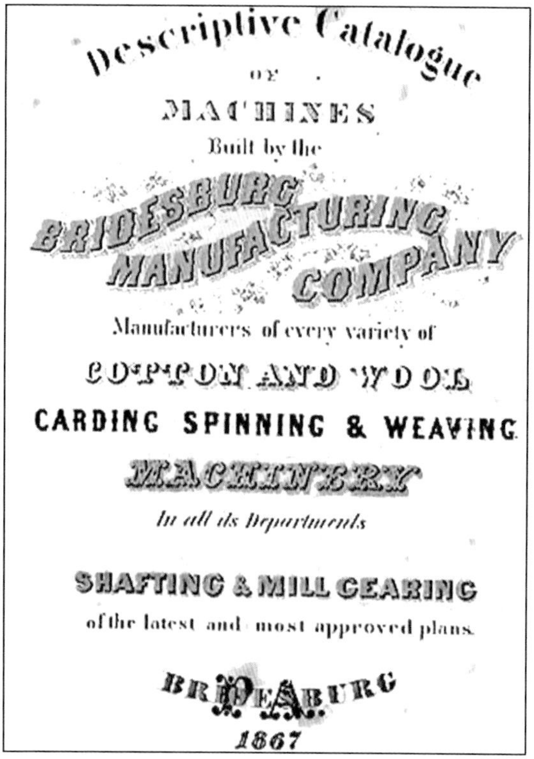

Descriptive Catalogue

OF

MACHINES

Built by the

BRIDESBURG MANUFACTURING COMPANY

Manufacturers of every variety of

COTTON AND WOOL

CARDING SPINNING & WEAVING

MACHINERY

In all its Departments

SHAFTING & MILL GEARING

of the latest and most approved plans.

BRIDESBURG PA.

1867

Shown here is the cover of the 1867 Bridesburg Manufacturing Company descriptive catalog. An original of this document can be found in the business school library of Harvard University.

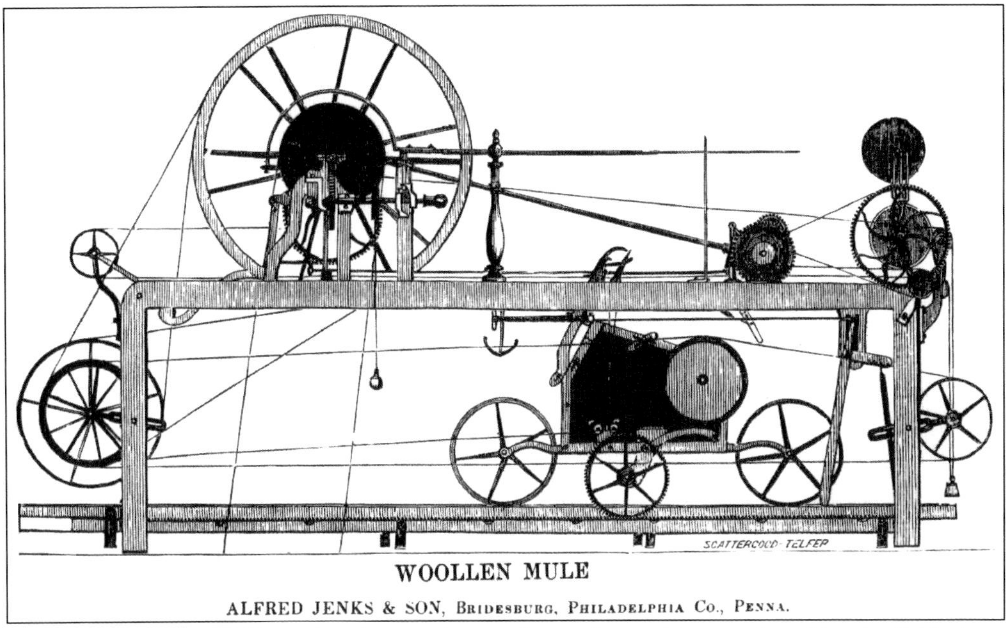

This page from the 1867 catalog depicts the woolen mule machine produced by the Bridesburg Manufacturing Company. The machine simultaneously draws and twists fiber into woolen yarn or thread.

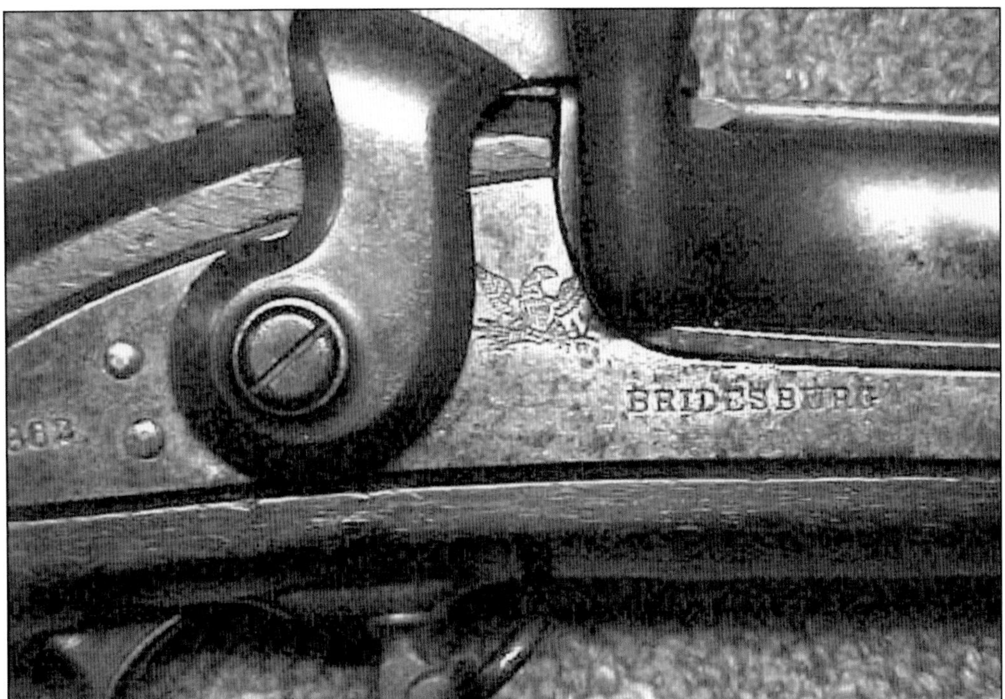

In view shows the lock plate of a musket manufactured at the Bridesburg Manufacturing Company in 1863. The company produced 95,000 muskets for the Civil War action. A few of the muskets are still available as collectors' items.

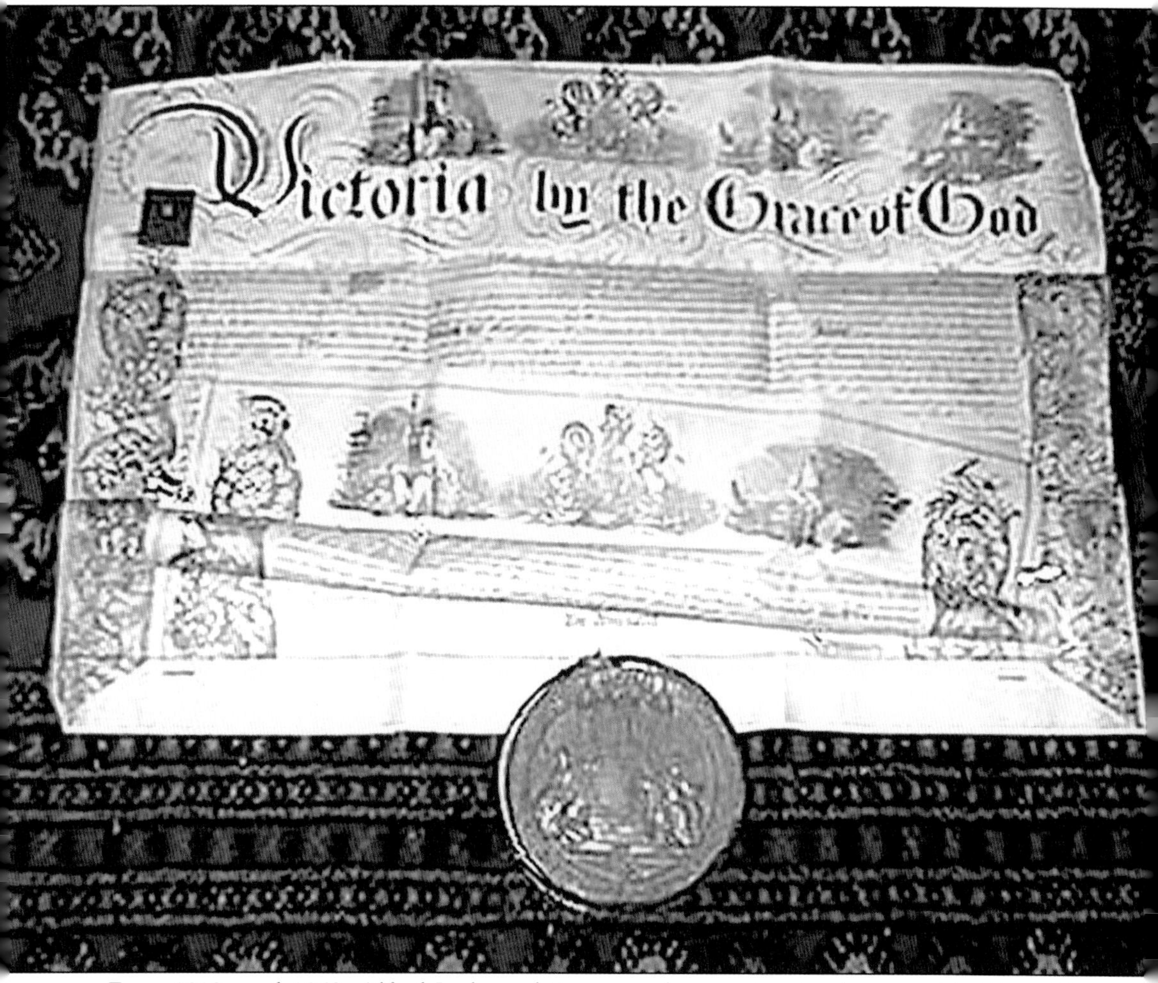

From 1810 until 1863, Alfred Jenks and Sons was the premier developer and builder of fine knitting and weaving machines. The company's equipment was considered among the finest made in the United States, as well as in Great Britain. Queen Victoria granted the business the patent pictured here.

Five

PRIDE AND PATRIOTISM

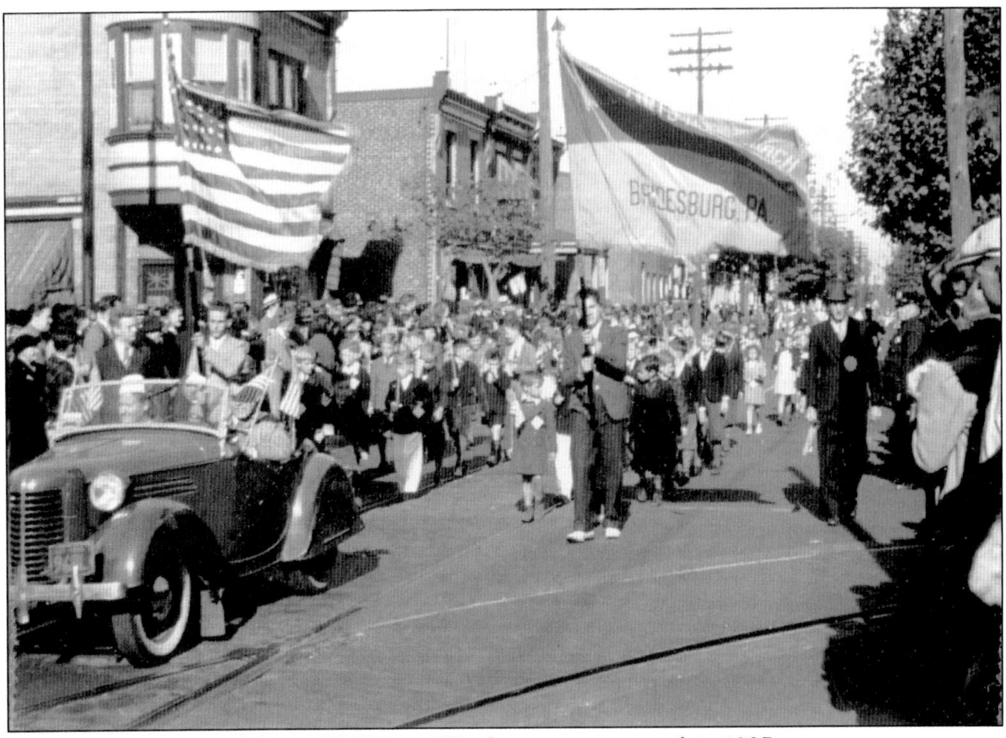

A parade is held to celebrate Old Home Week, an event started in 1937.

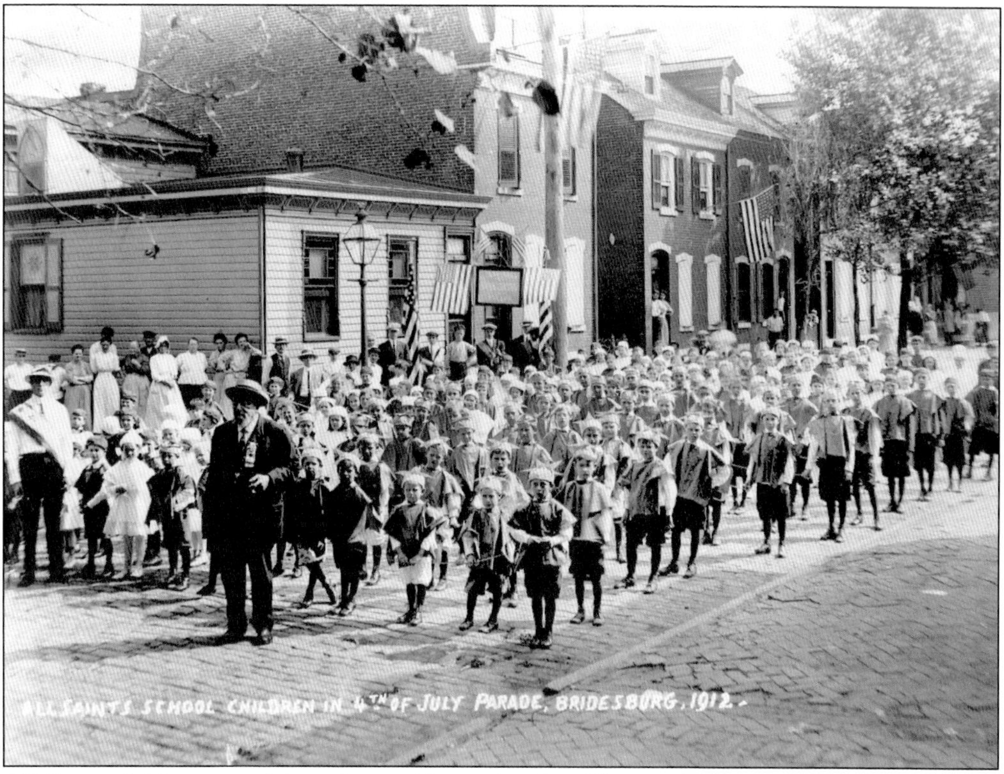

All Saints children assemble in front of their school on Thompson Street for the Fourth of July parade in 1912.

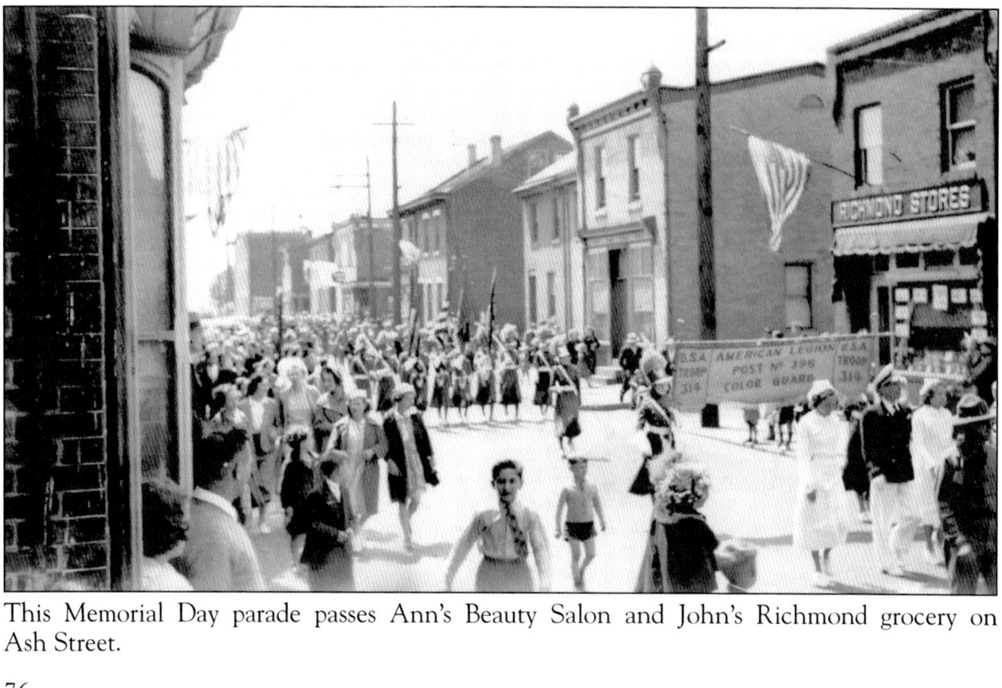

This Memorial Day parade passes Ann's Beauty Salon and John's Richmond grocery on Ash Street.

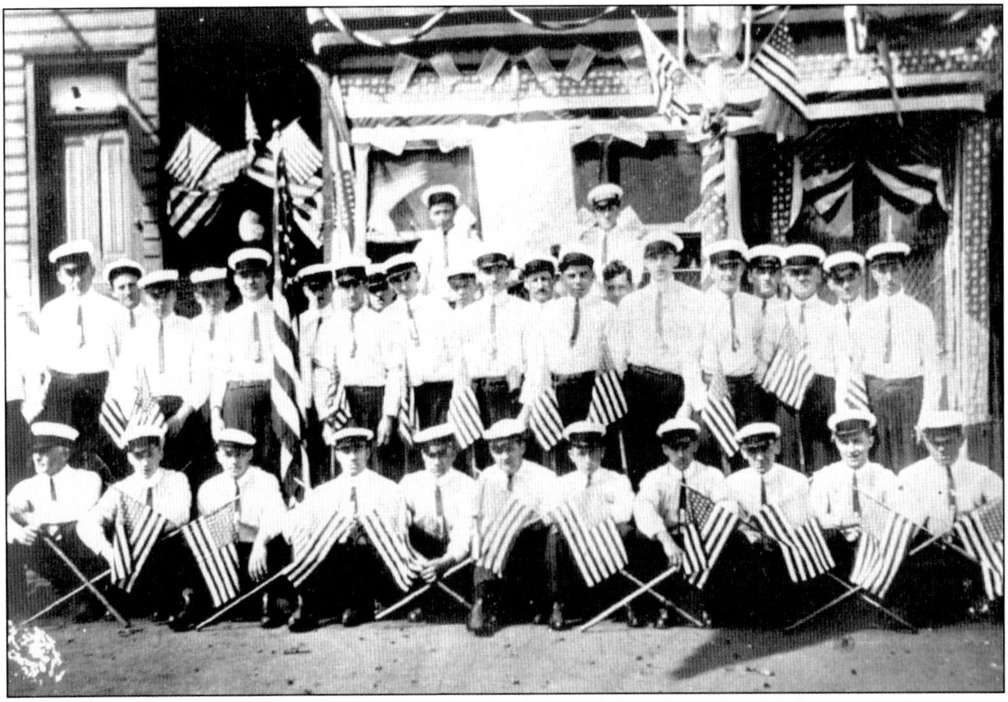

Members of the Mayflower Club are pictured in front of their Fourth of July parade float.

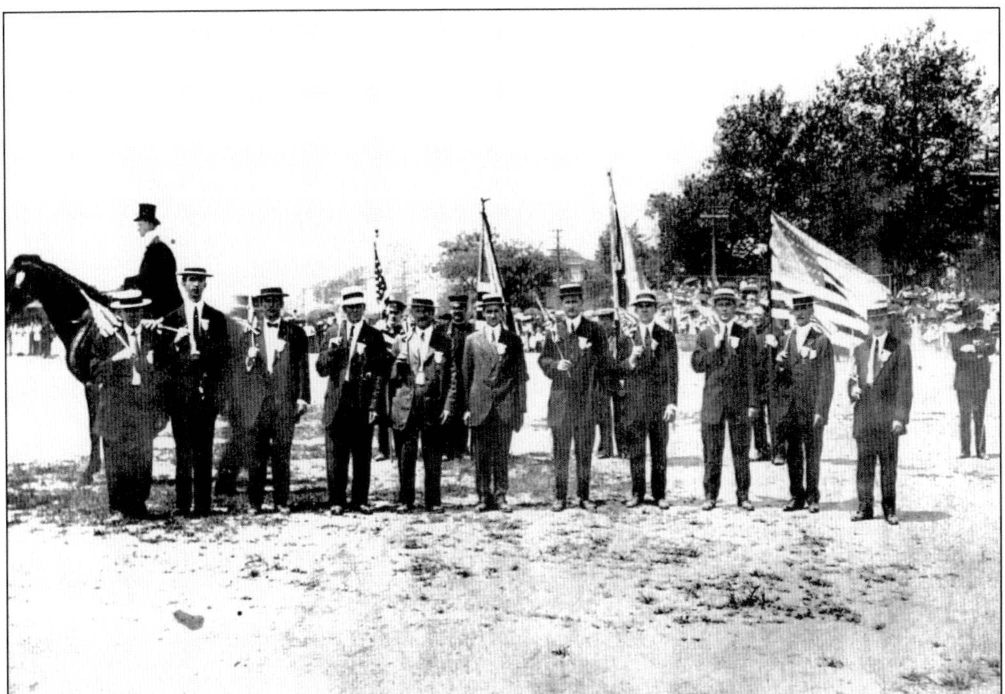

Citizens gather at the Bridesburg Park for a Fourth of July parade c. 1917.

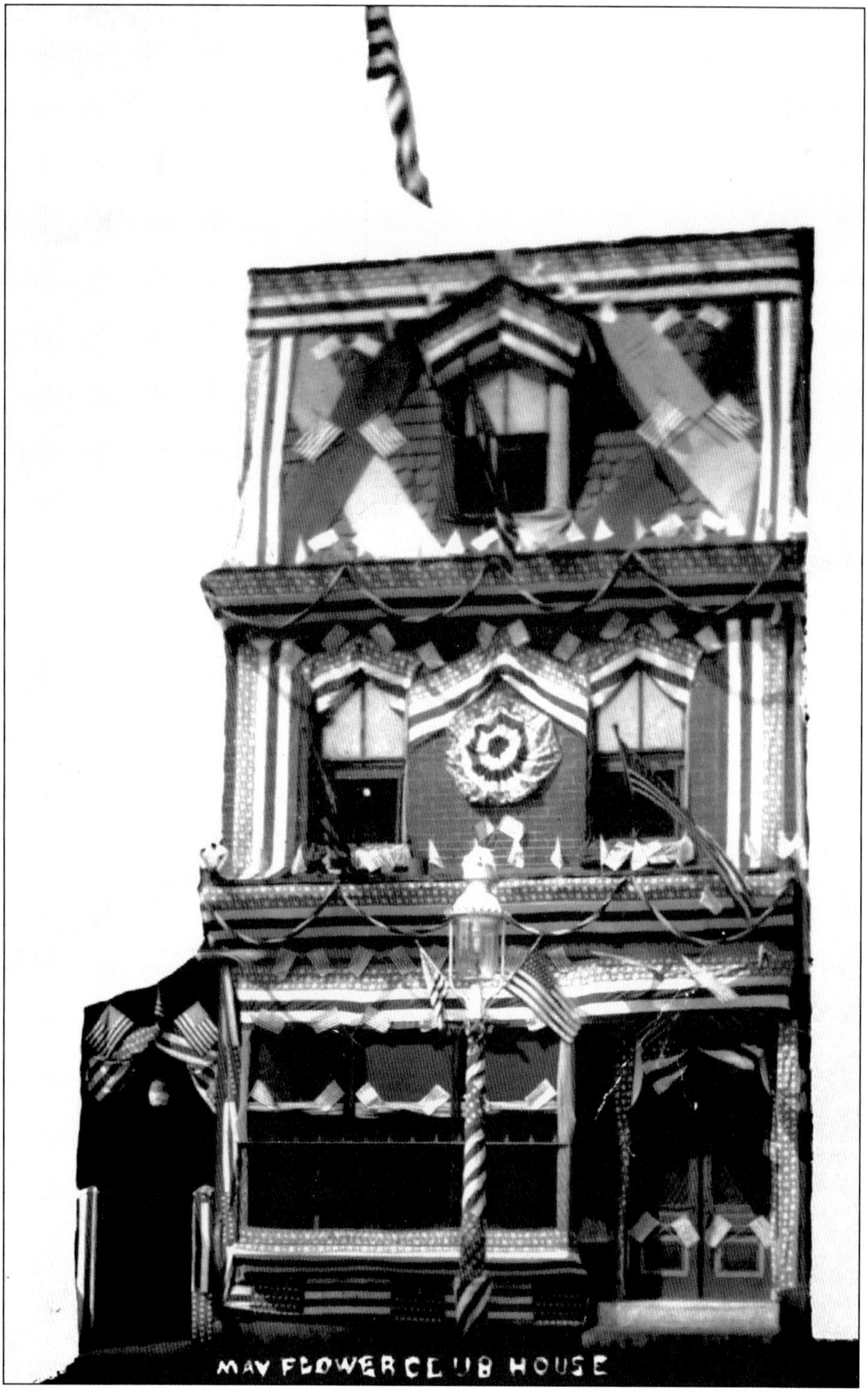

The original home of the Mayflower Club on Bridge Street is decorated for the Fourth of July *c.* 1917.

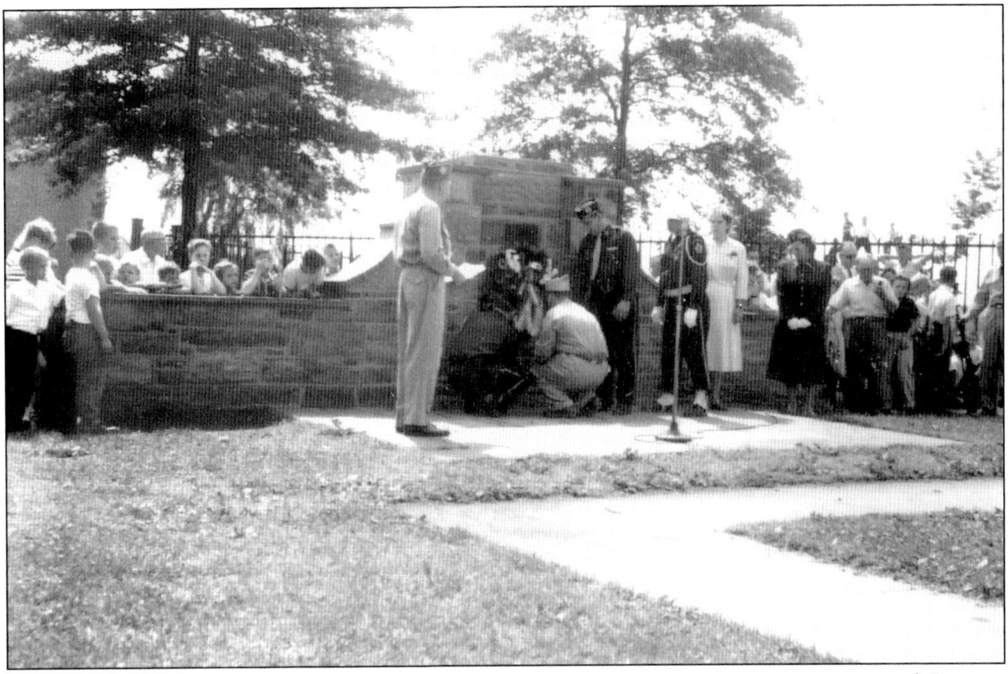

A wreath is placed at the All Wars Memorial at Bridesburg Park on a 1950s Memorial Day.

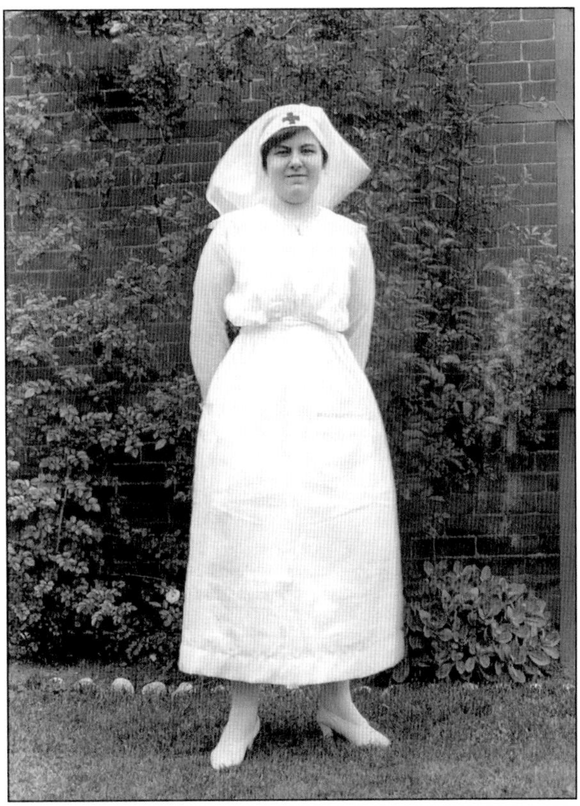

Elaine Conley served her country as a nurse during World War I.

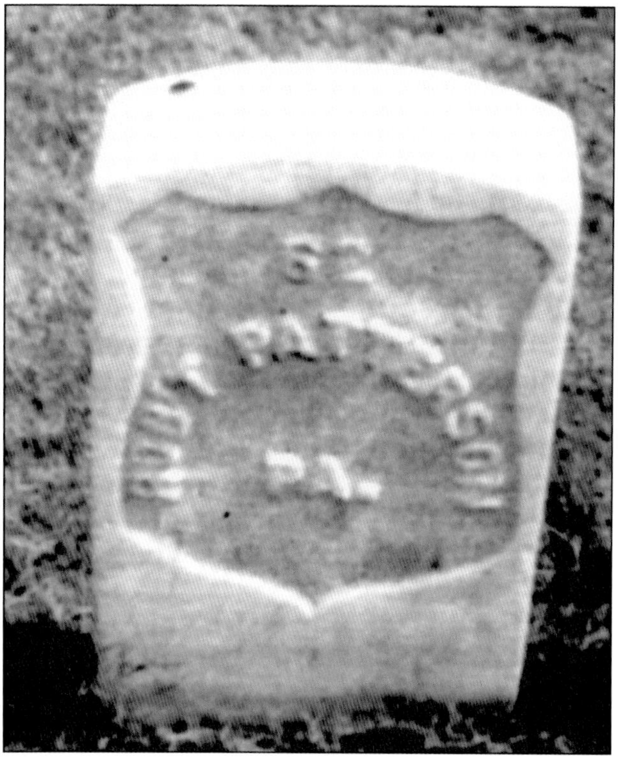

Pvt. Robert Patterson, one of the boys from the Irving School, enlisted in the Union army at age 15. Wounded at Bull Run and captured in Virginia, he was eventually taken to Andersonville Prison, where he died and was buried in 1864. This is his grave marker.

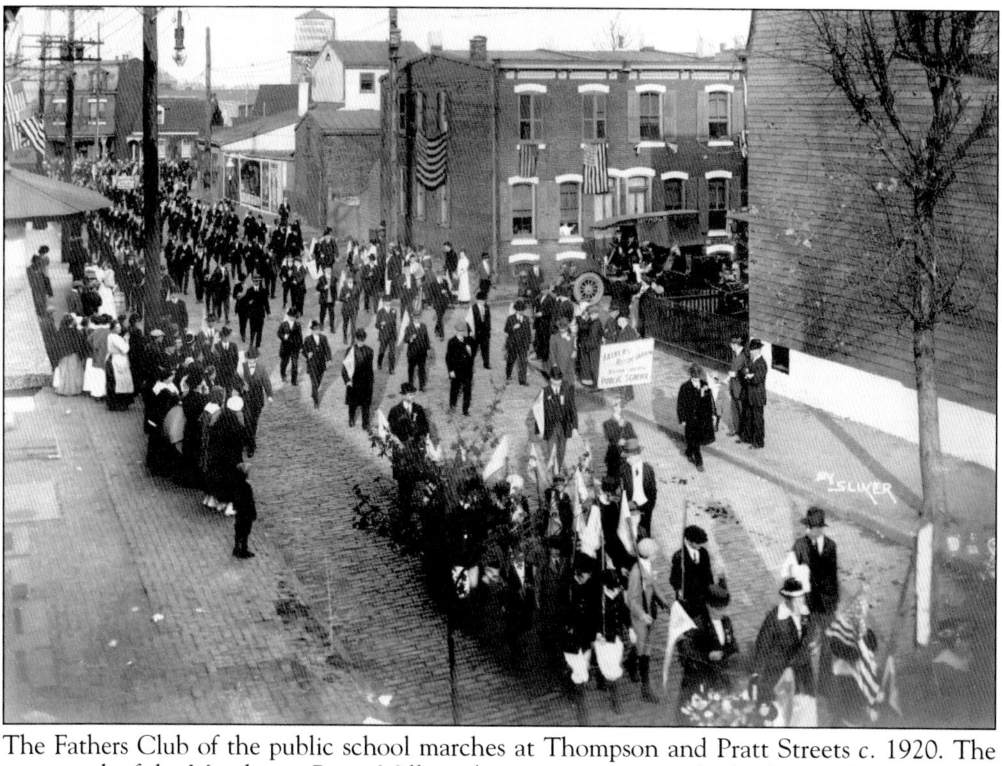

The Fathers Club of the public school marches at Thompson and Pratt Streets c. 1920. The water tank of the Morehouse Paper Mill can be seen towering in the background.

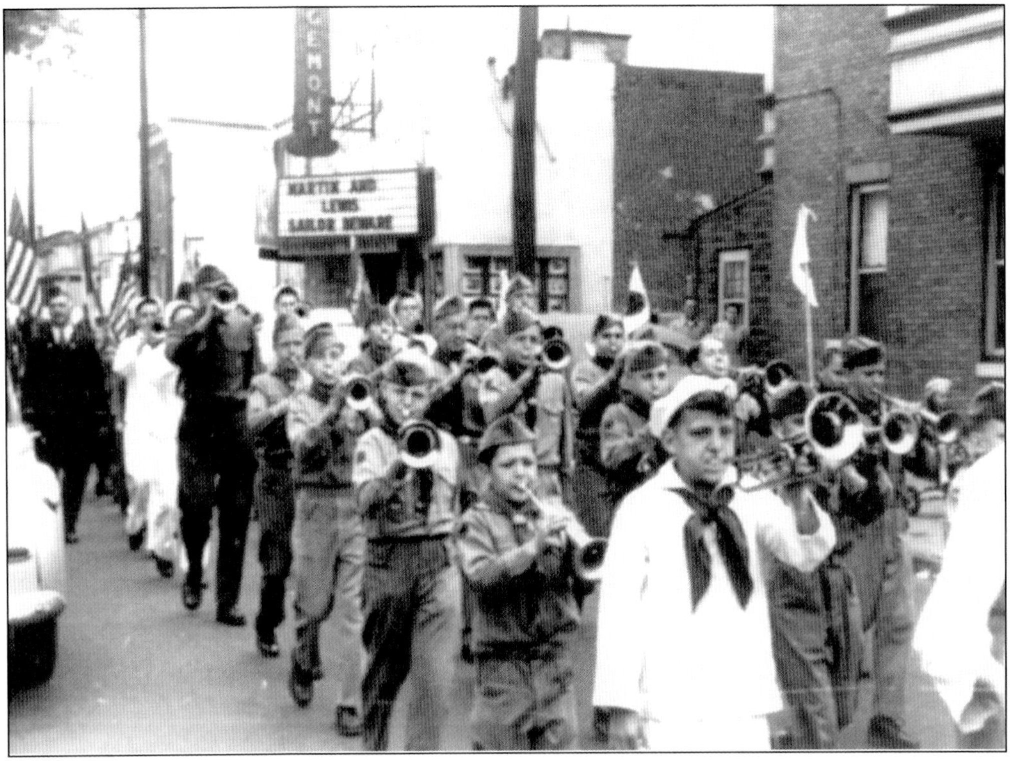

Boy Scouts and Sea Scouts march down Edgemont, approaching Orthodox Street, on Memorial Day. The Edgemont Theater marquee lists Dean Martin and Jerry Lewis in the film *Sailor Beware*.

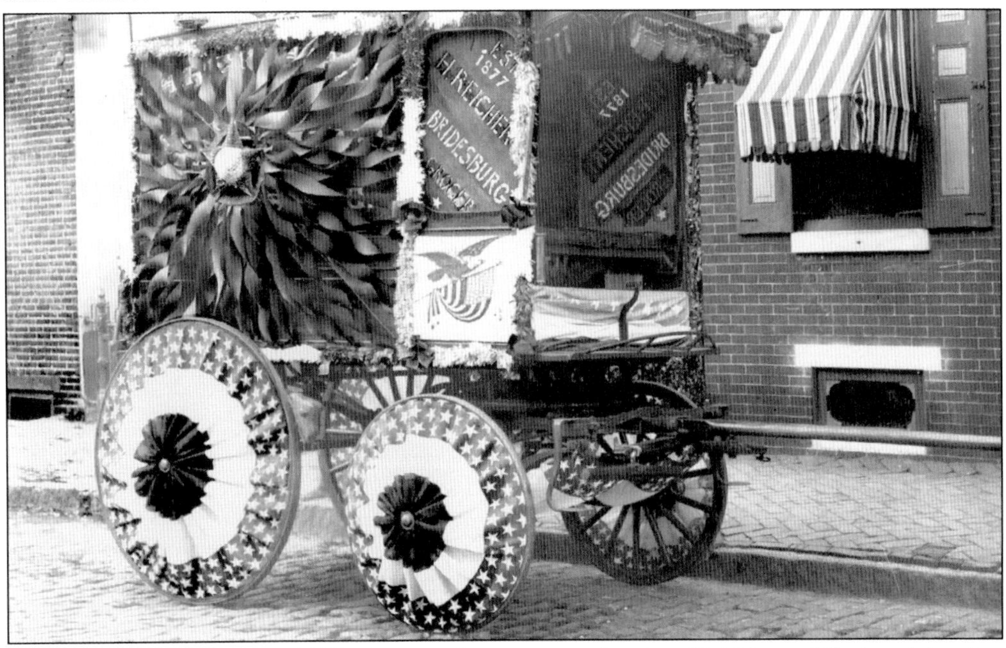

Reichert's, established in 1877, decorated its wagon for the Old Home Week celebration in 1909.

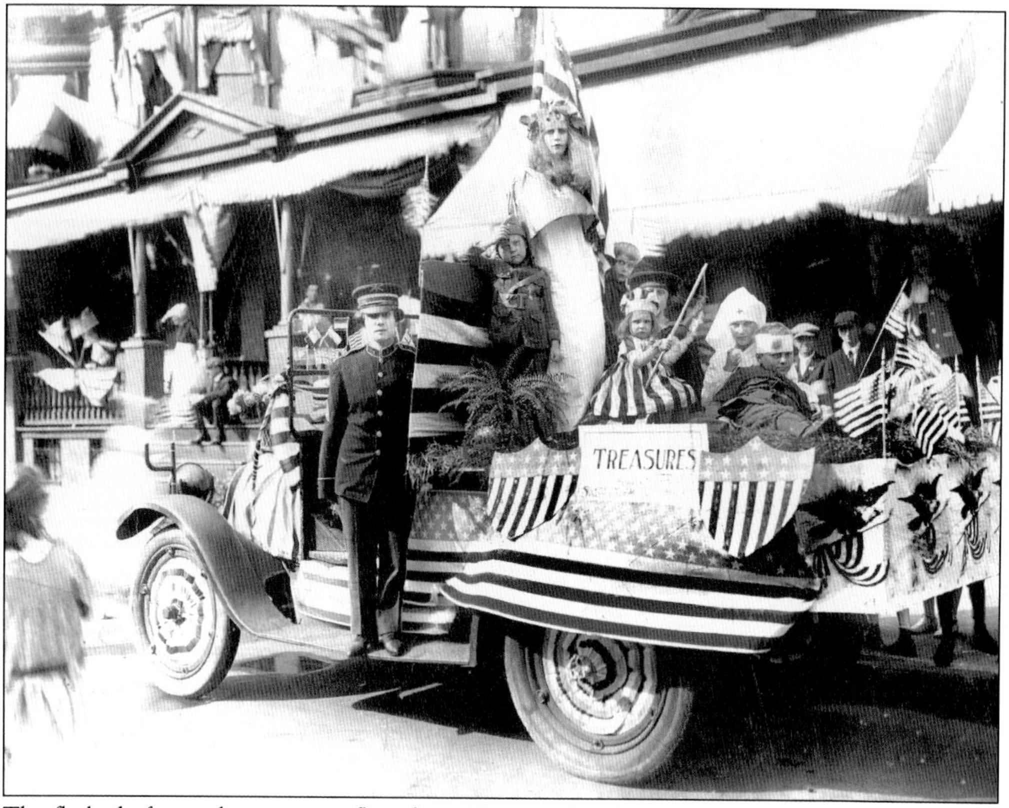

The flatbed of a truck serves as a float for a 1918 war bond rally on Orthodox Street.

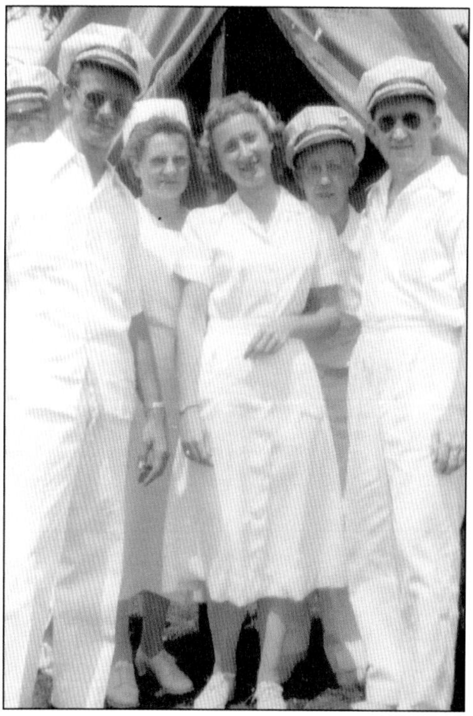

Pictured here in the 1950s are members of the Bridesburg Ambulance Corps, part of the Bridesburg Civic Association.

A rally for Associated Relief Through the Bridesburg Churches is viewed from the Van Dusen property on Richmond Street, facing the Bridesburg School, in the 1930s.

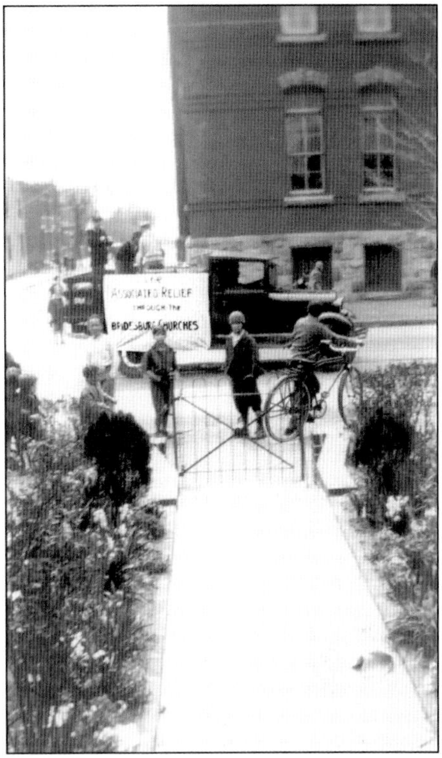

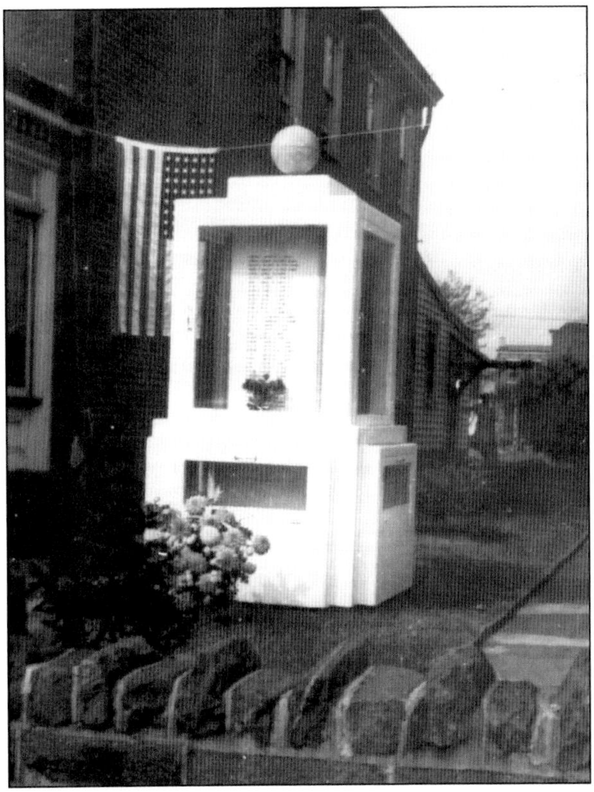

This World War II honor roll, erected by Edward R. Franecke, was located at 4482 Richmond Street and, unfortunately, no longer exists. The Bridesburg Historical Society maintains the information on its All Wars Memorial.

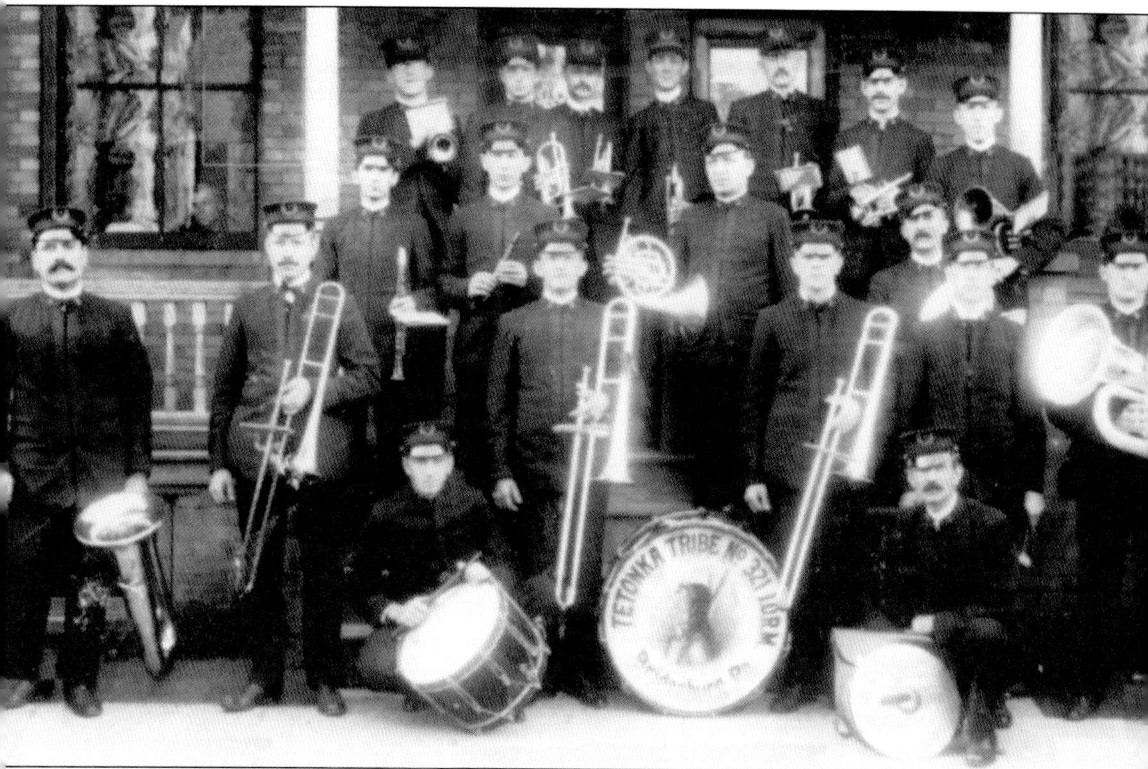

The marching band of Tetonka Tribe 321 of the International Order of Redmen is shown here in the early 20th century. This group met in Tetonka Hall on Haworth Street, once the Washington Irving School and now the home of the Trilby String Band.

Six

Religion and Education

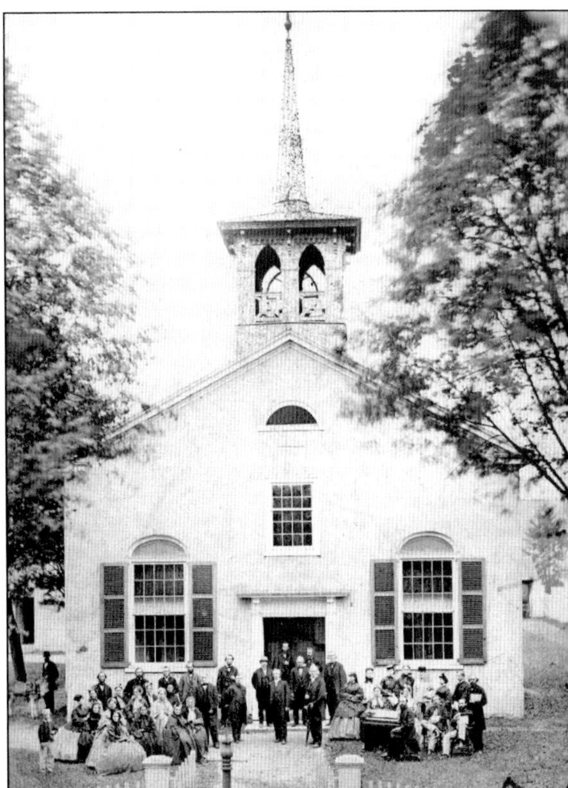

The Bridesburg Presbyterian Church congregation gathers outside the church in 1862.

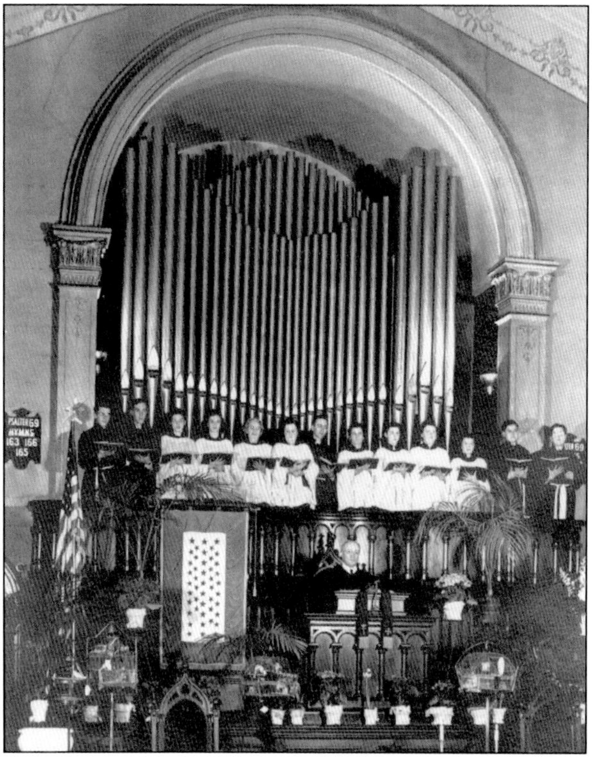

Members of the Presbyterian choir raise their voices at the altar to celebrate Easter Sunday in 1943.

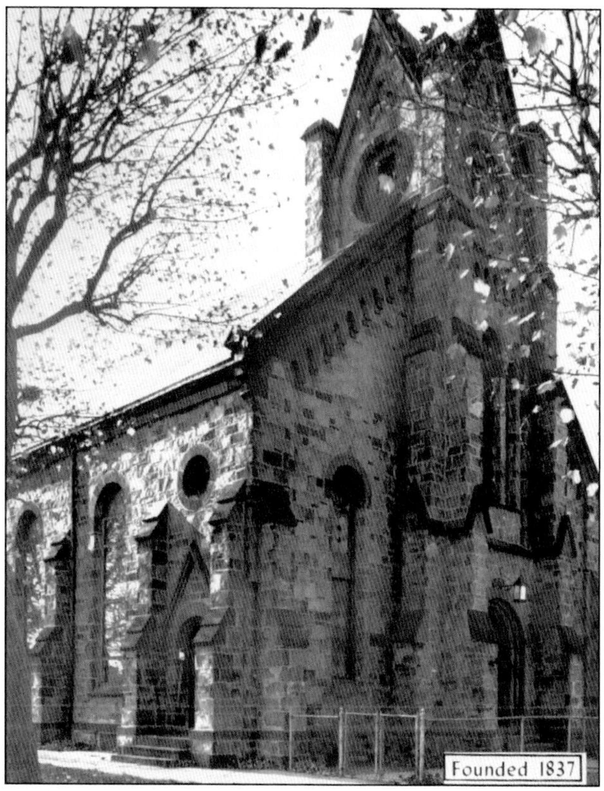

This photograph was taken in 1997 to mark the 150th anniversary of the founding of the Bridesburg Presbyterian Church.

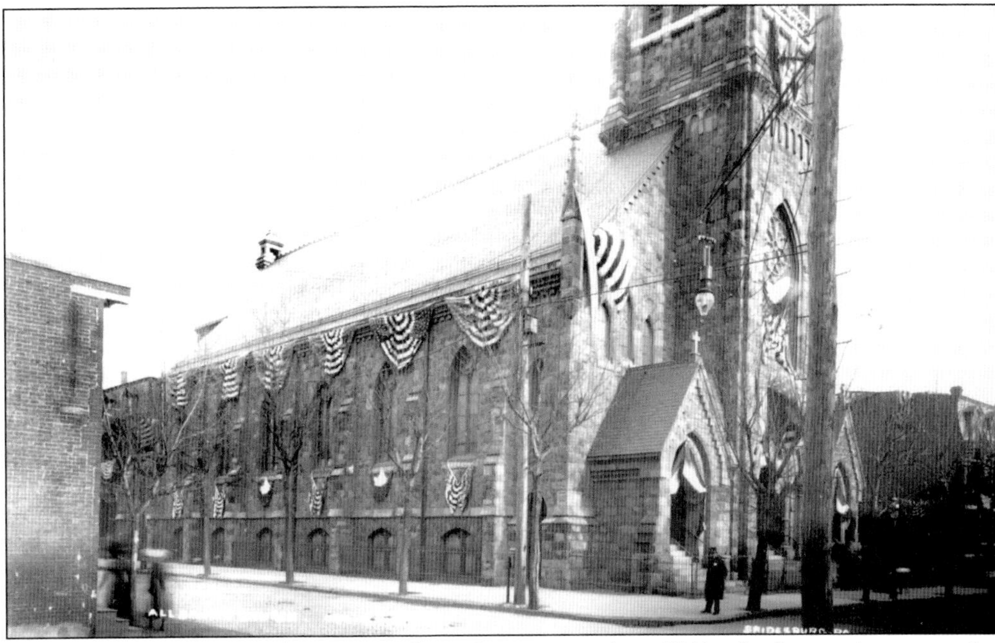

All Saints Catholic Church was started as a German parish in 1861, after having been served as a mission by the Redemptorist Fathers for 13 years. The original church building, now known as Marian Hall, still stands on Edgemont Street.

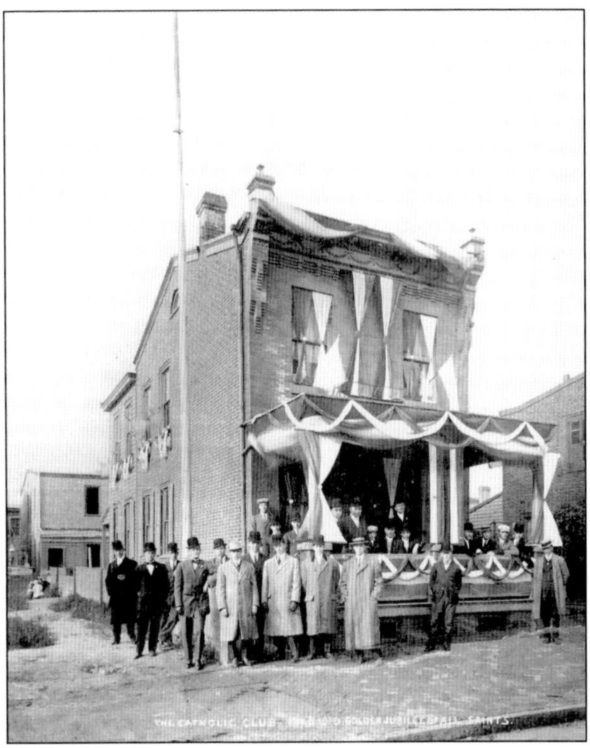

Religious societies and social clubs are a part of every church. In 1910, members of All Saints Catholic Club pose in front of their clubhouse. The building is gaily festooned for a special occasion.

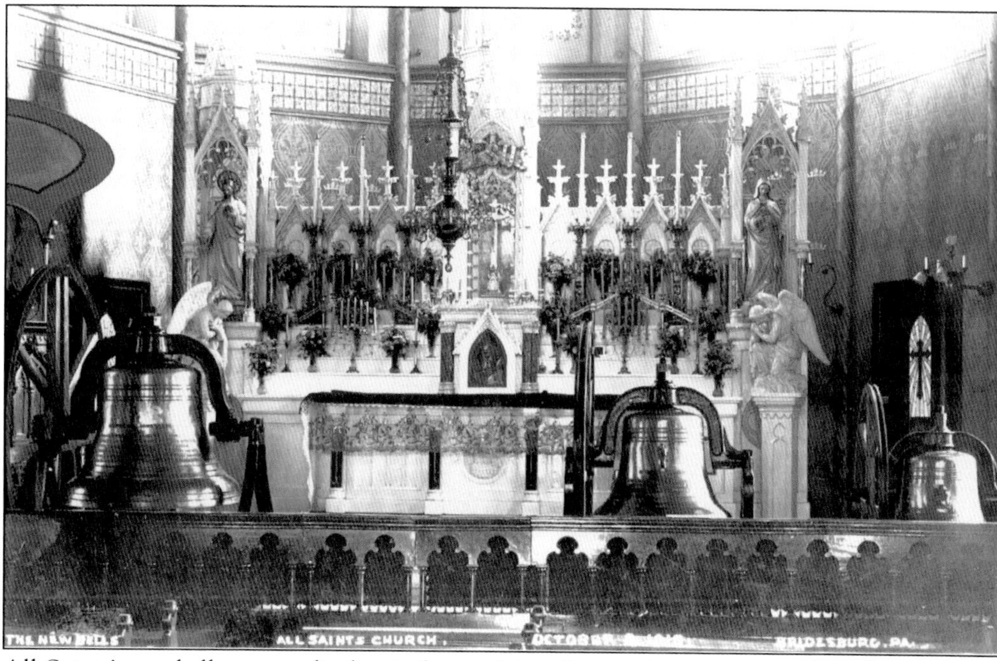

All Saints' new bells are on display in front of the altar in the sanctuary. This photograph is dated October 2, 1910. The raised pulpit with its soundboard, the elaborate altar trim and rail, as well as the angels kneeling in adoration, were replaced in later years.

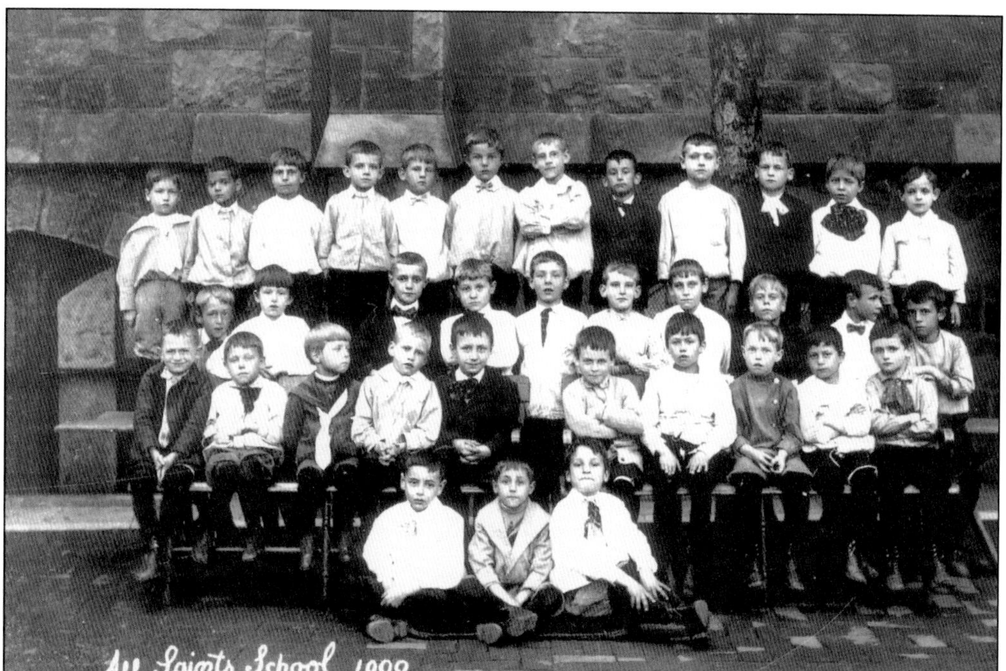

Schoolboys from All Saints pose by the church for a class photograph in 1909. Classes were held in the convent building on Thompson Street, which was the original parish school. School was taught by the Sisters of St. Francis.

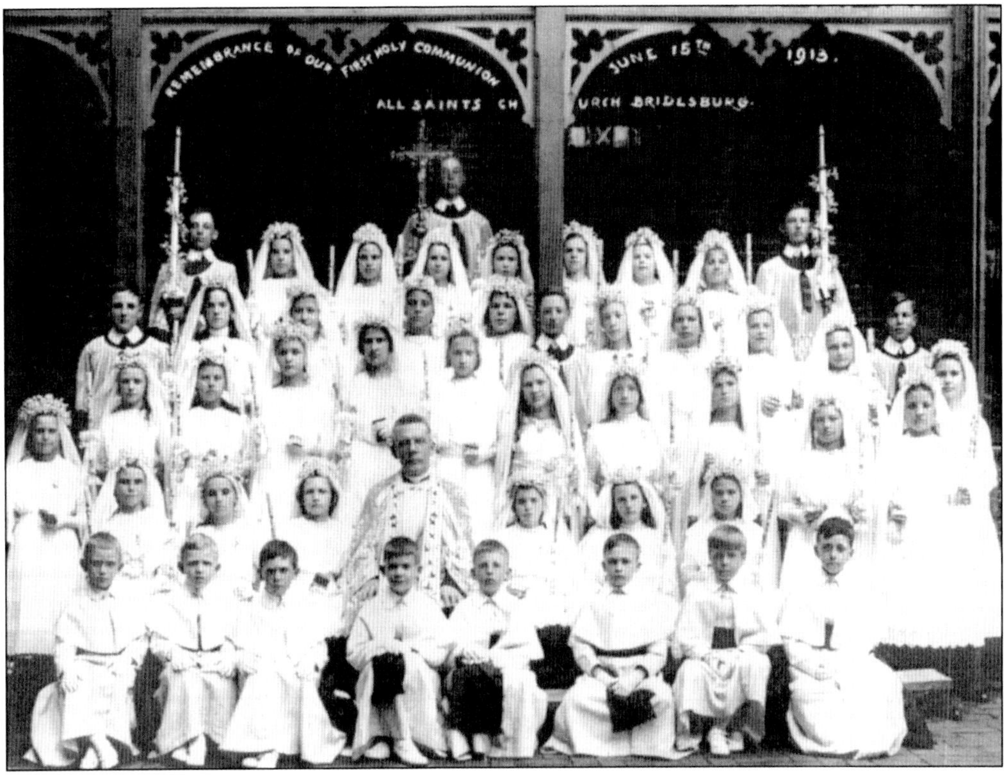

The 1913 first holy communion class of the All Saints school stands with the altar boys and the pastor, Rev. Ernest Deham, alongside the convent. Note the elaborate gingerbread work adorning the side porch.

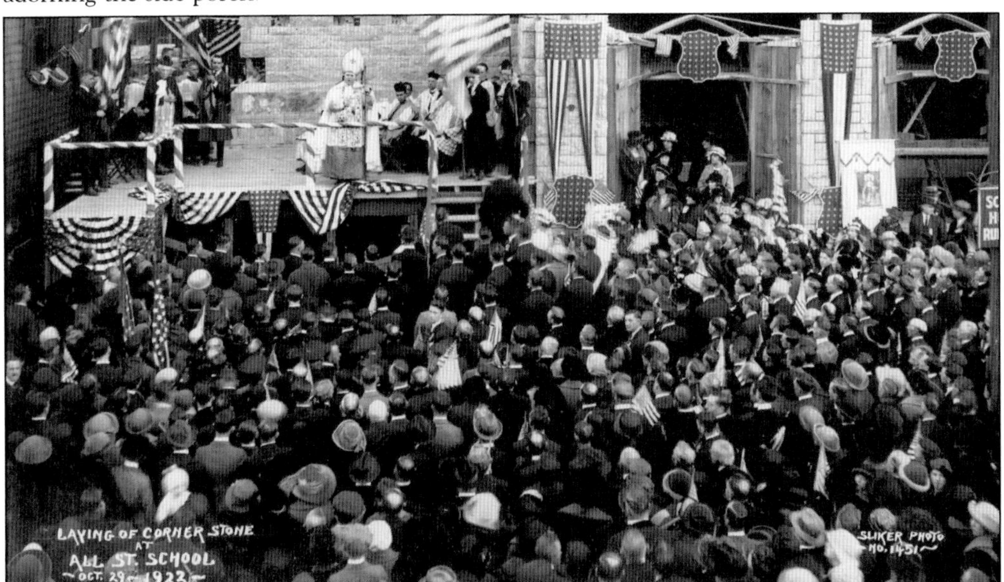

On October 23, 1922, Cardinal Dougherty was present for the laying of the cornerstone of the new school building for All Saints Church, on Thompson Street next to the convent. Parishioners gathered to celebrate this momentous occasion.

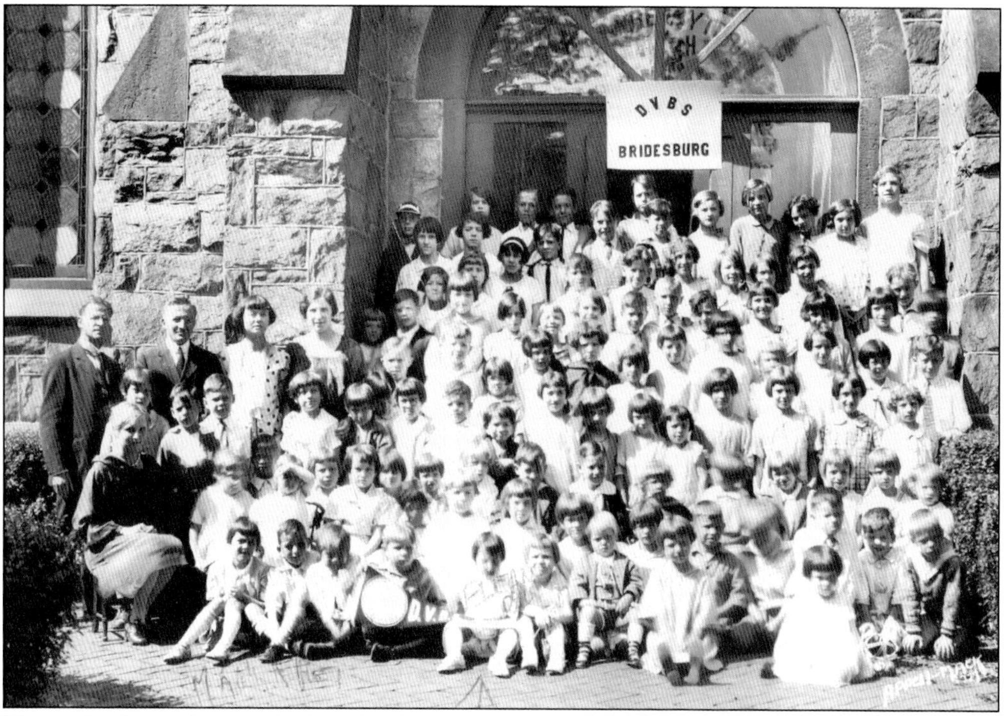

These children, along with their Bible study teachers, stand outside the Presbyterian church in 1927.

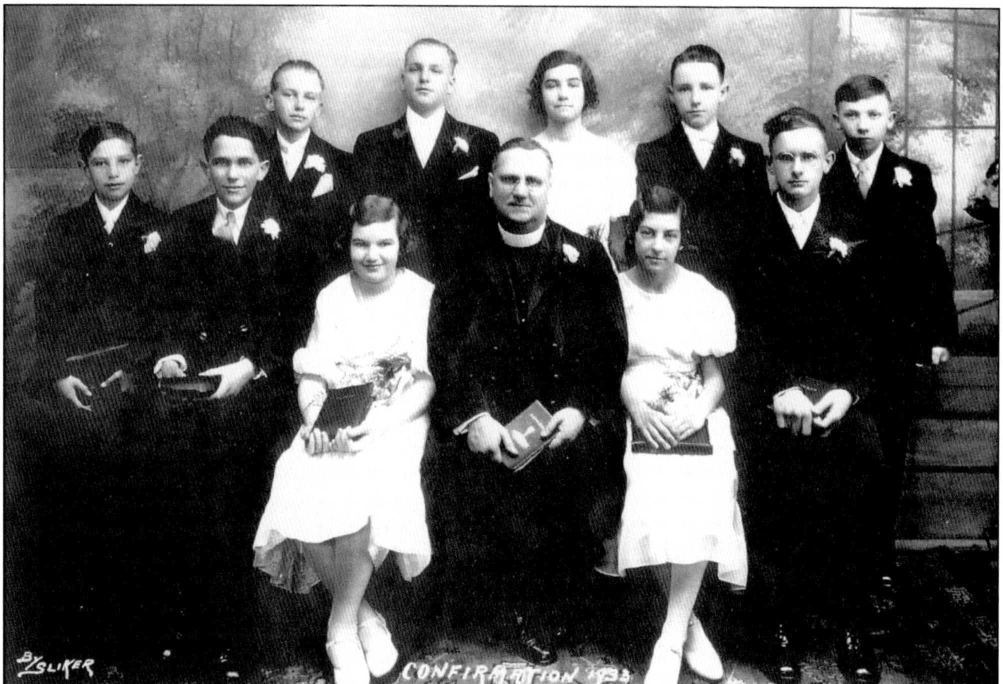

Confirmation is an important milestone in religious life. Seen here with the pastor is a group of young people who were confirmed in the Emanuel German Reformed Church in 1933.

The German Protestant population of Bridesburg formed the Emanuel German Reformed Church, entering the synod in 1862. By 1864, they had dedicated their new church building, located on Filmore Street near Almond. This church is now known as the Emanuel Evangelical United Church of Christ.

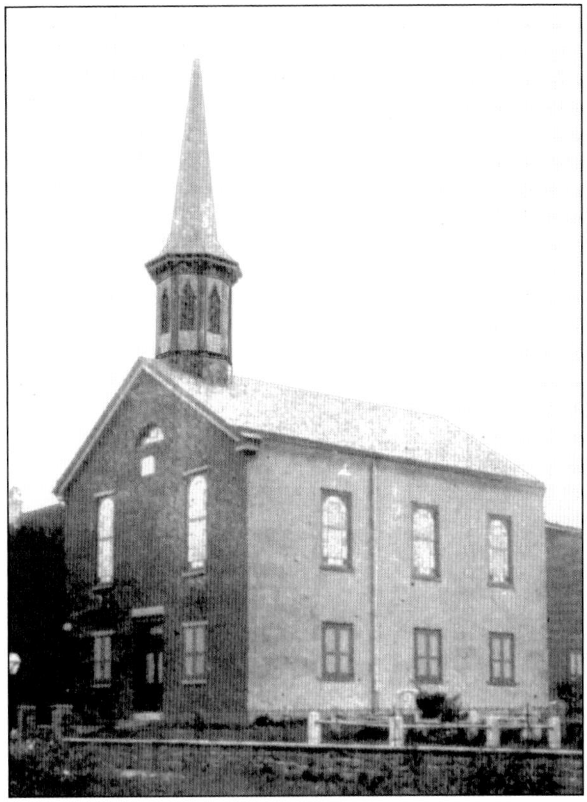

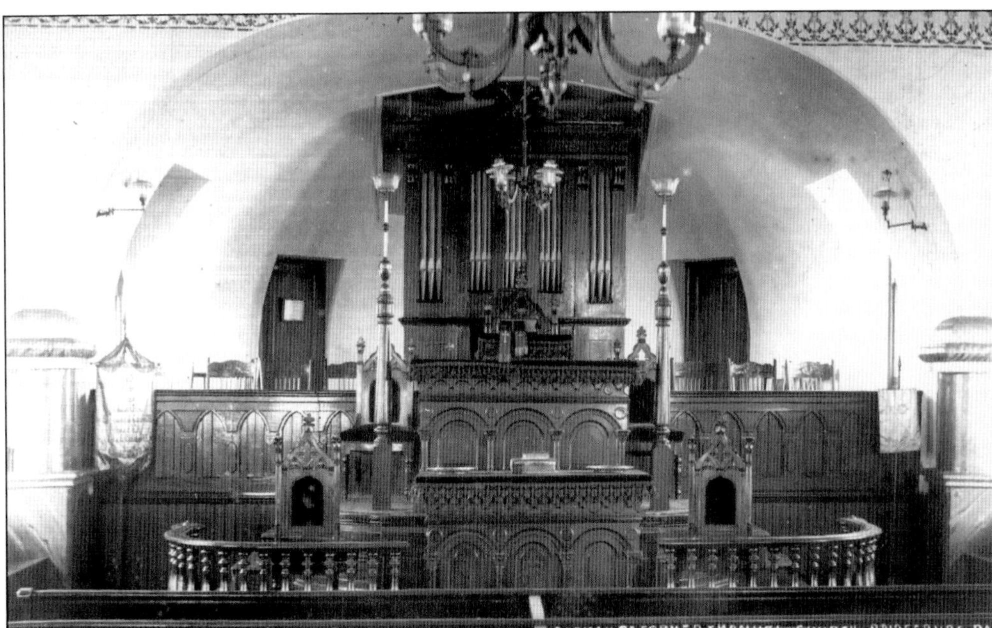

This detailed photograph of the altar of the German Reformed Emanuel Church highlights the beautiful woodwork and lighting fixtures.

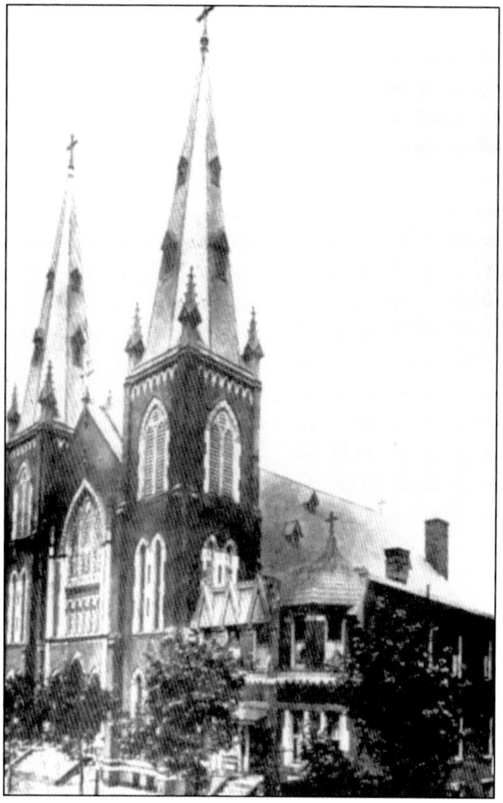

In 1892, the Polish families of Bridesburg and Frankford met to organize a Roman Catholic church to serve the community. By 1893, the new parish of St. John Cantius had erected its first church. The building, which now serves as a chapel, stands to the left of the twin-spired church in this photograph. The beautiful twin-spired structure was built in 1899 to serve the growing population.

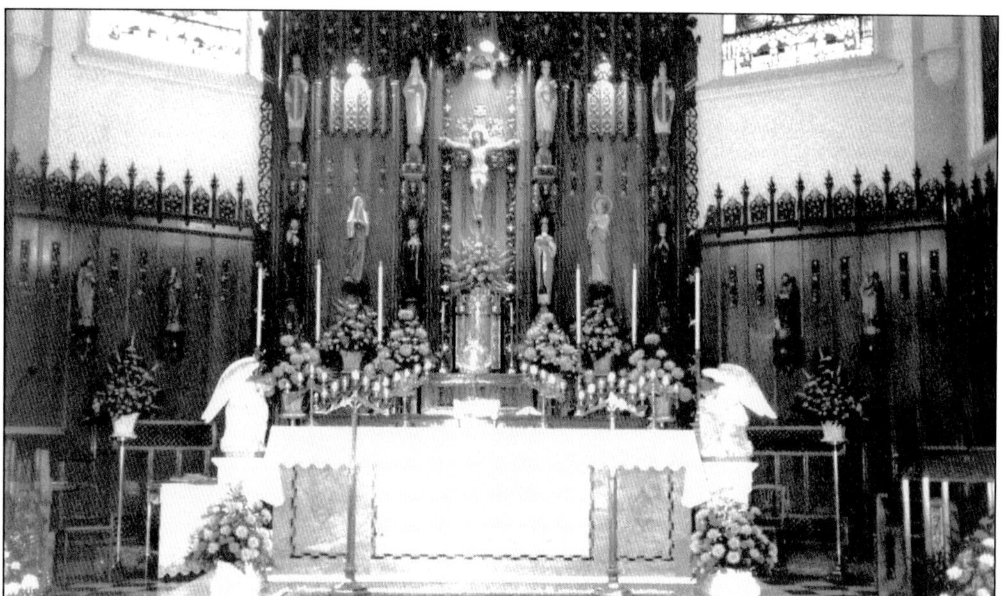

The sanctuary of St. John Cantius holds statues of many saints of the church, including patron saints of Poland. The main altar is reminiscent of many of the grand altars of European churches.

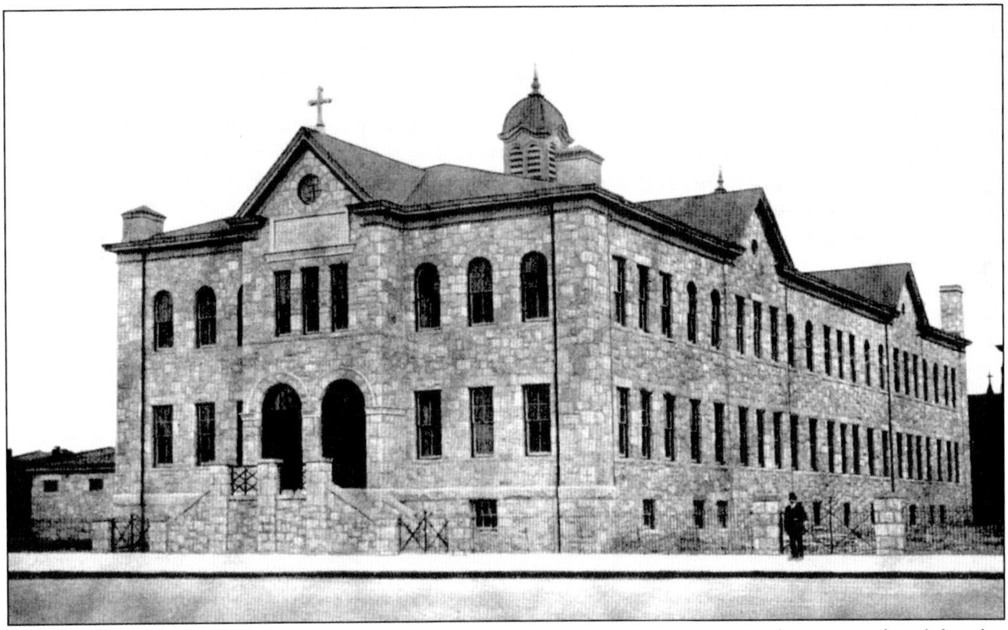

This large, impressive building was erected on Almond Street in 1907 to house a school for the children of the St. John Cantius parish. The Sisters of the Holy Family of Nazareth undertook the task of educating their charges in religious studies and the Polish language, in addition to the standard curriculum.

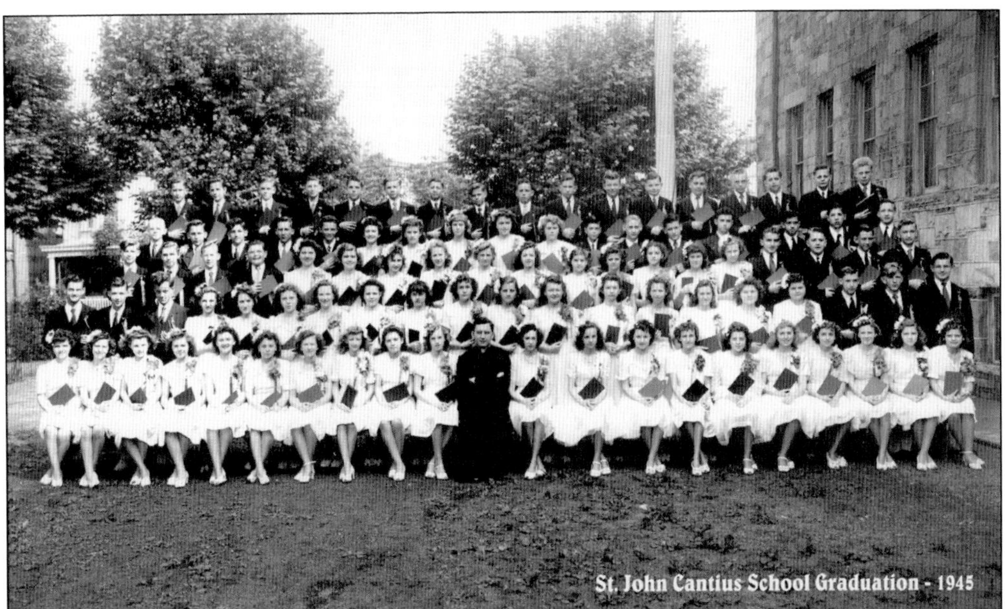

The graduating class of 1945 bears witness to the large number of students educated at St. John Cantius.

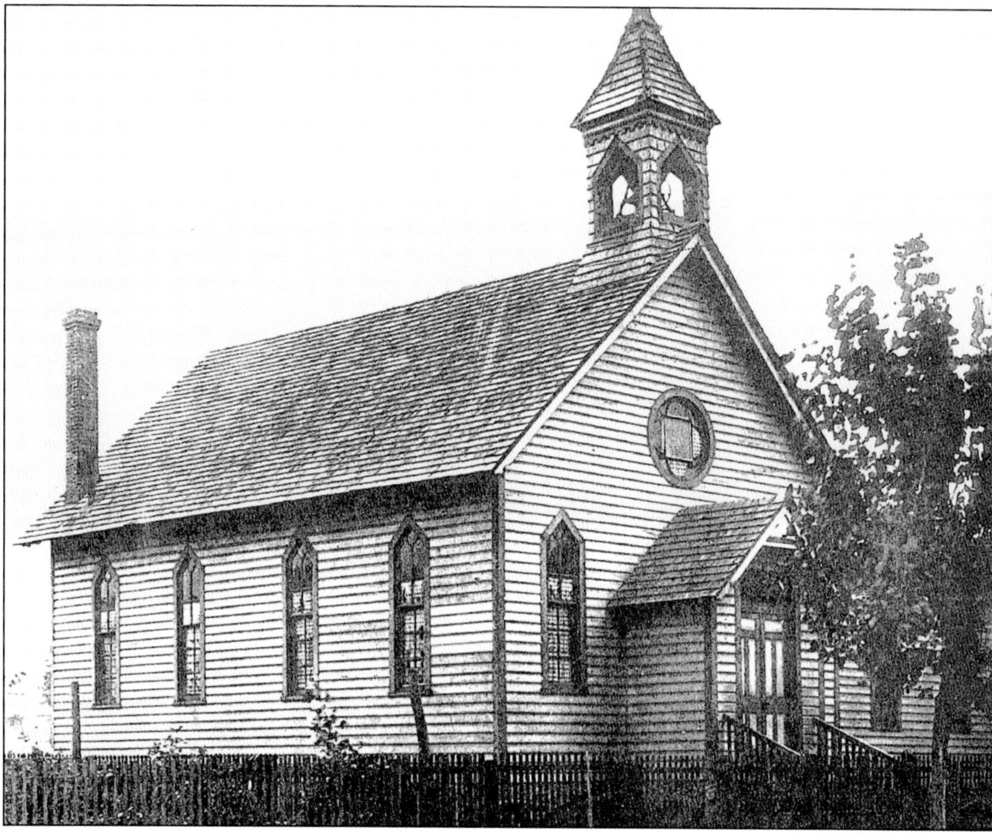

In 1899, a Baptist congregation began meetings in Holly Hall, under the leadership of William Moritz. The present church building, on Lefevre Street near Salmon, was dedicated in 1901.

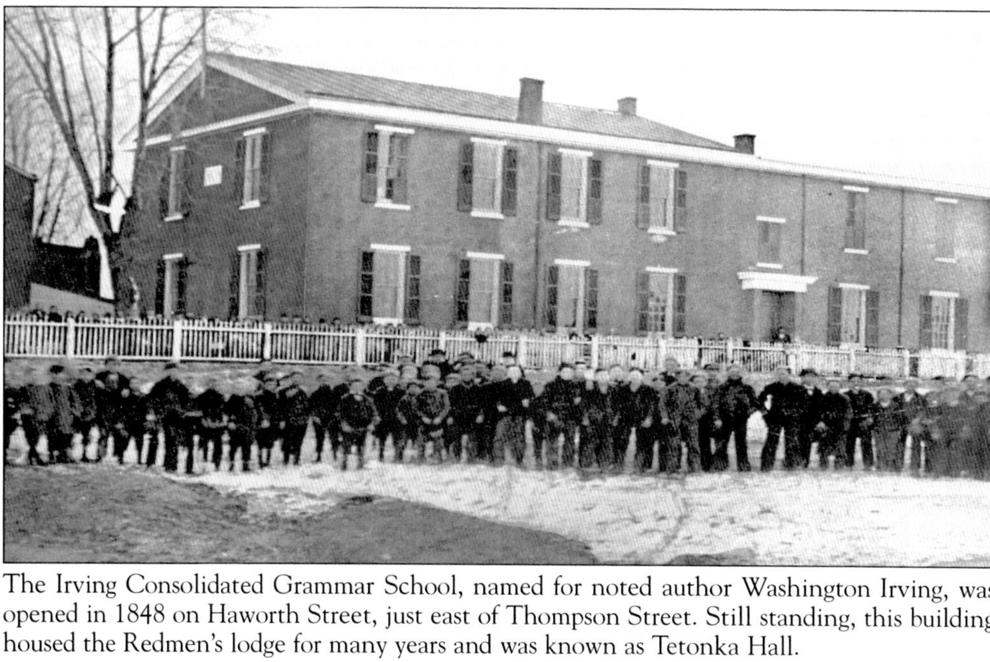

The Irving Consolidated Grammar School, named for noted author Washington Irving, was opened in 1848 on Haworth Street, just east of Thompson Street. Still standing, this building housed the Redmen's lodge for many years and was known as Tetonka Hall.

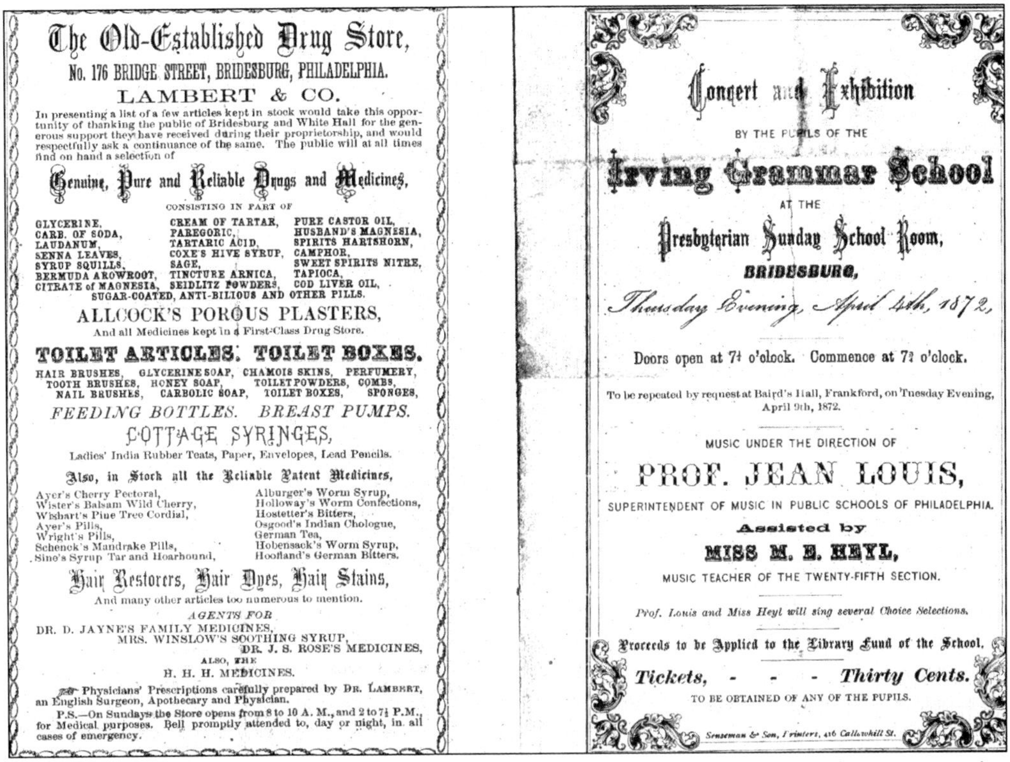

The Old-Established Drug Store,

No. 176 BRIDGE STREET, BRIDESBURG, PHILADELPHIA.

LAMBERT & CO.

In presenting a list of a few articles kept in stock would take this opportunity of thanking the public of Bridesburg and White Hall for the generous support they have received during their proprietorship, and would respectfully ask a continuance of the same. The public will at all times find on hand a selection of

Genuine, Pure and Reliable Drugs and Medicines,

CONSISTING IN PART OF

GLYCERINE, CARB. OF SODA, LAUDANUM, SENNA LEAVES, SYRUP SQUILLS, BERMUDA AROWROOT, CITRATE of MAGNESIA, CREAM OF TARTAR, PAREGORIC, TARTARIC ACID, COXE'S HIVE SYRUP, SAGE, TINCTURE ARNICA, SEIDLITZ POWDERS, PURE CASTOR OIL, HUSBAND'S MAGNESIA, SPIRITS HARTSHORN, CAMPHOR, SWEET SPIRITS NITRE, TAPIOCA, COD LIVER OIL,

SUGAR-COATED, ANTI-BILIOUS AND OTHER PILLS.

ALLCOCK'S POROUS PLASTERS,

And all Medicines kept in a First-Class Drug Store.

TOILET ARTICLES. TOILET BOXES.

HAIR BRUSHES, GLYCERINE SOAP, CHAMOIS SKINS, PERFUMERY, TOOTH BRUSHES, HONEY SOAP, TOILET POWDERS, COMBS, NAIL BRUSHES, CARBOLIC SOAP, TOILET BOXES, SPONGES,

FEEDING BOTTLES. BREAST PUMPS.

COTTAGE SYRINGES,

Ladies' India Rubber Teats, Paper, Envelopes, Lead Pencils.

Also, in Stock all the Reliable Patent Medicines,

Ayer's Cherry Pectoral, Wister's Balsam Wild Cherry, Wishart's Pine Tree Cordial, Ayer's Pills, Wright's Pills, Schenck's Mandrake Pills, Sine's Syrup Tar and Hoarhound, Alburger's Worm Syrup, Holloway's Worm Confections, Hostetter's Bitters, Osgood's Indian Chologue, German Tea, Hobensack's Worm Syrup, Hoofland's German Bitters.

Hair Restorers, Hair Dyes, Hair Stains,

And many other articles too numerous to mention.

AGENTS FOR

DR. D. JAYNE'S FAMILY MEDICINES,
MRS. WINSLOW'S SOOTHING SYRUP,
DR. J. S. ROSE'S MEDICINES,
ALSO, THE
H. H. H. MEDICINES.

☞ Physicians' Prescriptions carefully prepared by DR. LAMBERT, an English Surgeon, Apothecary and Physician.

P.S.—On Sundays the Store opens from 8 to 10 A. M., and 2 to 7½ P.M., for Medical purposes. Bell promptly attended to, day or night, in all cases of emergency.

Concert and Exhibition

BY THE PUPILS OF THE

Irving Grammar School

AT THE

Presbyterian Sunday School Room,

BRIDESBURG,

Thursday Evening, April 4th, 1872,

Doors open at 7¼ o'clock. Commence at 7¾ o'clock.

To be repeated by request at Baird's Hall, Frankford, on Tuesday Evening, April 9th, 1872.

MUSIC UNDER THE DIRECTION OF

PROF. JEAN LOUIS,

SUPERINTENDENT OF MUSIC IN PUBLIC SCHOOLS OF PHILADELPHIA.

Assisted by

MISS M. E. HEYL,

MUSIC TEACHER OF THE TWENTY-FIFTH SECTION.

Prof. Louis and Miss Heyl will sing several Choice Selections.

Proceeds to be Applied to the Library Fund of the School.

Tickets, - - - Thirty Cents.

TO BE OBTAINED OF ANY OF THE PUPILS.

Sensenman & Son, Printers, 416 Callowhill St.

In 1872, the Irving Grammar School held a concert and exhibition at the Presbyterian Sunday school room. This program notes that funds were being raised for the school library.

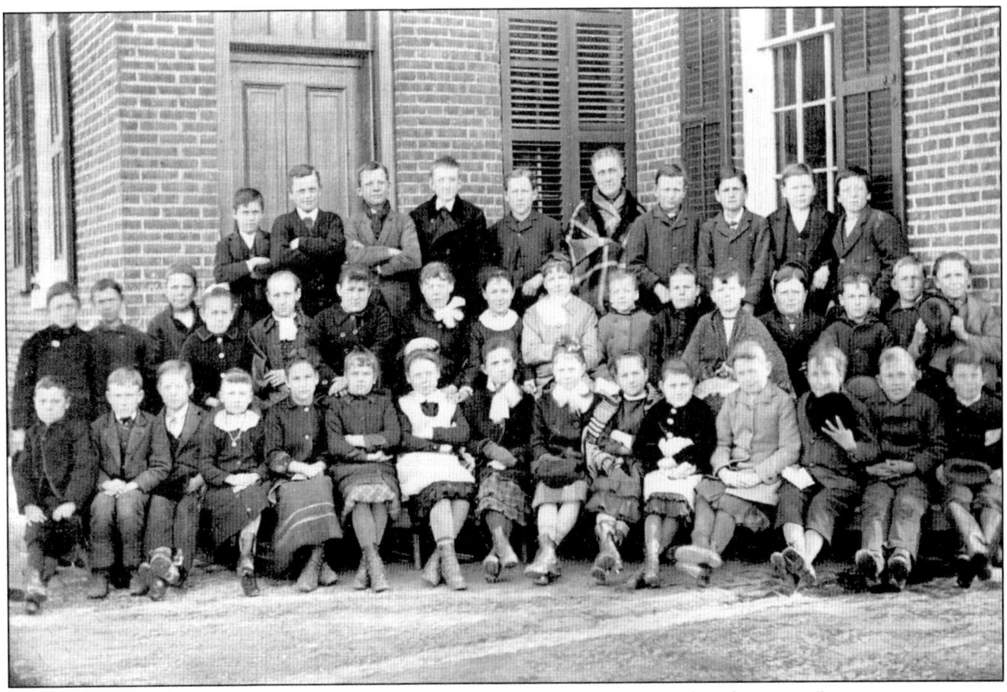

Students pose with their teacher outside the Irving Grammar School in 1885.

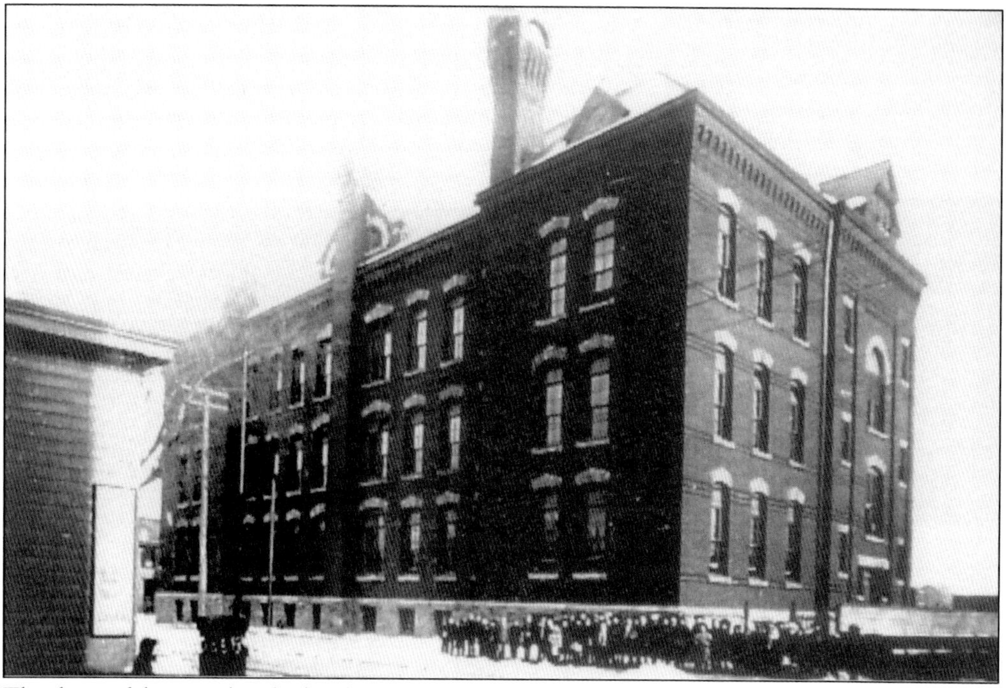

This beautiful example of school architecture of the period was opened in 1888 on the 4700 block of Richmond Street to house Bridesburg's public school students. Here, proud citizens of Bridesburg gather to celebrate this landmark occasion.

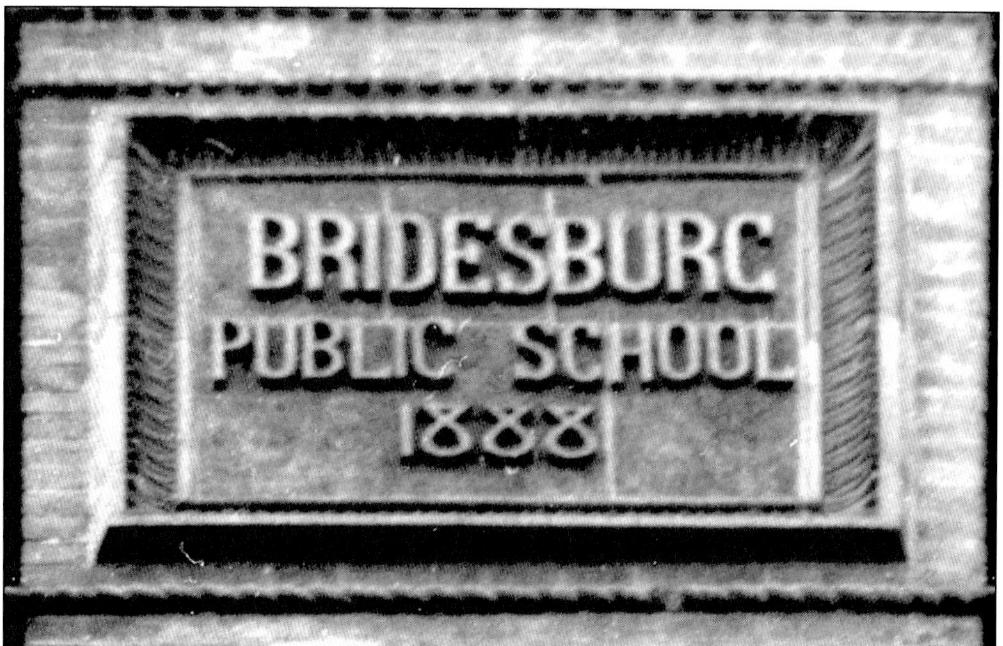

This stone marks the date of the building of the Bridesburg Public School on Richmond Street—1888. It also marks the date when the Irving School was closed and the student body moved to the new school.

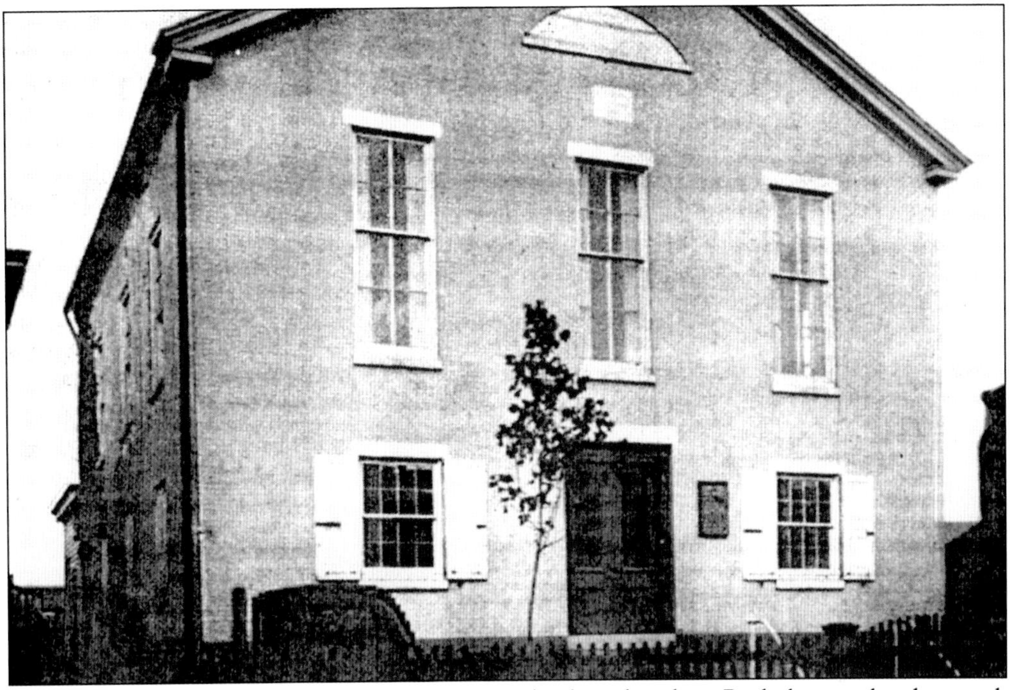

The Methodist Society, formalized in 1833, was the first church in Bridesburg to be chartered. Edwin Jenks, Alfred Jenks's brother, was among the founders. Services were held in the old town hall before the church was built in 1851. This photograph of the church was taken in 1910.

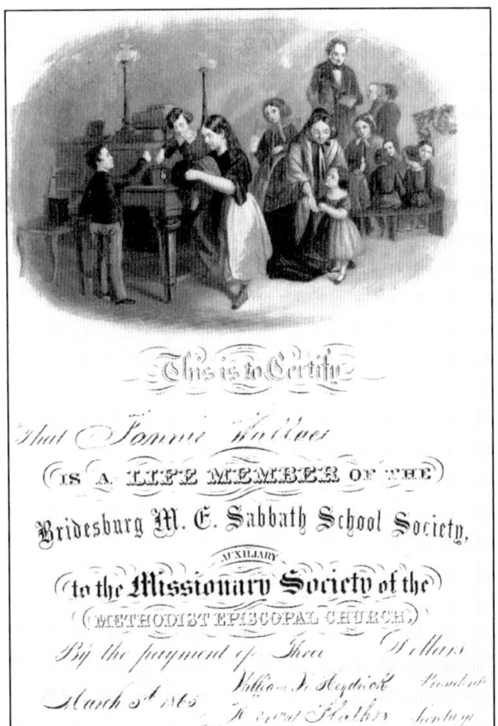

This is to Certify

That

is a LIFE MEMBER of the

Bridesburg M. E. Sabbath School Society,

AUXILIARY

to the Missionary Society of the

METHODIST EPISCOPAL CHURCH,

By the payment of Three Dollars

This beautifully illustrated certificate was issued to those attaining life membership in the Bridesburg Methodist Episcopal Sabbath School Society, auxiliary to the Missionary Society of the Methodist church.

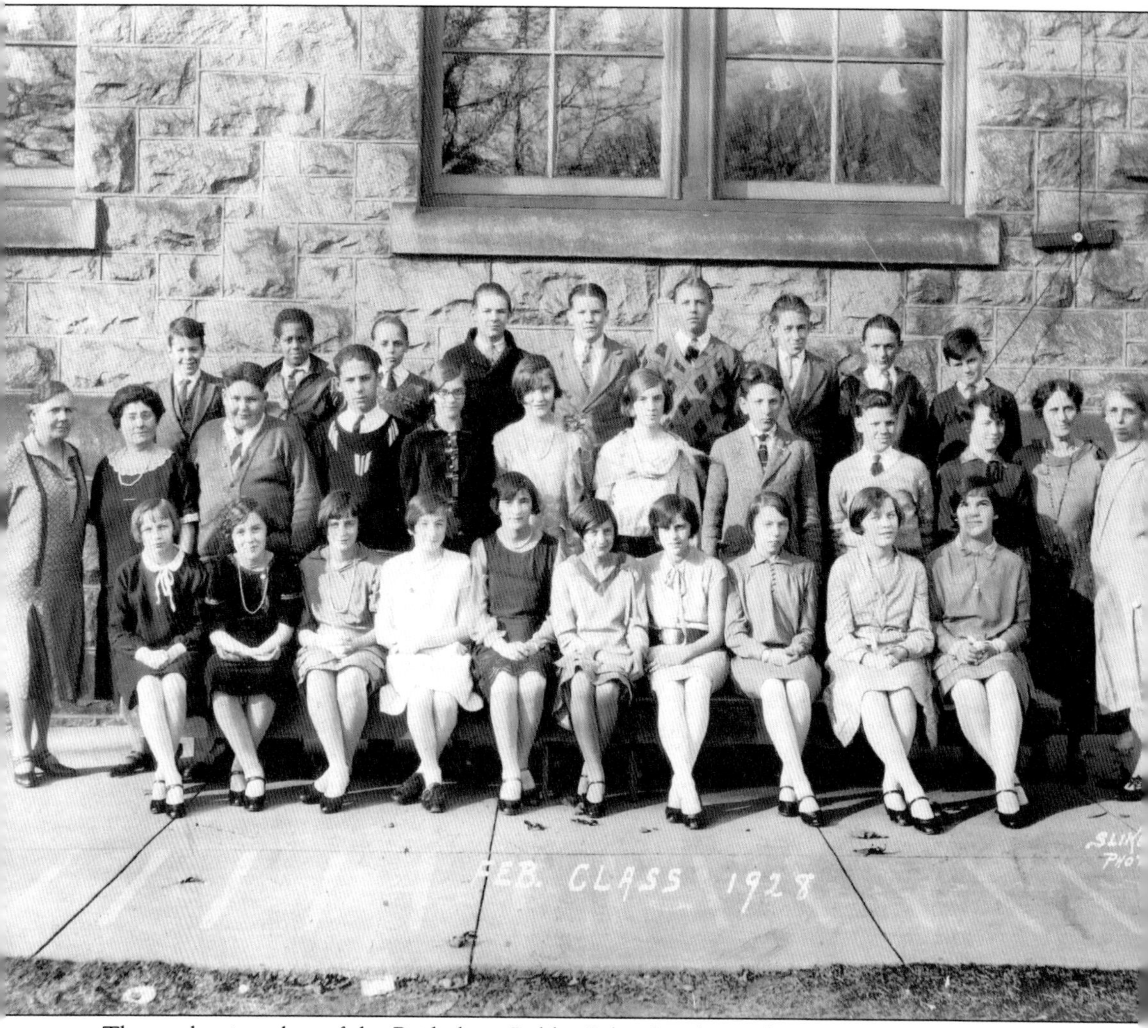

The graduating class of the Bridesburg Public School is shown here in February 1928.

Seven

THE 1909 BLIZZARD

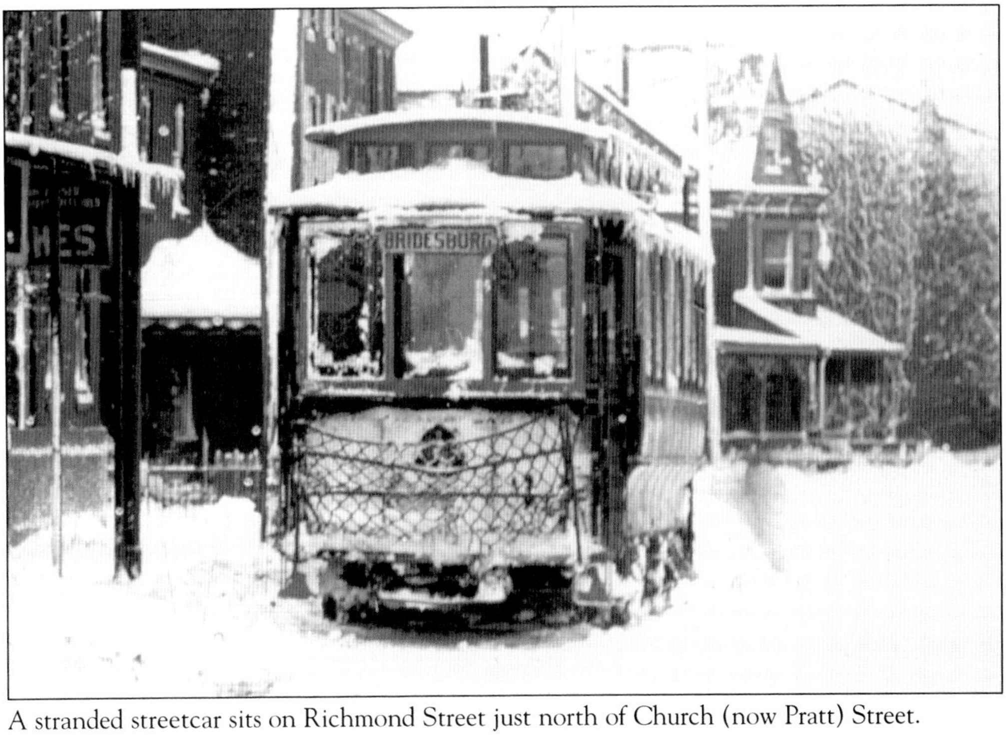

A stranded streetcar sits on Richmond Street just north of Church (now Pratt) Street.

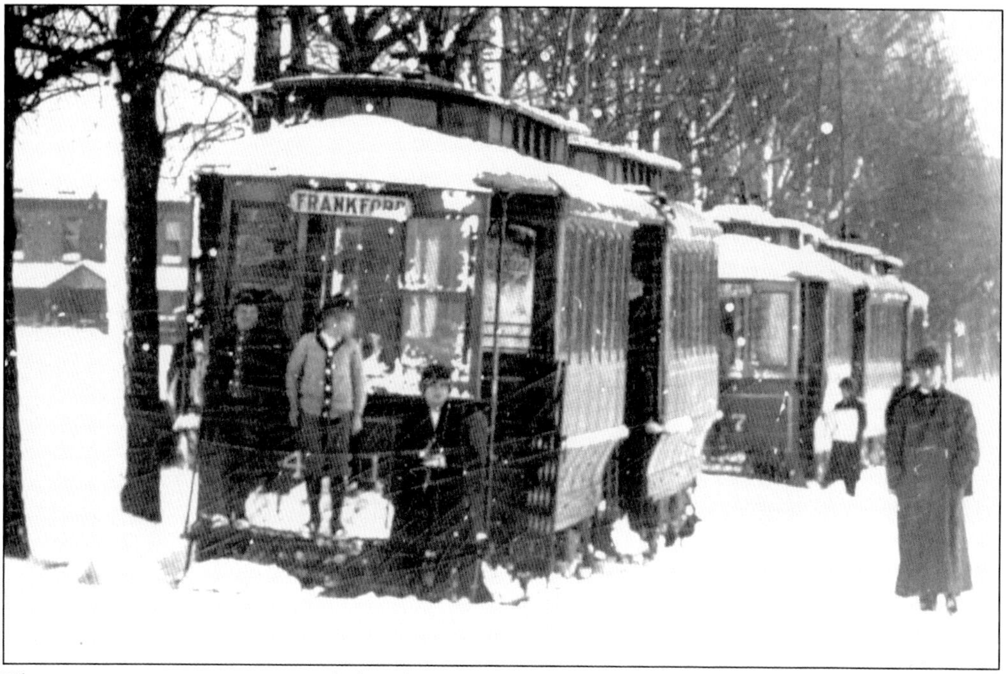

These two streetcars were stranded in front of St. John Cantius Roman Catholic Church. If not stranded by the snow, they would have been making their way west on Orthodox Street.

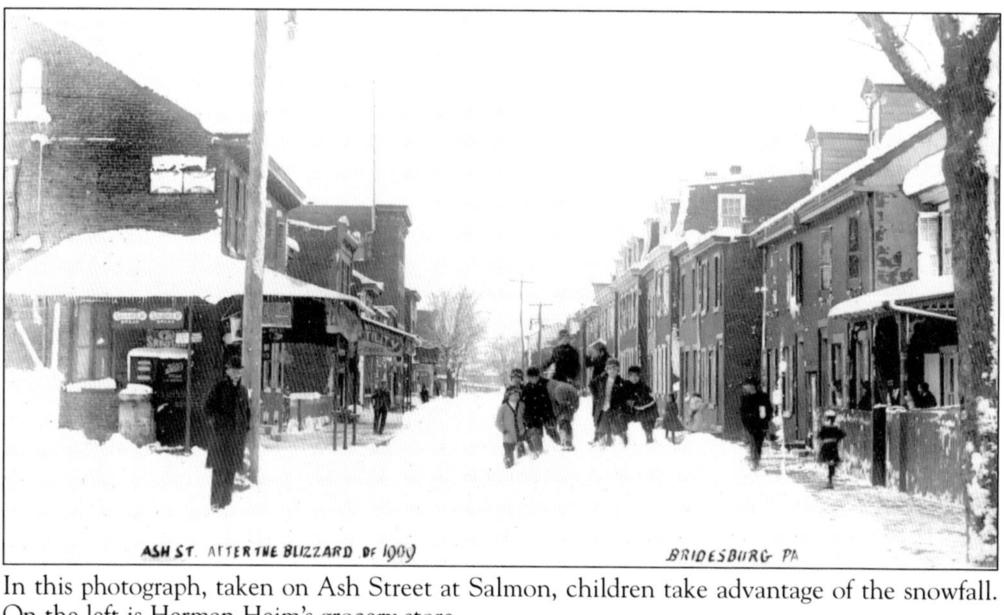

In this photograph, taken on Ash Street at Salmon, children take advantage of the snowfall. On the left is Herman Heim's grocery store.

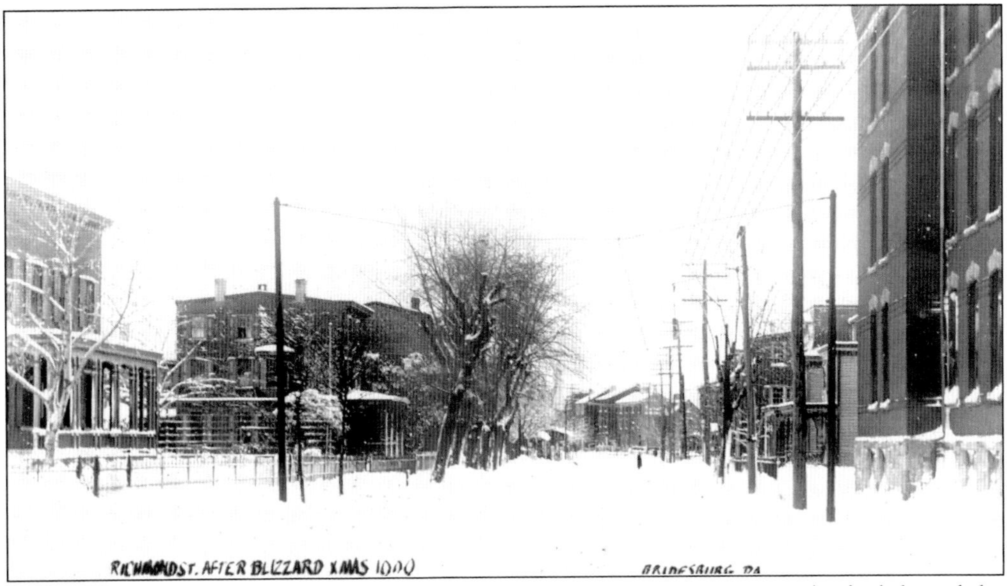

In this northward view of Richmond Street, the Van Dusen Mansion is on the far left, and the Bridesburg School is on the right.

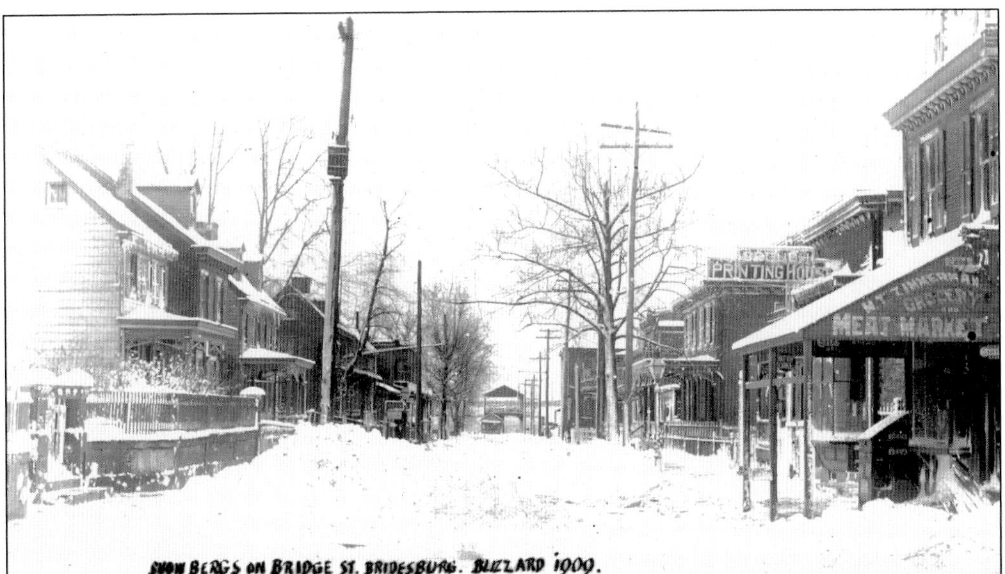

This view, looking east toward the Delaware River, reveals an impassable roadway. It is doubtful that many passengers made it to the pier for the boat ride to Center City.

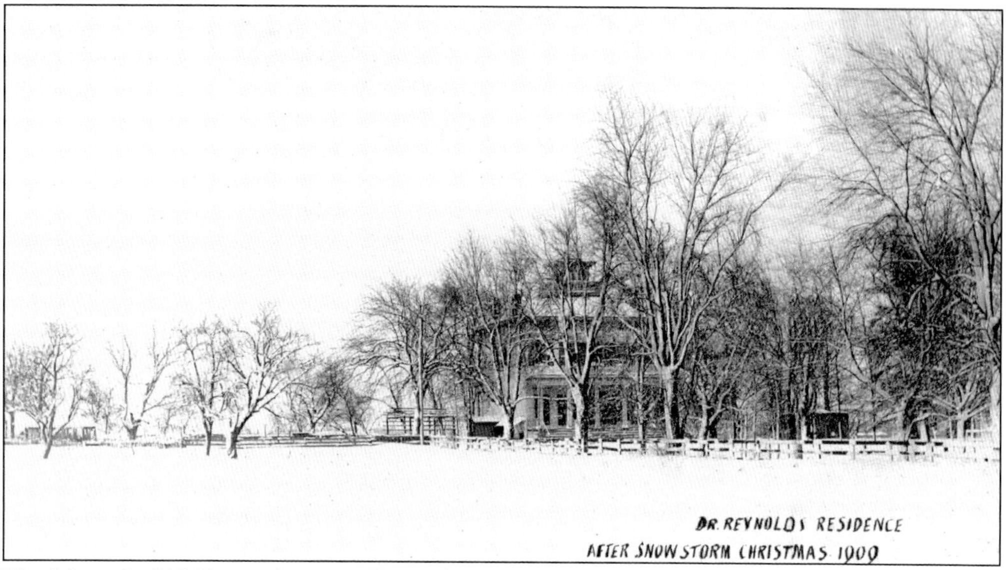

The blizzard of 1909 was the worst December snowstorm on record in Philadelphia, with more than 20 inches. This beautiful scene is of the Reynolds Mansion, on Richmond Street.

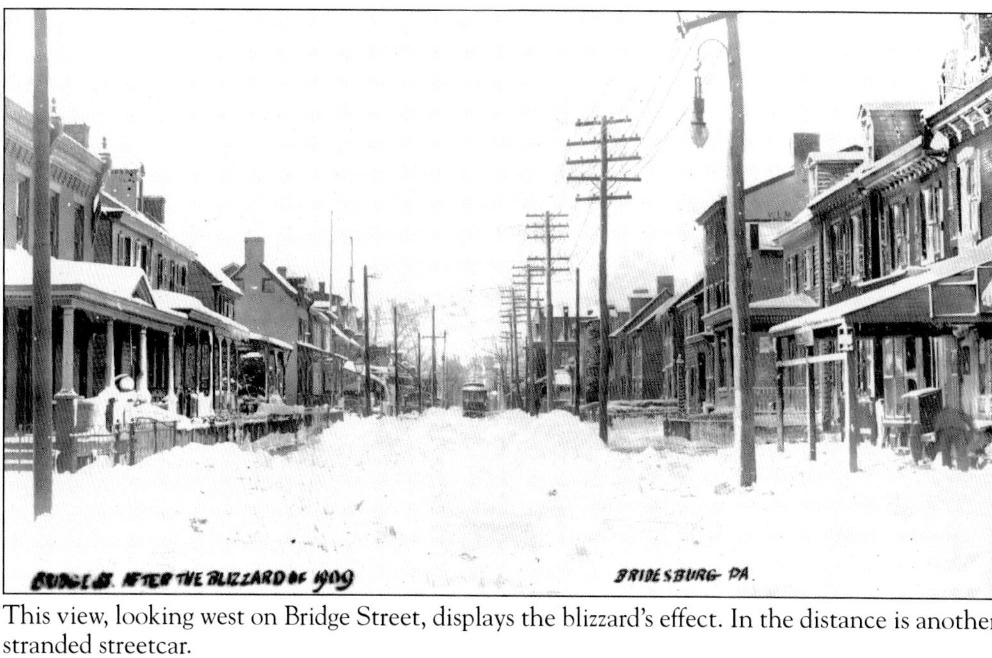

This view, looking west on Bridge Street, displays the blizzard's effect. In the distance is another stranded streetcar.

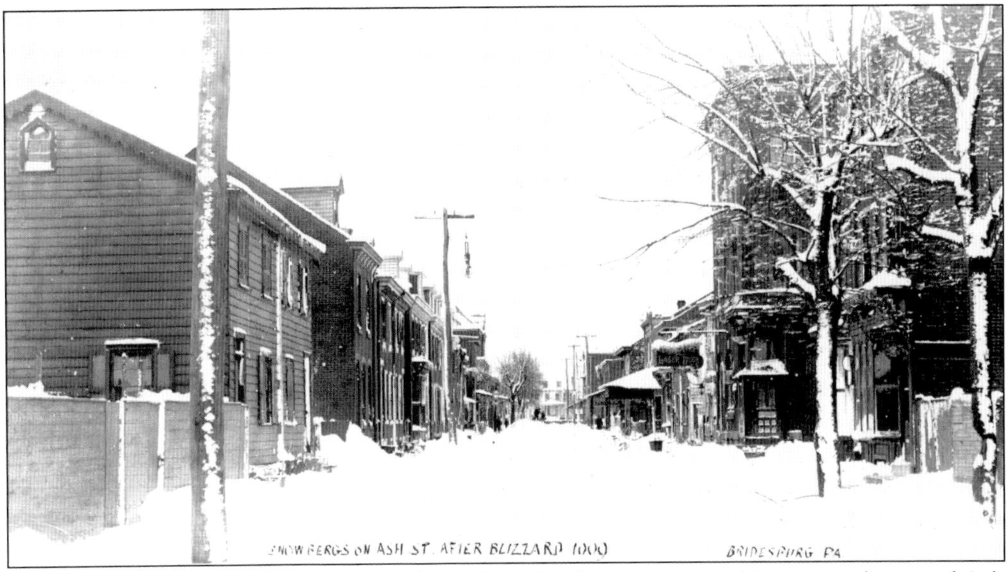

The Edgemont Hotel looms large on the right side of the street in this eastward view of Ash Street from Thompson.

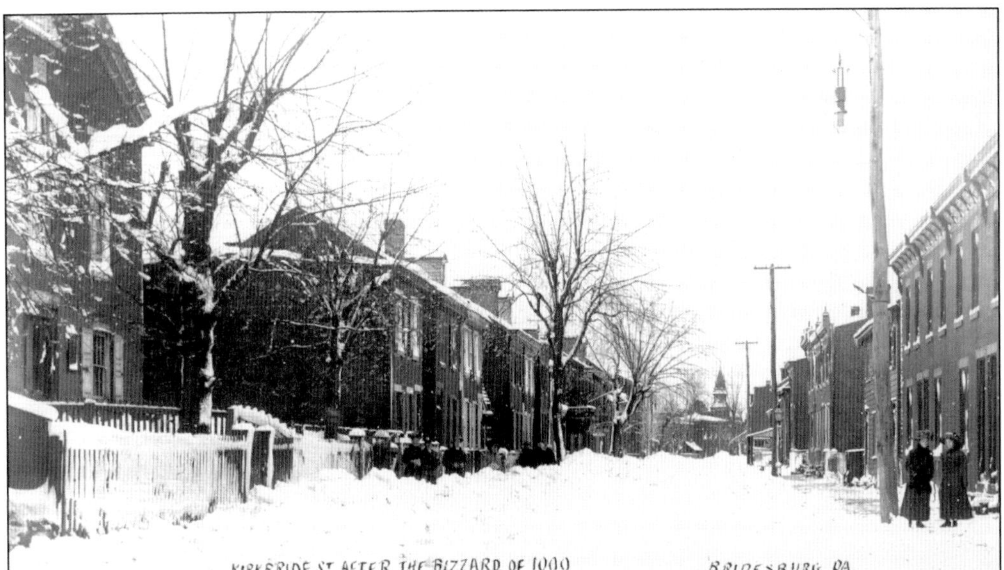

This photograph of Kirkbride Street was taken after the blizzard of 1909. The Methodist church is on the left, and at the end of the street is the old borough hall clock tower.

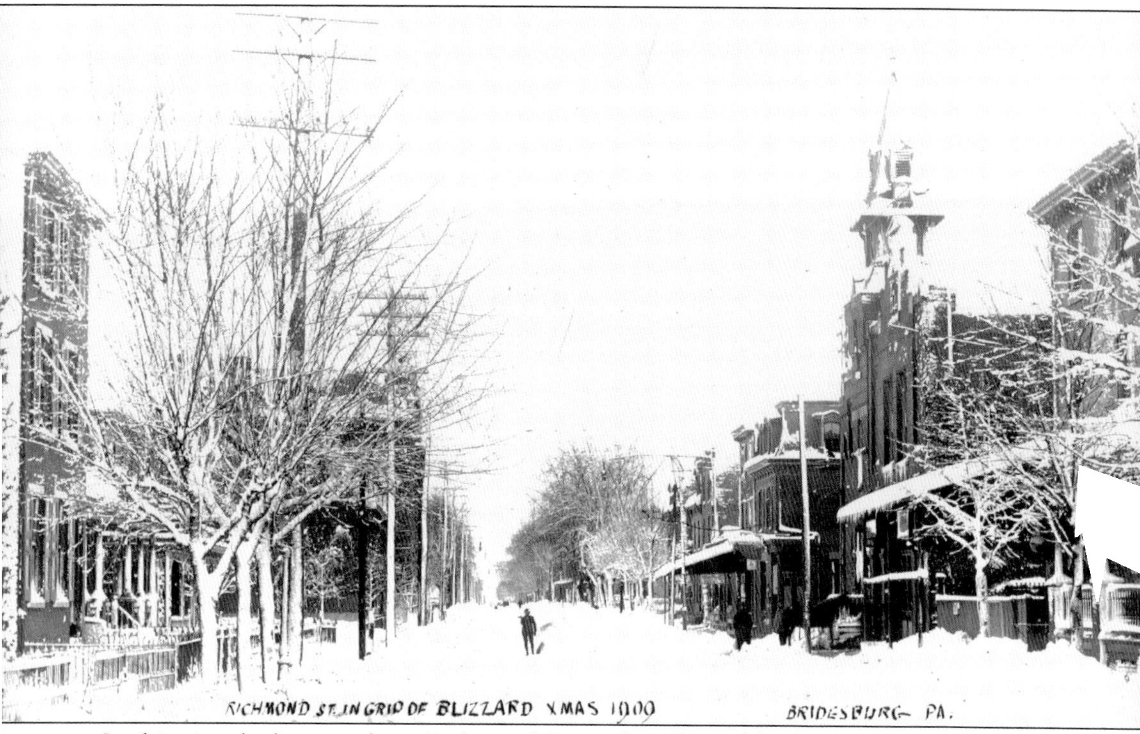

In this view, looking south on Richmond Street from Reynolds, the clock tower on the police station appears on the right.

Eight

THE RIVERFRONT

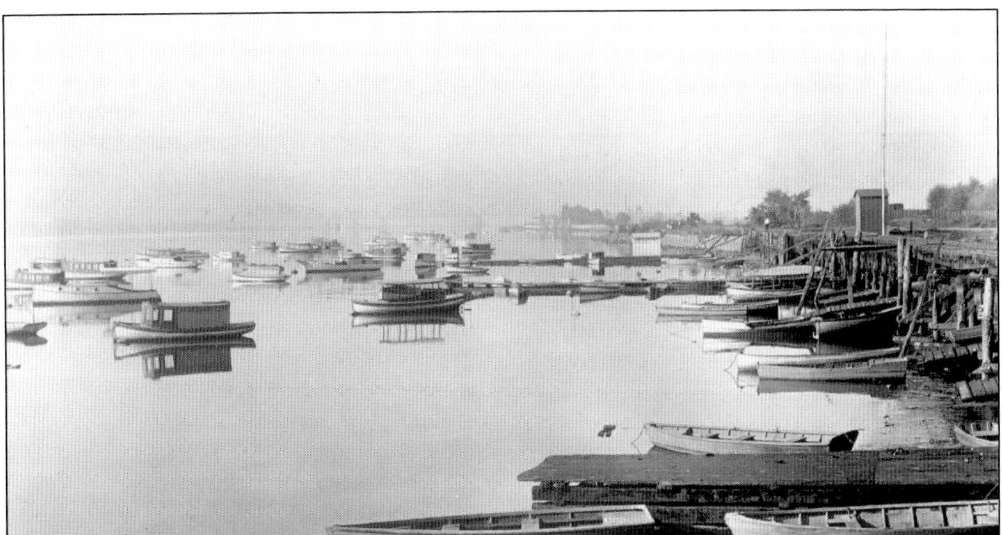

Bridesburg's riverfront was important to both the economy and the recreation of the community. This placid scene of boats and docks was a treasure for all.

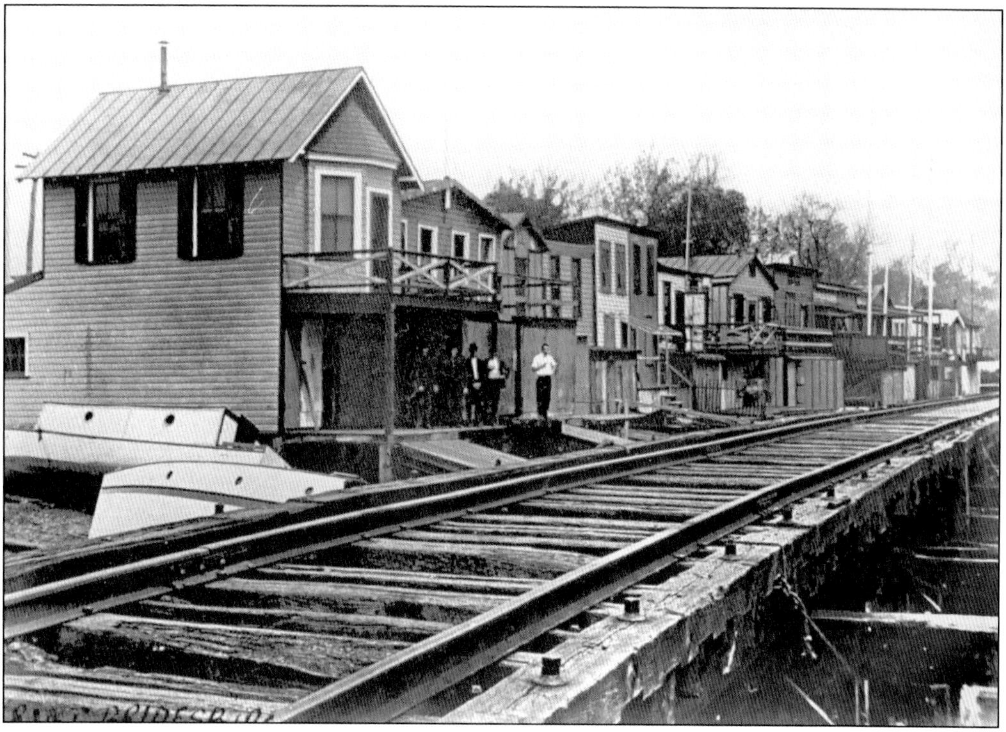

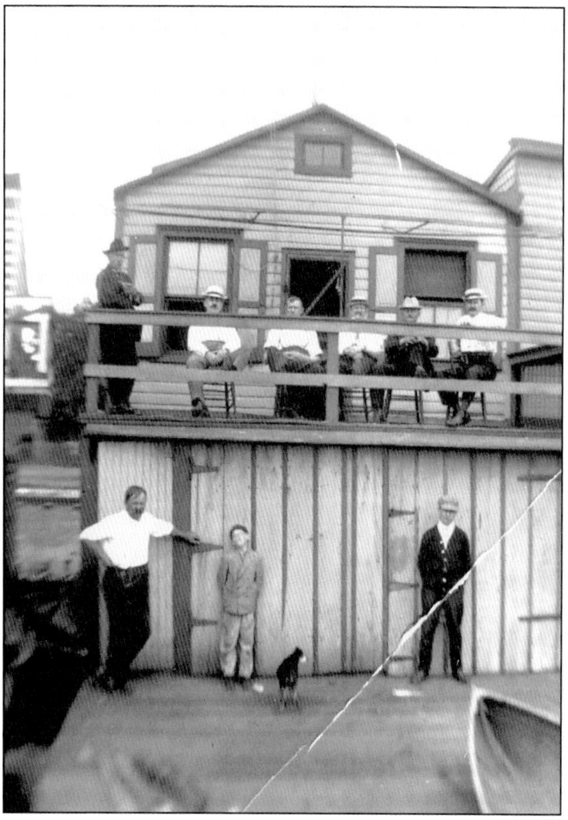

Fishermen built a series of two-story boathouses along the waterfront. The lower floor was used to store boats and gear. Ramps enabled boats to be moved in and out of the water. The upper floor was used for other recreation—making lunch, playing cards, and, perhaps, telling "fish stories." The porches made fine places to observe the river and to greet neighbors, as can be seen by the folks in these photographs.

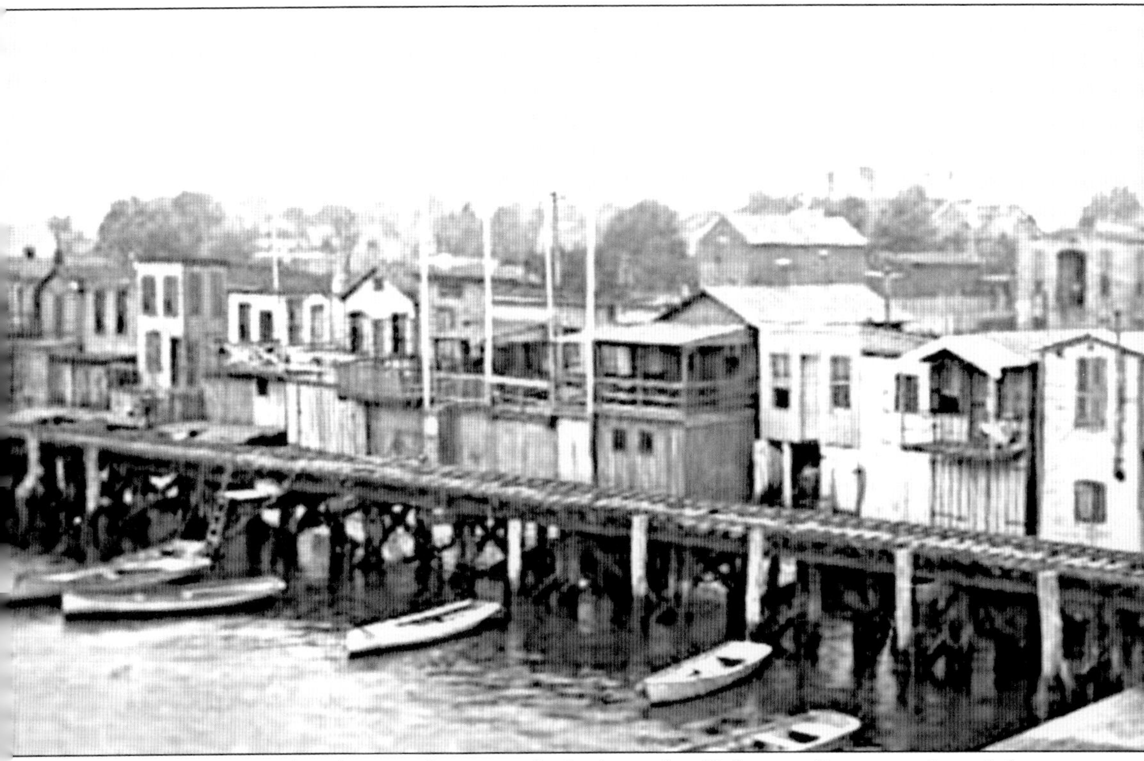

Shown here are the boathouses that stretched along the Delaware River southward from Bridge Street.

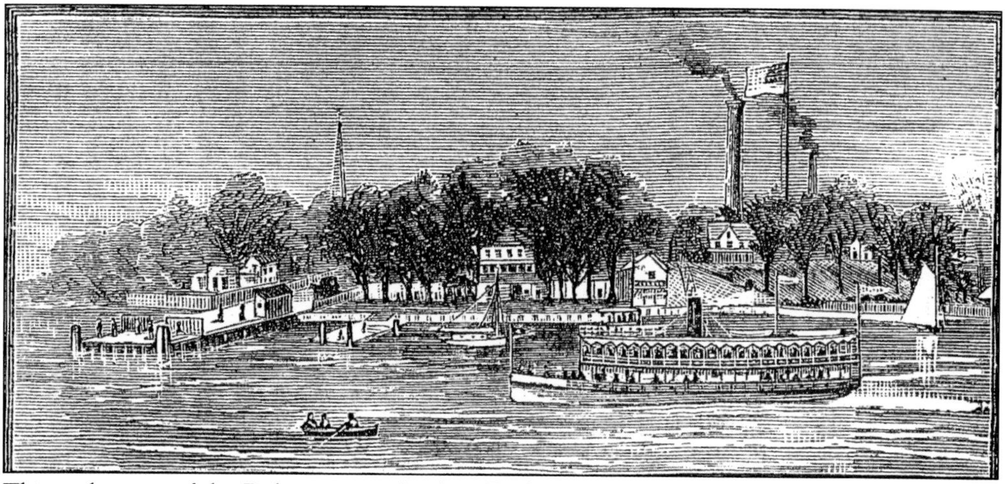

This early print of the Delaware riverbank at Bridge Street shows the Cedar Walk and Joseph Kirkbride's mansion. Note the Presbyterian church steeple in the background. These were landmarks for ships traversing the river.

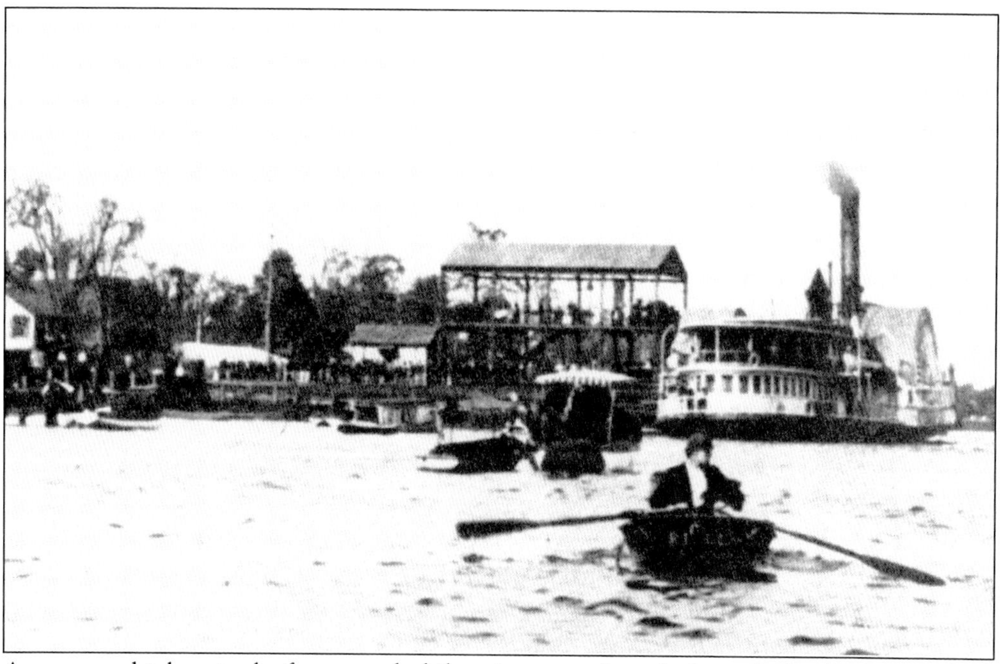

A man rows his boat in the foreground while a river steamboat docks at the Bridge Street wharf. This was one of the steamboats plying the Delaware and providing transportation to and from Center City, Philadelphia, in the early days. Bridesburg was one of several stops made between the Chestnut Street wharf and Bristol. Note the two-storied pier.

A timetable lists the departure and arrival schedules of the *Columbia* from Bristol to Philadelphia.

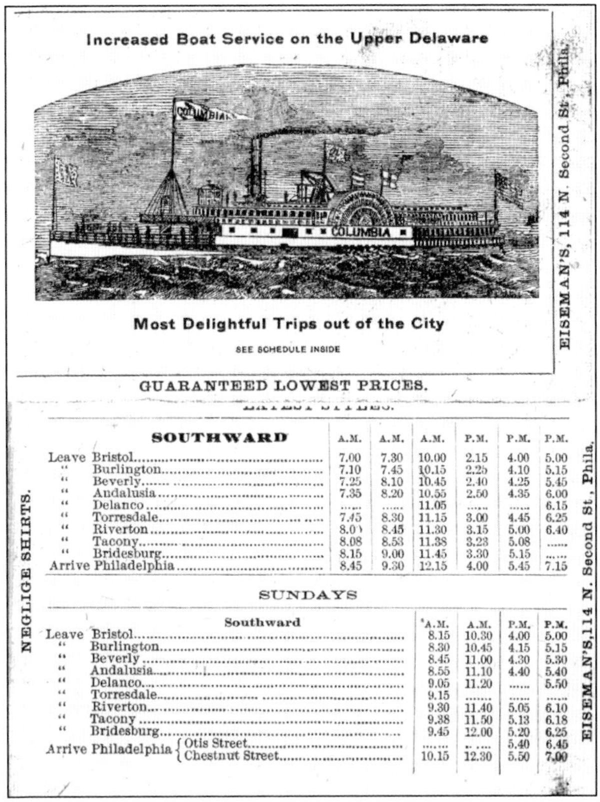

Increased Boat Service on the Upper Delaware

Most Delightful Trips out of the City

SEE SCHEDULE INSIDE

EISEMAN'S, 114 N. Second St., Phila.

GUARANTEED LOWEST PRICES.

SOUTHWARD	A.M.	A.M.	A.M.	P.M.	P.M.	P.M.
Leave Bristol	7.00	7.30	10.00	2.15	4.00	5.00
" Burlington	7.10	7.45	10.15	2.25	4.10	5.15
" Beverly	7.25	8.10	10.45	2.40	4.25	5.45
" Andalusia	7.35	8.20	10.55	2.50	4.35	6.00
" Delanco	......	......	11.05	......	......	6.15
" Torresdale	7.45	8.30	11.15	3.00	4.45	6.25
" Riverton	8.0[illegible]	8.45	11.30	3.15	5.00	6.40
" Tacony	8.08	8.53	11.38	3.23	5.08	......
" Bridesburg	8.15	9.00	11.45	3.30	5.15	......
Arrive Philadelphia	8.45	9.30	12.15	4.00	5.45	7.15

SUNDAYS

Southward	A.M.	A.M.	P.M.	P.M.
Leave Bristol	8.15	10.30	4.00	5.00
" Burlington	8.30	10.45	4.15	5.15
" Beverly	8.45	11.00	4.30	5.30
" Andalusia	8.55	11.10	4.40	5.40
" Delanco	9.05	11.20	......	5.50
" Torresdale	9.15	......	......	......
" Riverton	9.30	11.40	5.05	6.10
" Tacony	9.38	11.50	5.13	6.18
" Bridesburg	9.45	12.00	5.20	6.25
Arrive Philadelphia { Otis Street	......	......	5.40	6.45
Arrive Philadelphia { Chestnut Street	10.15	12.30	5.50	7.00

NEGLIGE SHIRTS.

EISEMAN'S, 114 N. Second St., Phila.

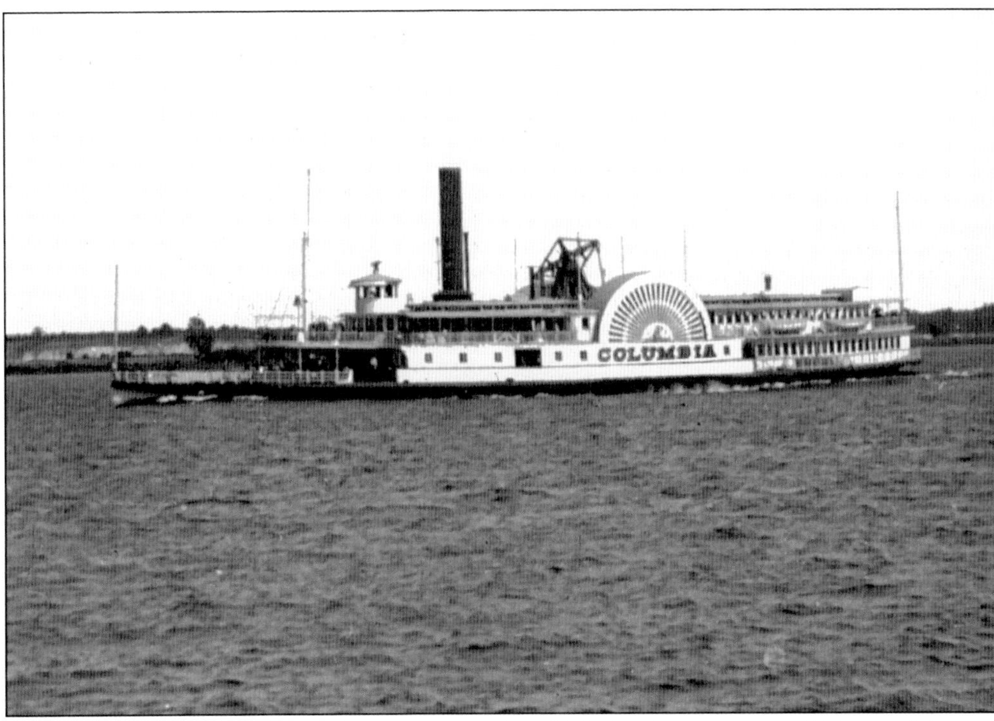

The paddle-wheel *Columbia* is shown on one of its "delightful trips" on the Delaware River.

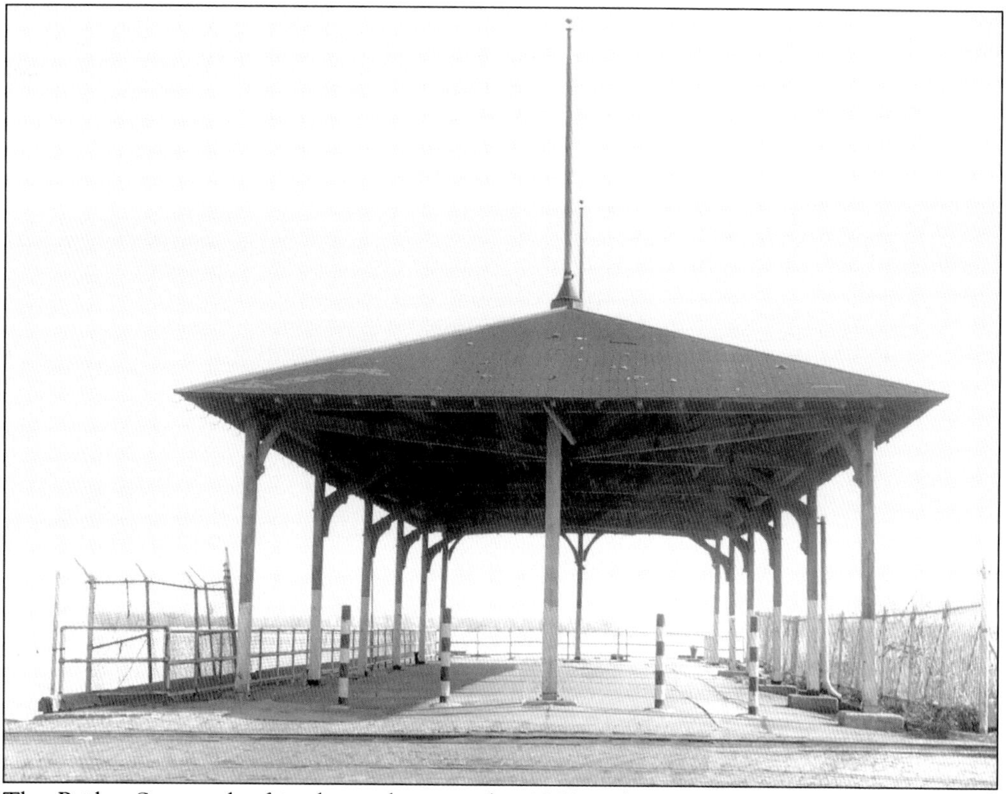

The Bridge Street wharf is shown here in the 1950s. This structure replaced the original double-decked pier standing for many years on the site. Although no longer used for passenger transportation, the wharf was still a popular spot with residents for river watching.

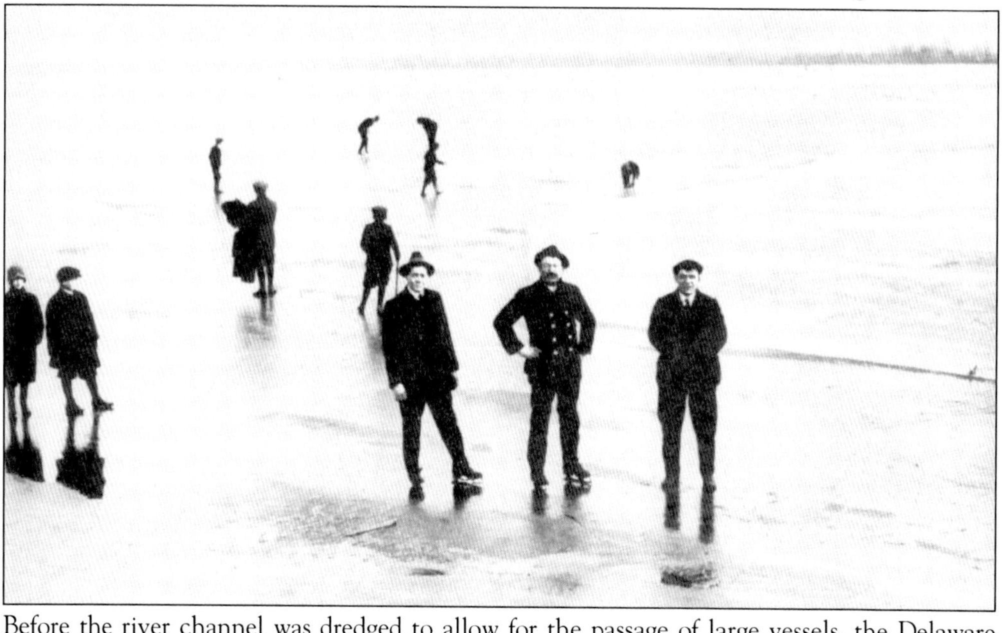

Before the river channel was dredged to allow for the passage of large vessels, the Delaware often froze over in the winter, providing an opportunity for recreation on the ice.

The dolphin exhibited here by three local fishermen was caught in the Delaware River.

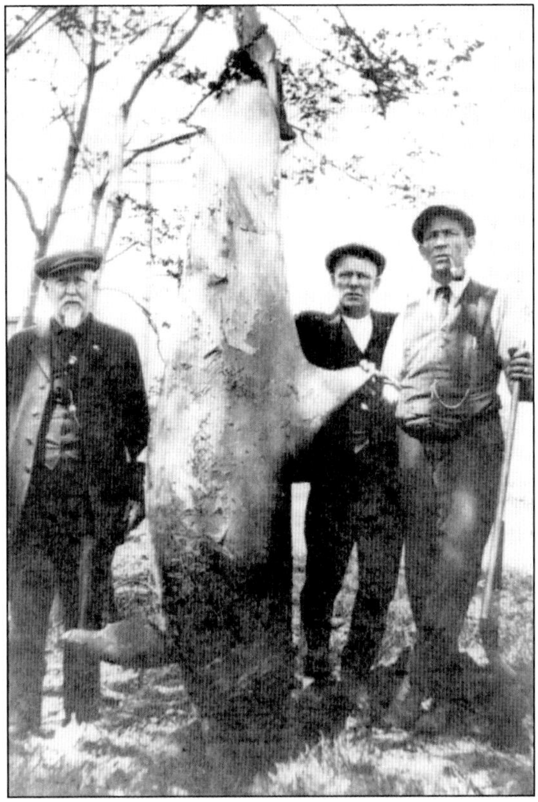

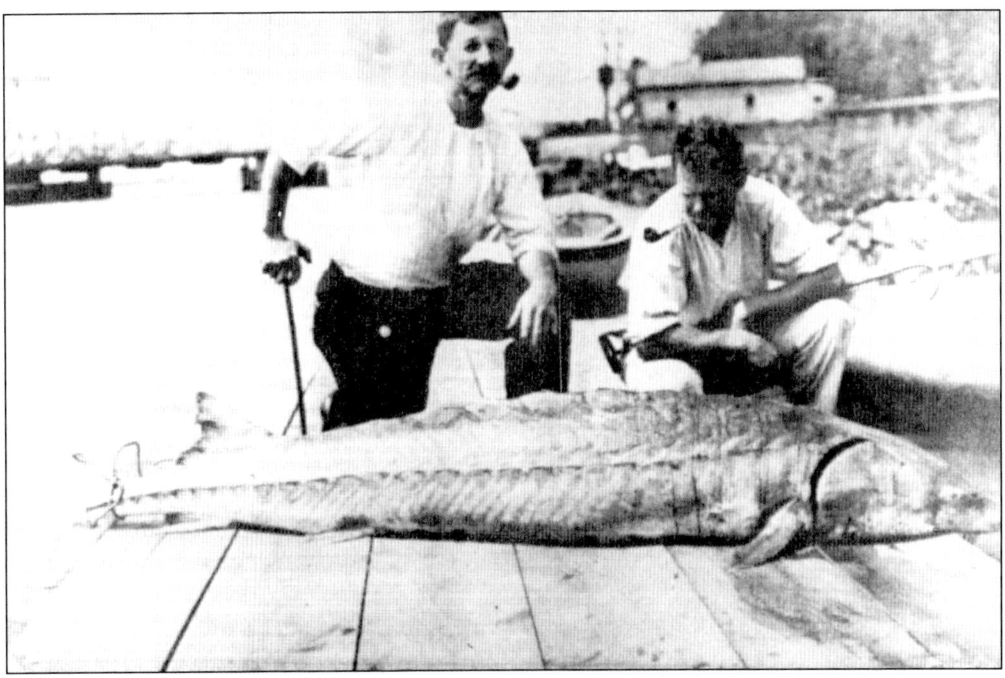

These proud fishermen display their catch of sturgeon along the banks of the Delaware.

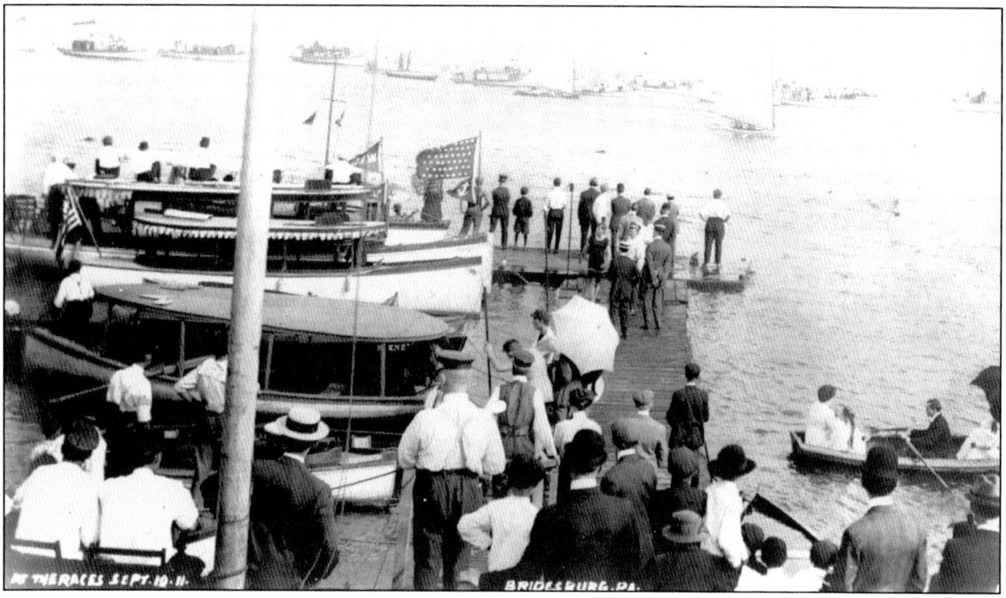

Crowds gather to watch the sailboat races on the river on September 10, 1911.

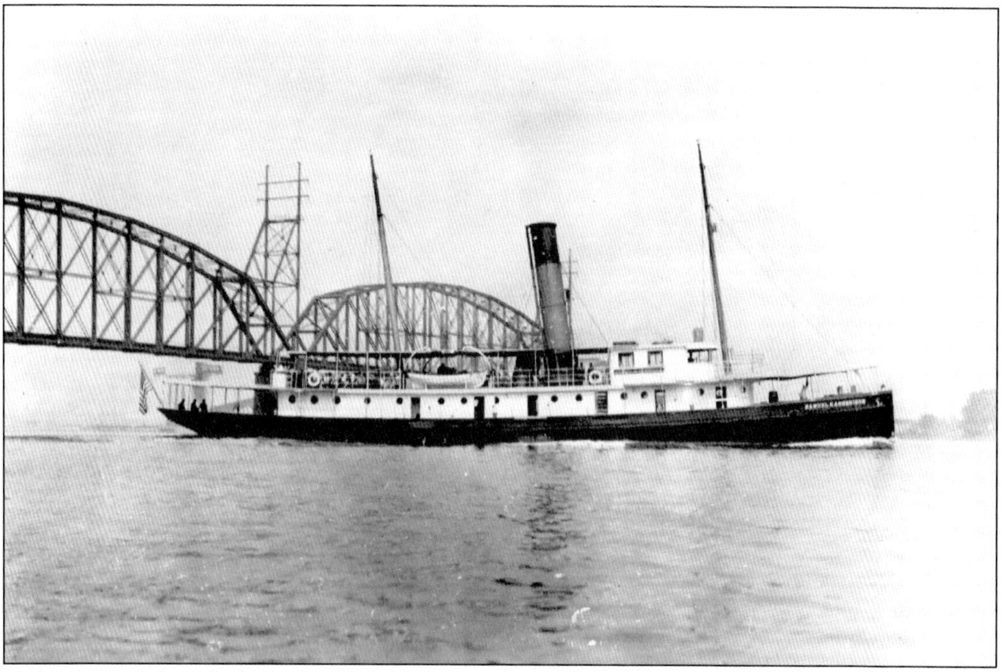
A ship passes the Black Bridge, which carried railroad trains across the Delaware River at the southern end of Bridesburg.

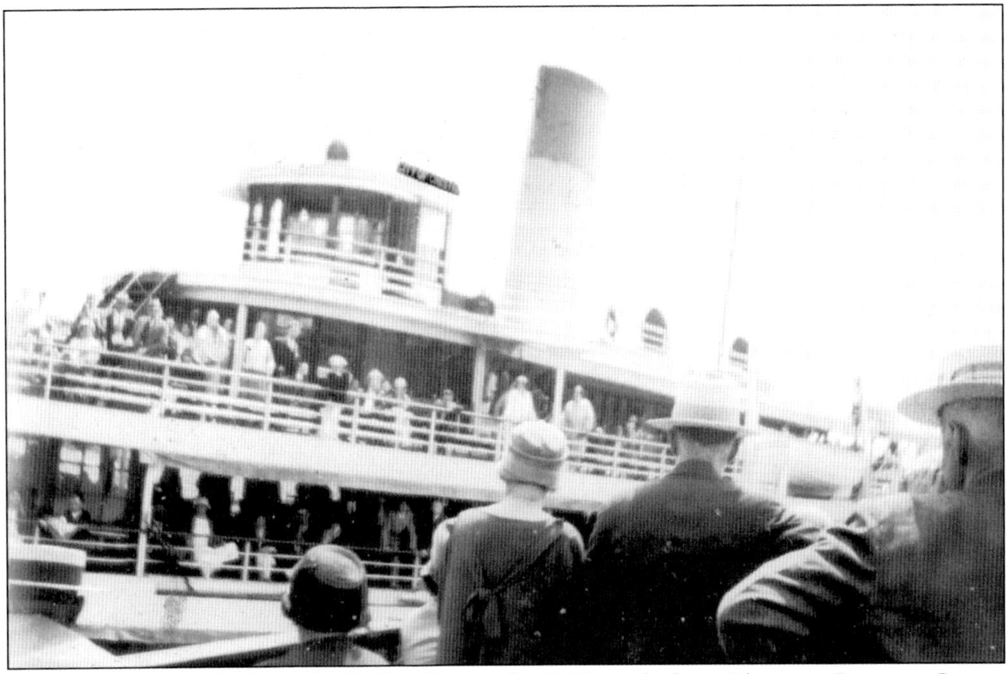

A river steamboat docks at the Bridge Street wharf. The ride from Chestnut Street in Center City to Bridesburg took 30 minutes and ran six times a day, Monday through Saturday, and four times on Sunday.

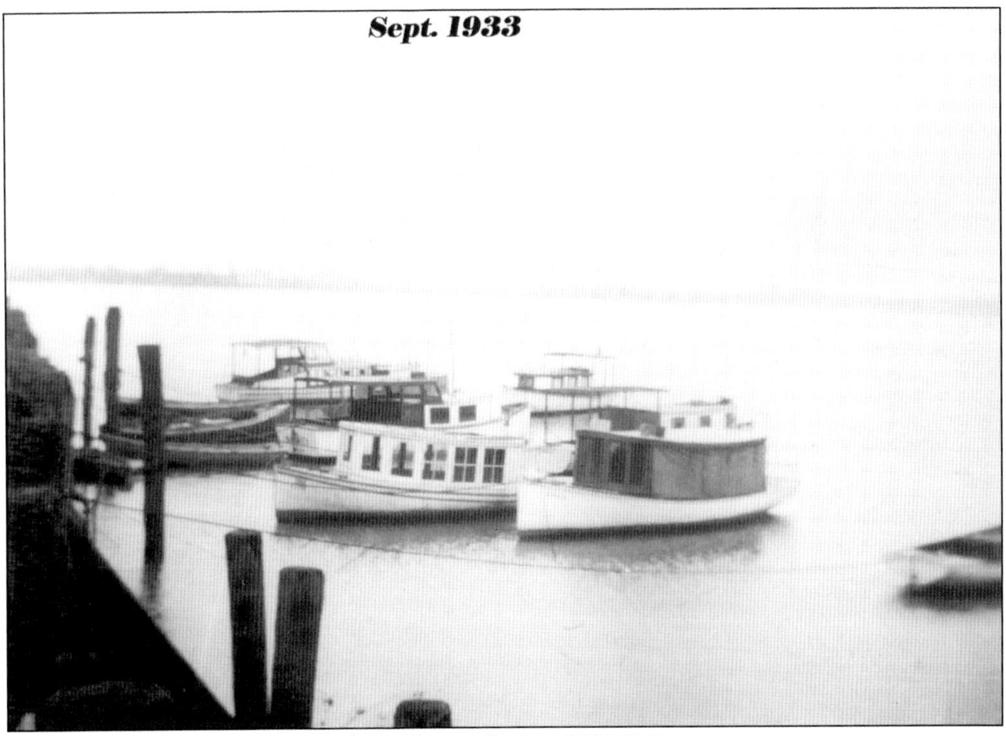

Several boats ride at anchor in the Delaware River off Bridesburg.

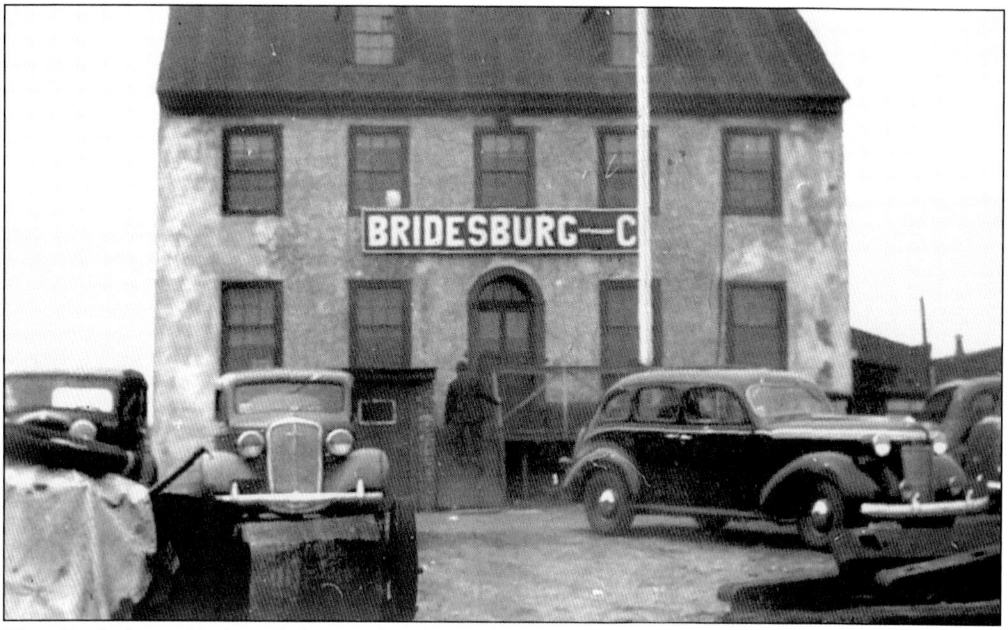

The Bridesburg Yacht Club stands along the river. In the background, the Bridesburg Manufacturing Company can be seen.

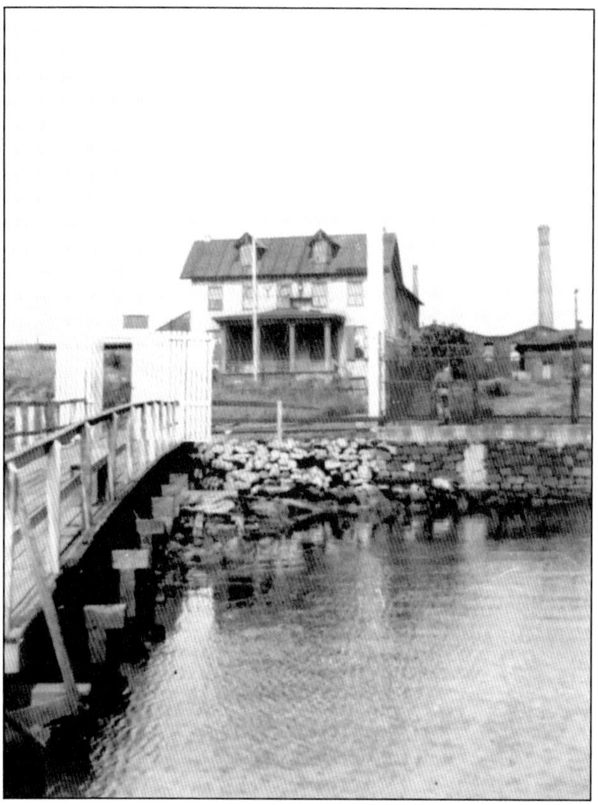

The Columbia Yacht Club sports a fine porch and a long pier that extends out into the river.

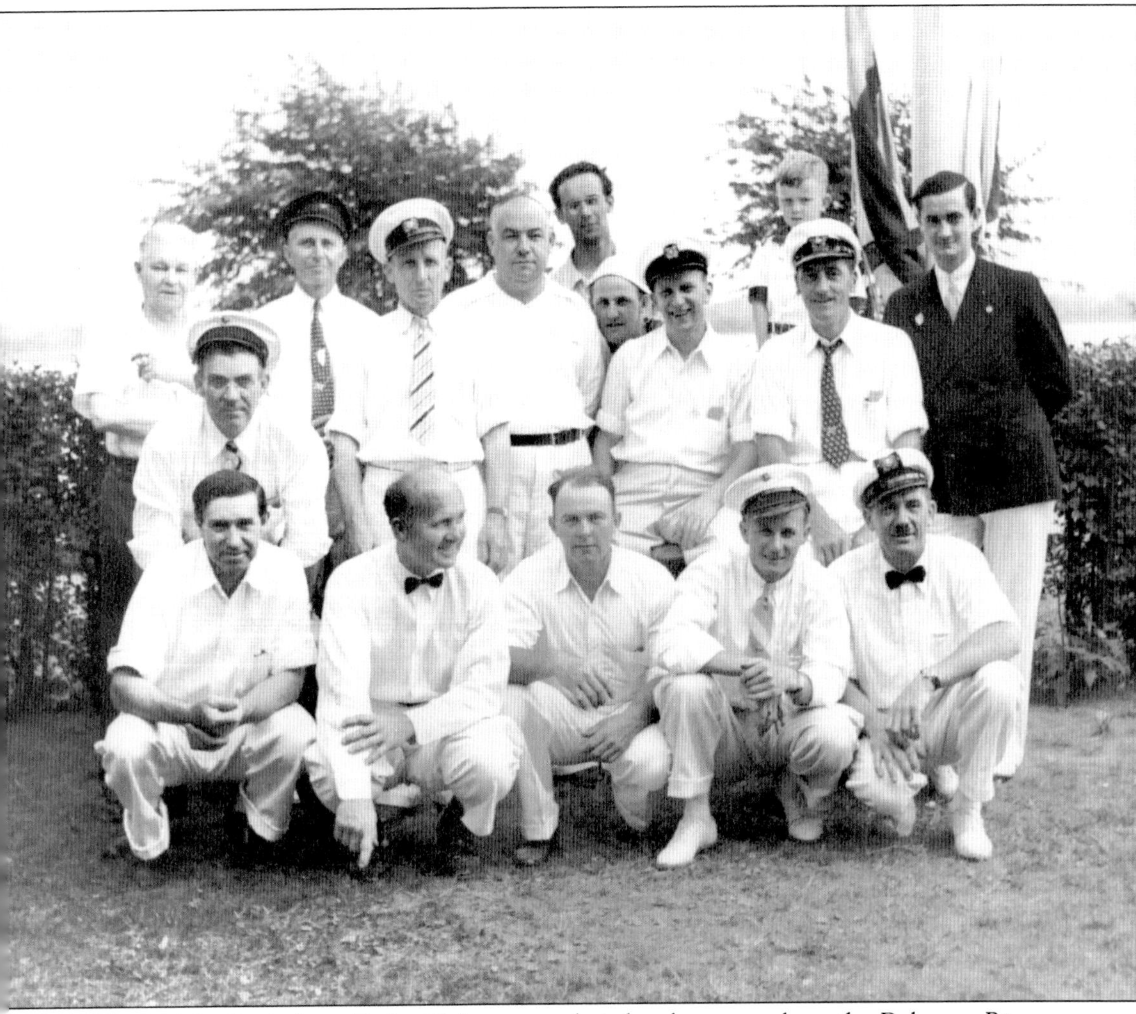

Members of the Bridesburg Yacht Club pose at their headquarters along the Delaware River. Edward Ludwig, Bridesburg's favorite mailman, is seen second from the left in the first row.

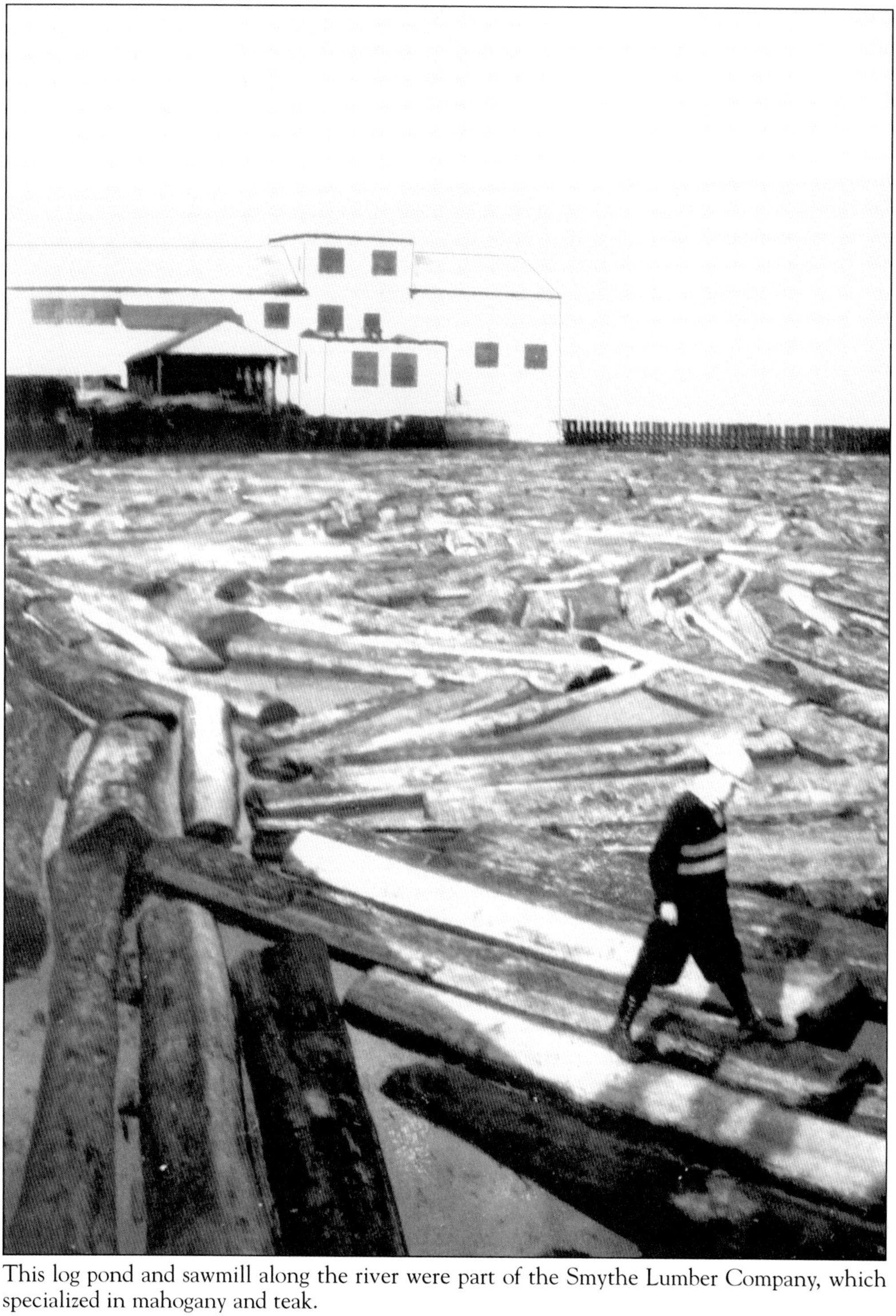

This log pond and sawmill along the river were part of the Smythe Lumber Company, which specialized in mahogany and teak.

Nine

Our Sports Heritage

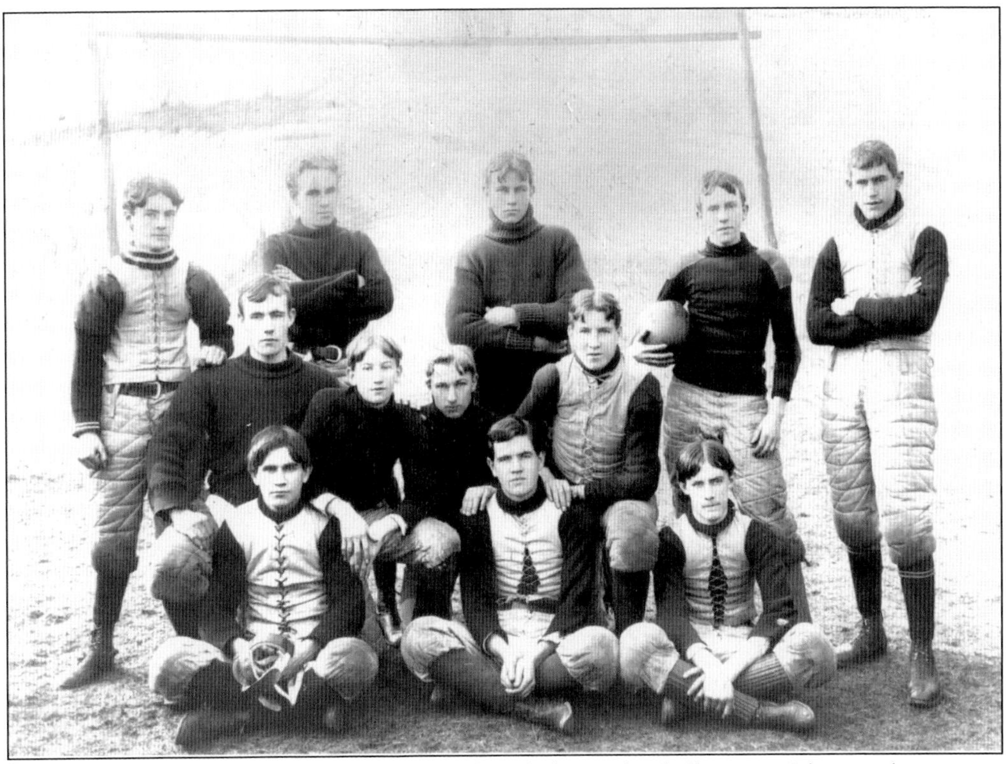

This 1899 photograph is the oldest of one of Bridesburg's football teams. Of particular interest is the style of uniform.

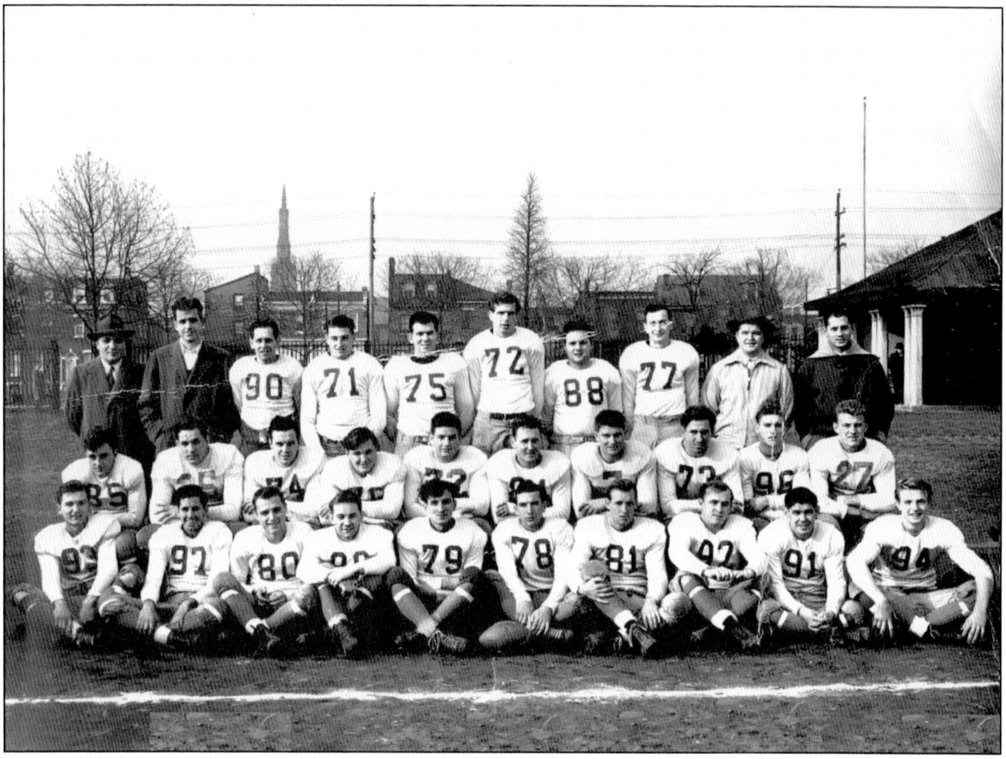

During the period of 1935 to 1950, Bridesburg had two semiprofessional football leagues: Ward A. A. and the Bridesburg Eagles. This photograph shows the 1946 football champions, the Bridesburg Eagles.

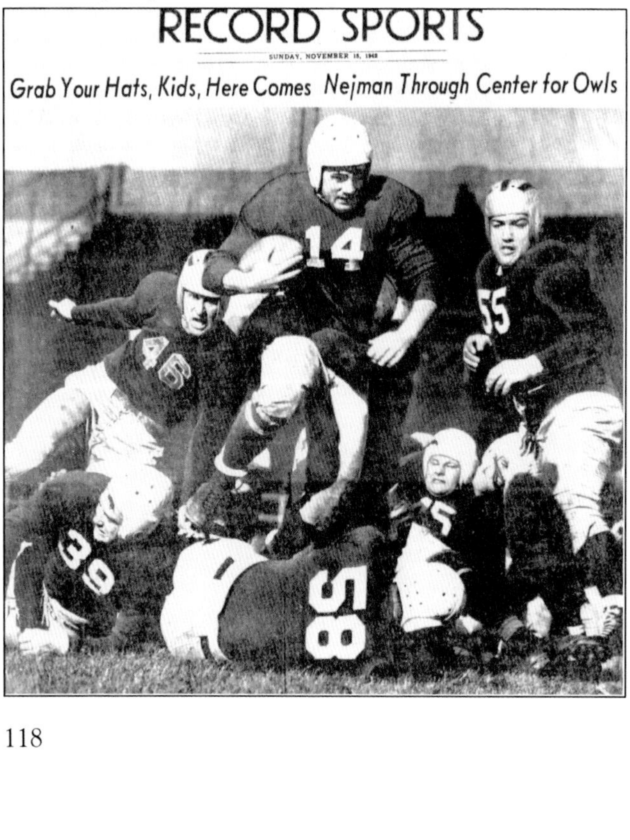

This clipping from the *Philadelphia Record* shows running back Joe Nejman, an alumnus of Frankford High School. He continued as an outstanding back at Temple University. The photograph caption in the newspaper says it all.

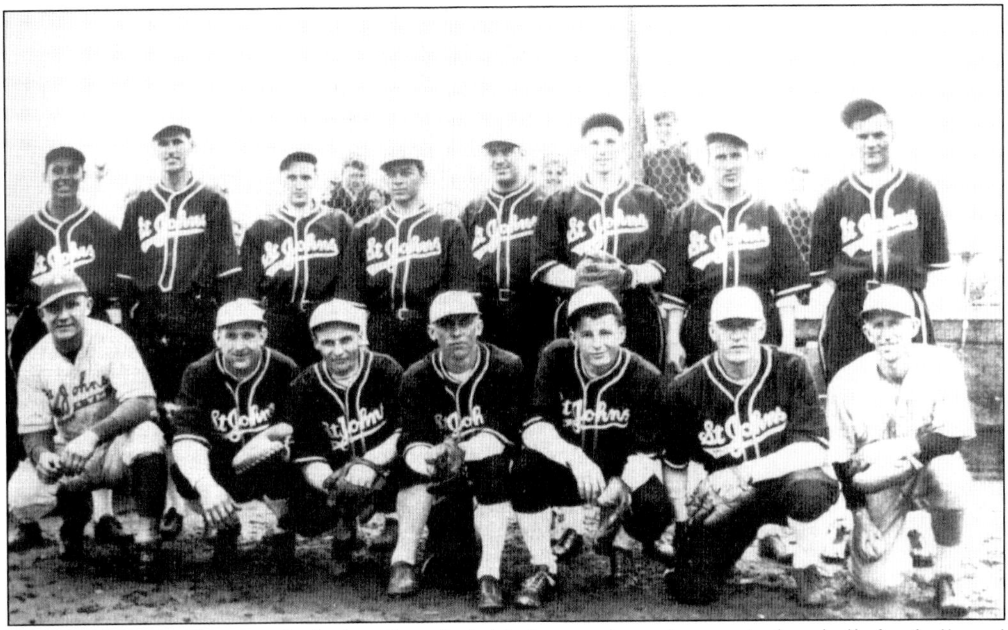

St. John Cantius Roman Catholic Church fielded a number of teams in baseball, football, and basketball. This is a photograph of one of St. John's baseball teams.

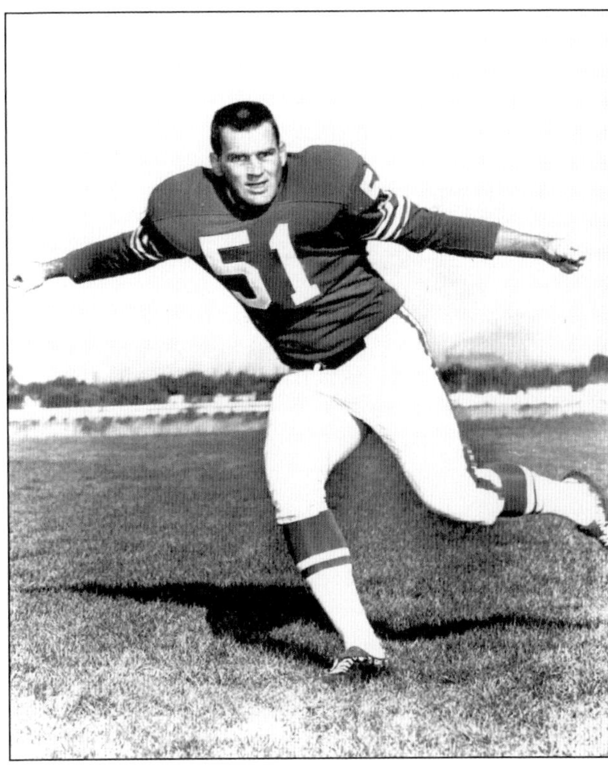

John Tracey was one of a number of young Bridesburg men who performed well in sports. He started his career playing basketball at the Bridesburg Boys Club, before being encouraged to give football a try by Temple University's Joe Nejman. Tracey played football at Texas A&M, then professionally for seven years with the Buffalo team.

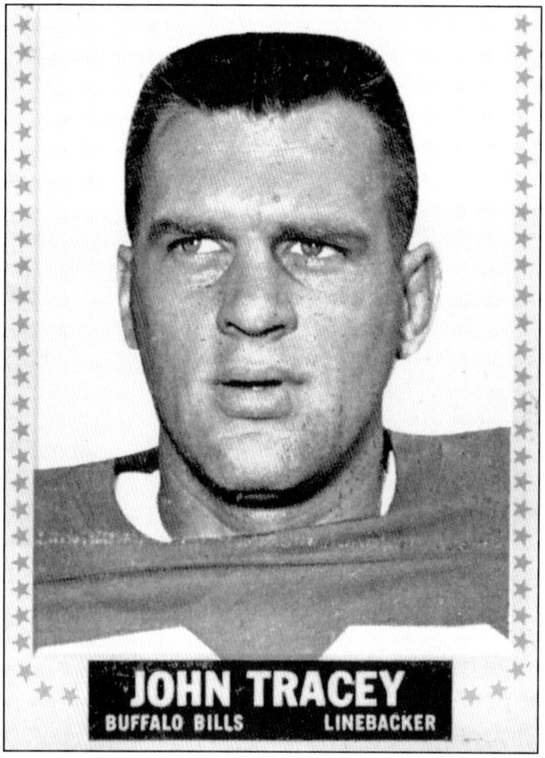

The front of this Topps bubble gum card honors Bridesburg's John Tracey.

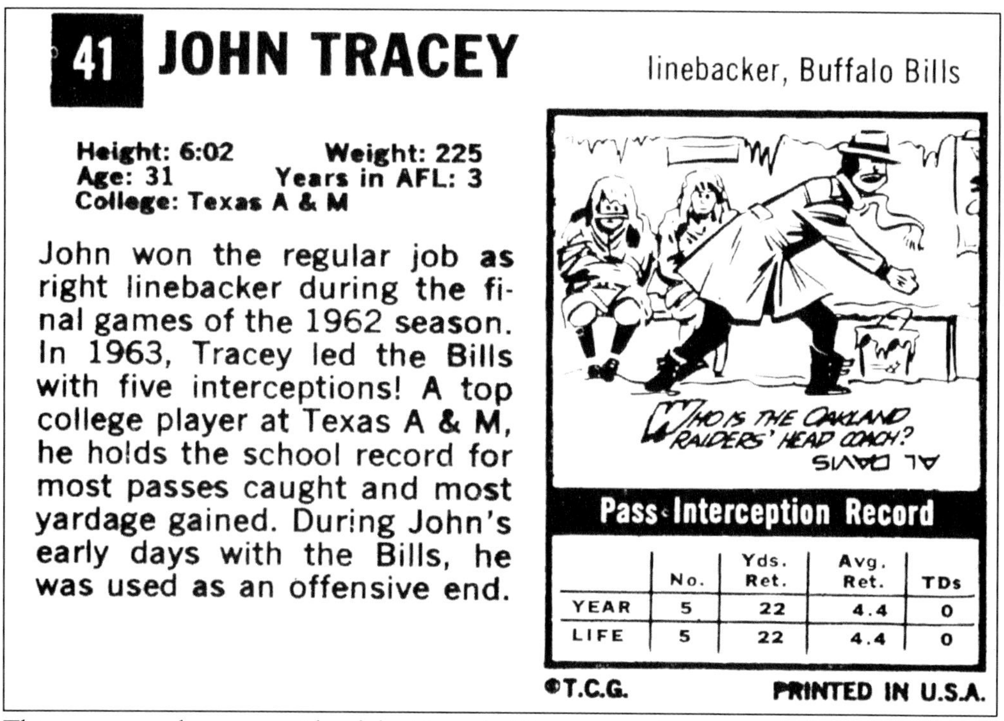

41 JOHN TRACEY

linebacker, Buffalo Bills

Height: 6:02 **Weight: 225**
Age: 31 **Years in AFL: 3**
College: Texas A & M

John won the regular job as right linebacker during the final games of the 1962 season. In 1963, Tracey led the Bills with five interceptions! A top college player at Texas A & M, he holds the school record for most passes caught and most yardage gained. During John's early days with the Bills, he was used as an offensive end.

WHO IS THE OAKLAND RAIDERS' HEAD COACH?
AL DAVIS

Pass Interception Record

	No.	Yds. Ret.	Avg. Ret.	TDs
YEAR	5	22	4.4	0
LIFE	5	22	4.4	0

©T.C.G. PRINTED IN U.S.A.

This image, on the reverse side of the Topps bubble gum card, gives the history and statistics of John Tracey's career.

"Big Hank" Fijalkowski was another of the great players with the Bridesburg Eagles. He also played with the Ottowa Raiders in the Canadian leagues.

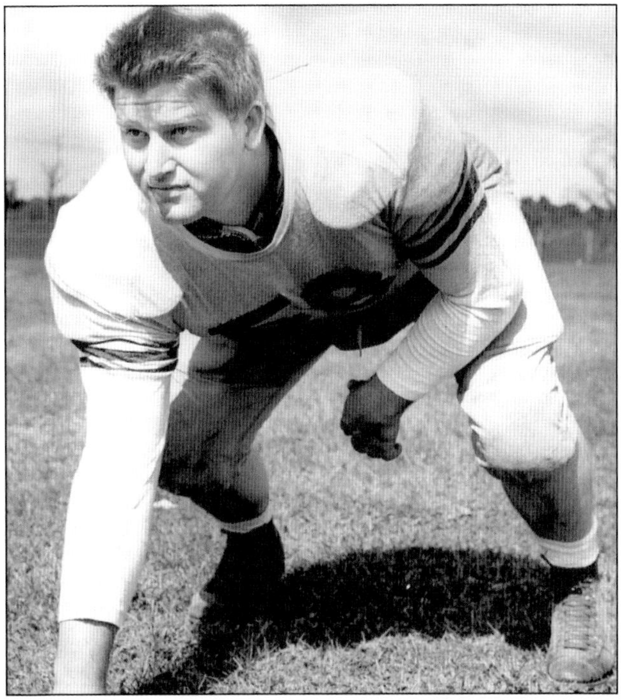

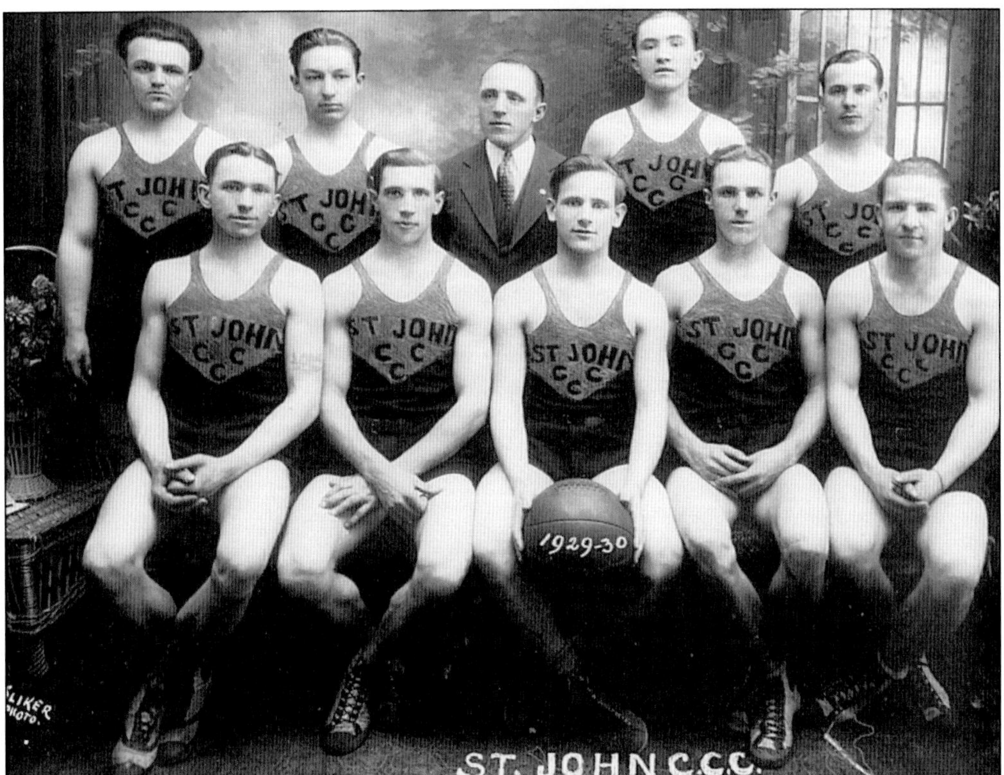

Bridesburg is relatively small in area, yet it had eight fields set aside for playing sports. This 1916 photograph shows another of the St. John Cantius teams.

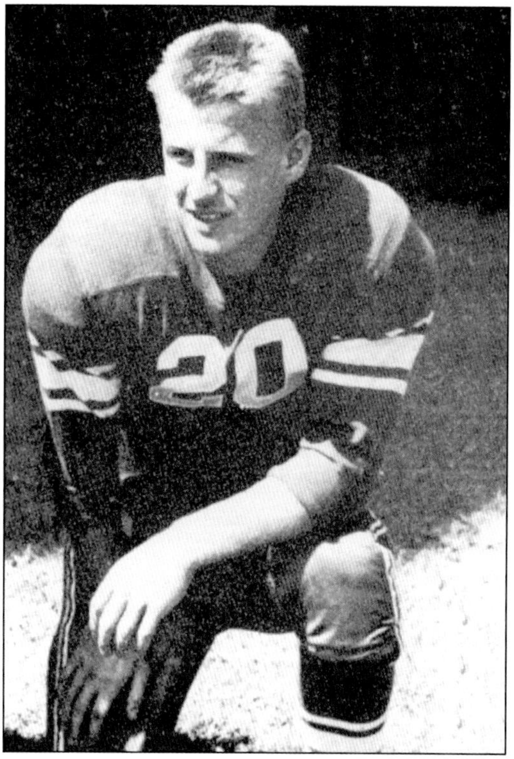

John Idzik began his sports endeavors in baseball but wound up as one of Bridesburg's most noted football athletes. He had outstanding records at the Northeast Catholic High School, the University of Maryland, and the Baltimore Orioles. He also spent a number of years coaching for the Philadelphia Eagles. Notably, Idzik holds a Super Bowl ring from his time with Baltimore, and his son John bears a Super Bowl ring from the 2003 winners, the Tampa Bay Buccaneers.

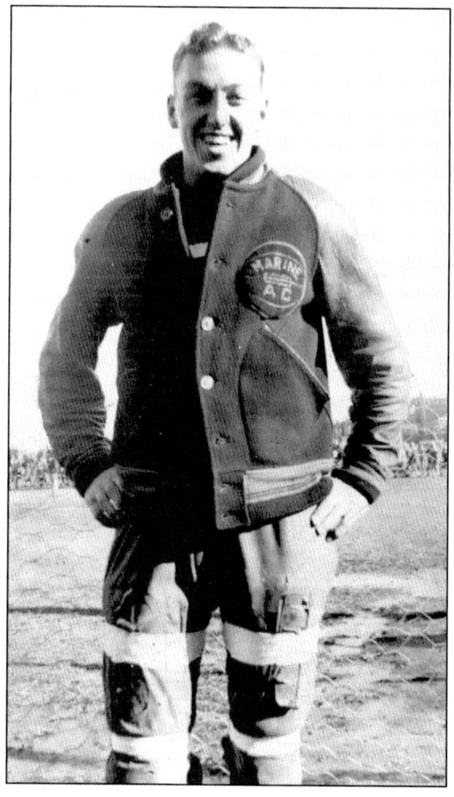

"Hack" Whittle was Bridesburg's all-around sportsman during the 1930s. He played baseball, football, and tennis and fought in the ring as well. He was a member of the 1938 all-star team, participating in the last game ever played in the Phillies' original home stadium, the Baker Bowl.

In the early 1900s, Bridesburg's sports activity was explosive. Every piece of ground that could hold a home plate and three bases became another baseball field. This 1903 photograph shows a young John Bendler Sr. wearing the uniform of the Bridesburg Athletic Club.

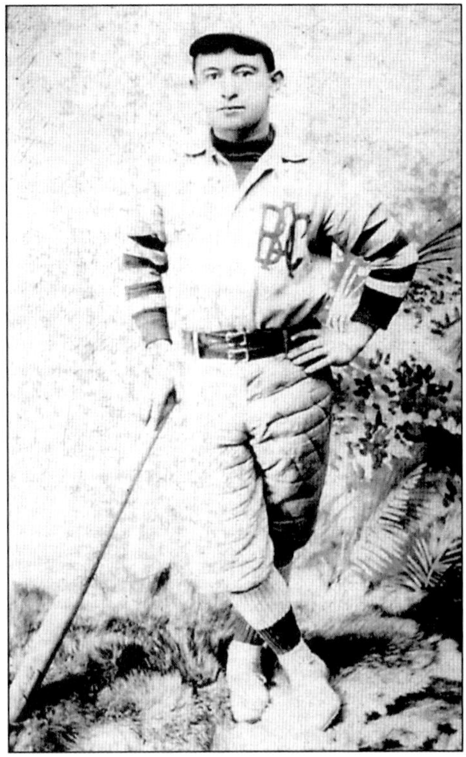

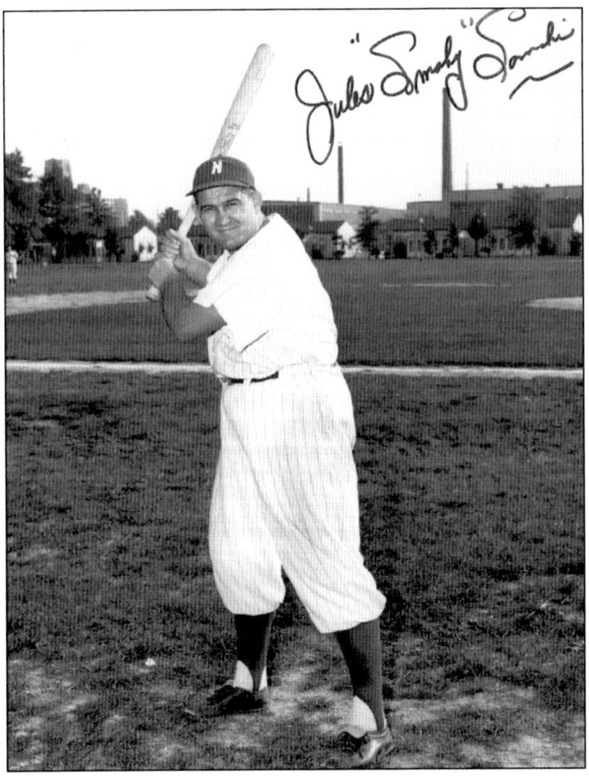

Jules "Smoky" Samocki, another young man from Bridesburg, did very well in baseball, playing in the Philadelphia Athletics organization.

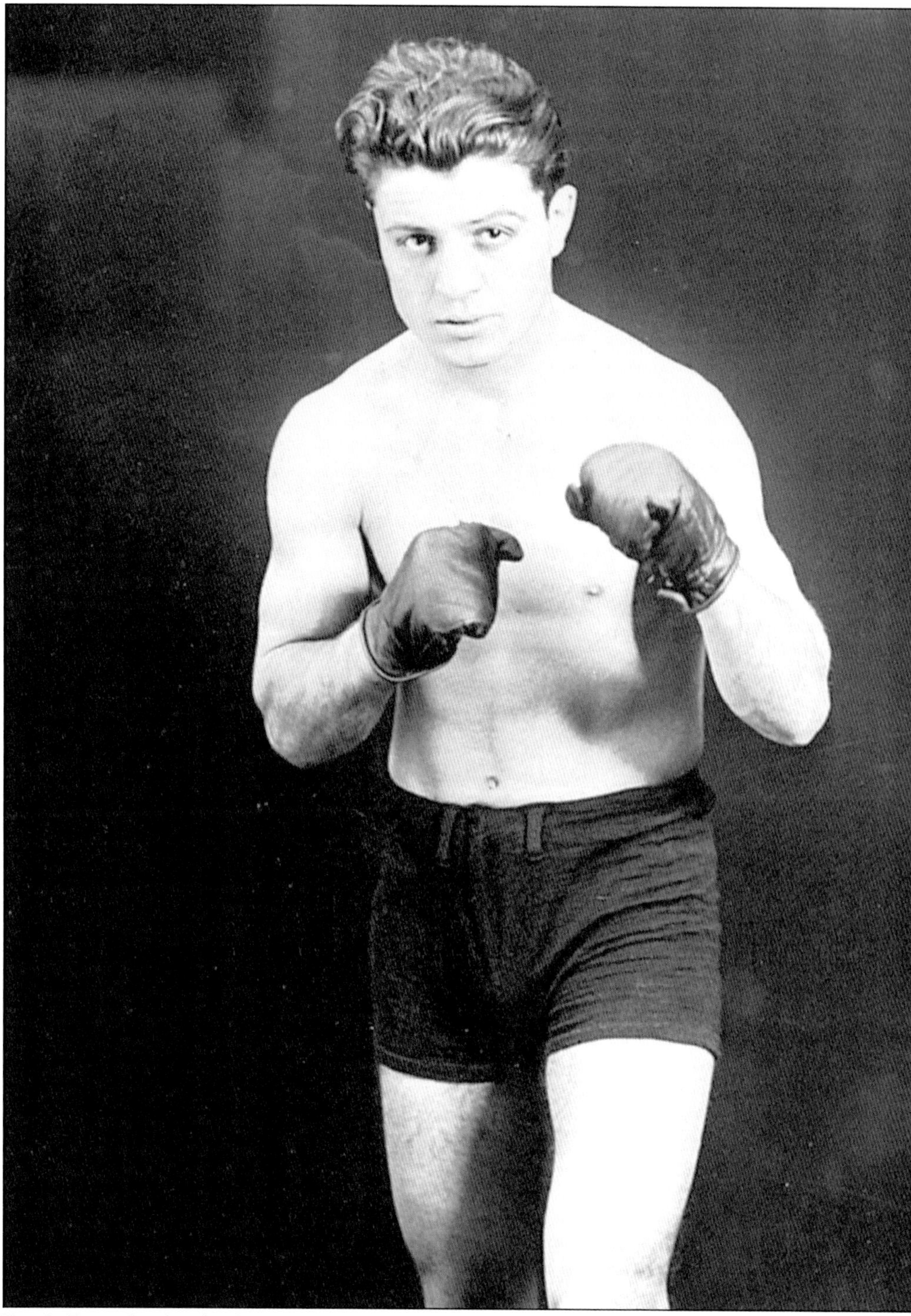

Frank Ferro fought the best contenders inside and outside the Philadelphia area during the 1920s. He fought as an amateur for two years and then spent ten years as a professional, pretty much on a monthly basis.

The Robinson brothers, Jimmy and Tommy, of Garden Street were competent boxers, both having won national AAU championships. Here, Jimmy fights in his 1941 exhibition bout in Milwaukee, with the famous world champion Joe Louis. Tommy went on to win 48 of 53 boxing career matches.

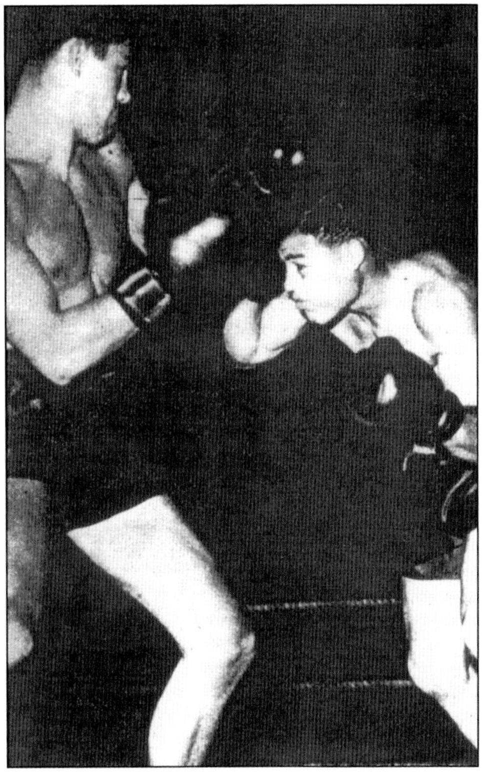

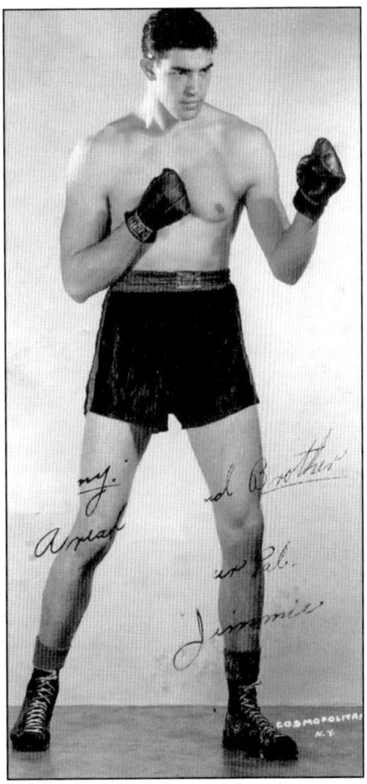

In formal boxing pose, Jimmy Robinson appears here early in his career.

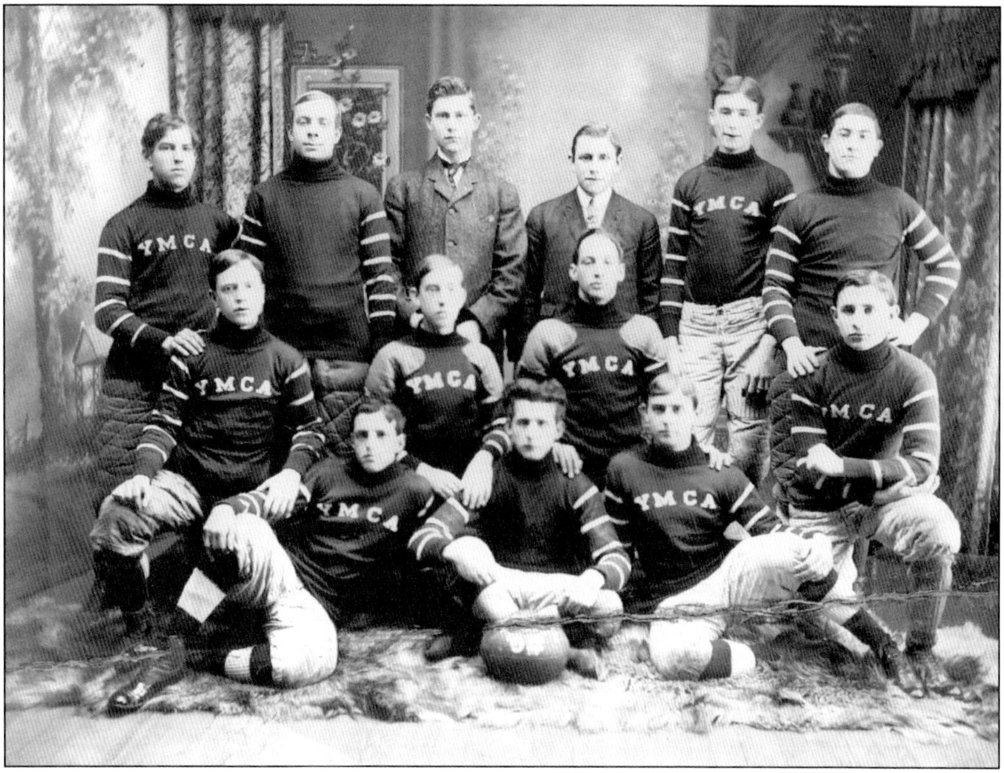

In the late 1800s, the Bridesburg YMCA sponsored this rugby team.

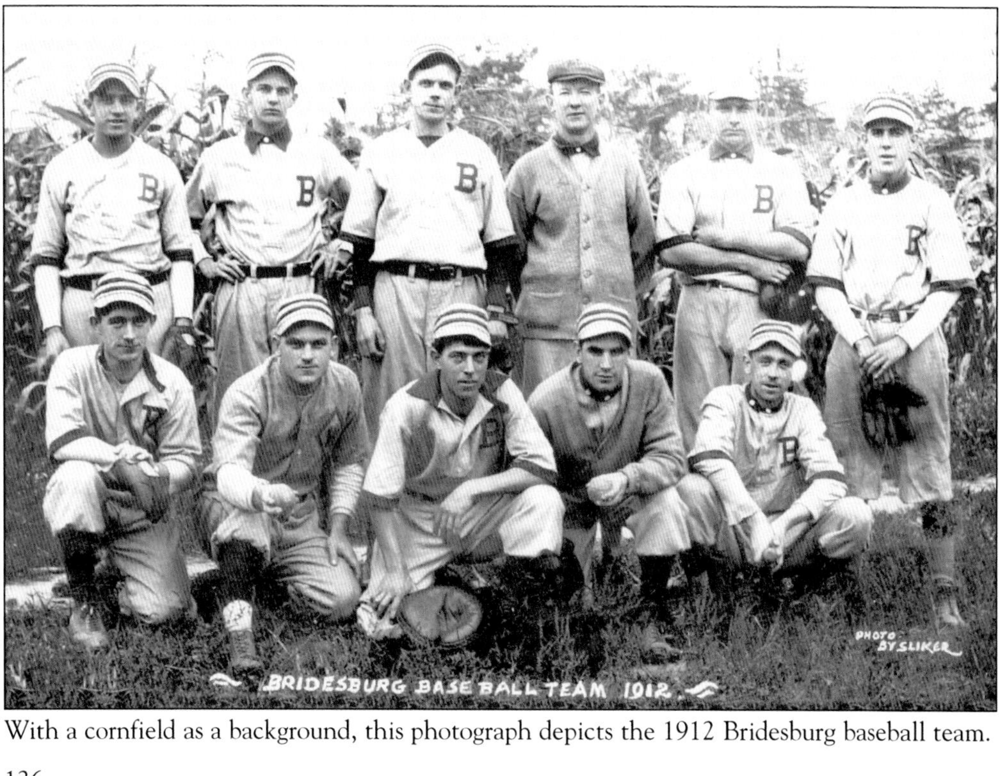

With a cornfield as a background, this photograph depicts the 1912 Bridesburg baseball team.

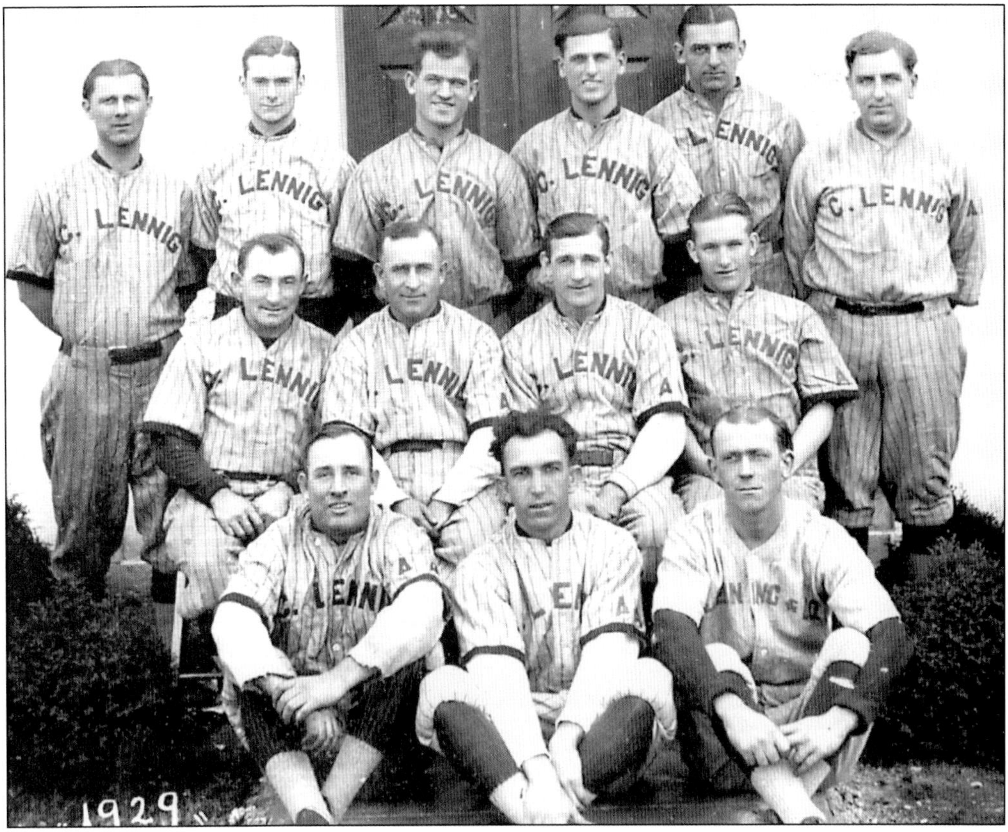

From the mid-1800s until the mid-1900s, Bridesburg maintained a very strong sports heritage. Teams sponsored by church athletic organizations and companies prevailed in all kinds of sports. This photograph shows the 1929 baseball team sponsored by the Charles F. Lennig Chemical Company.

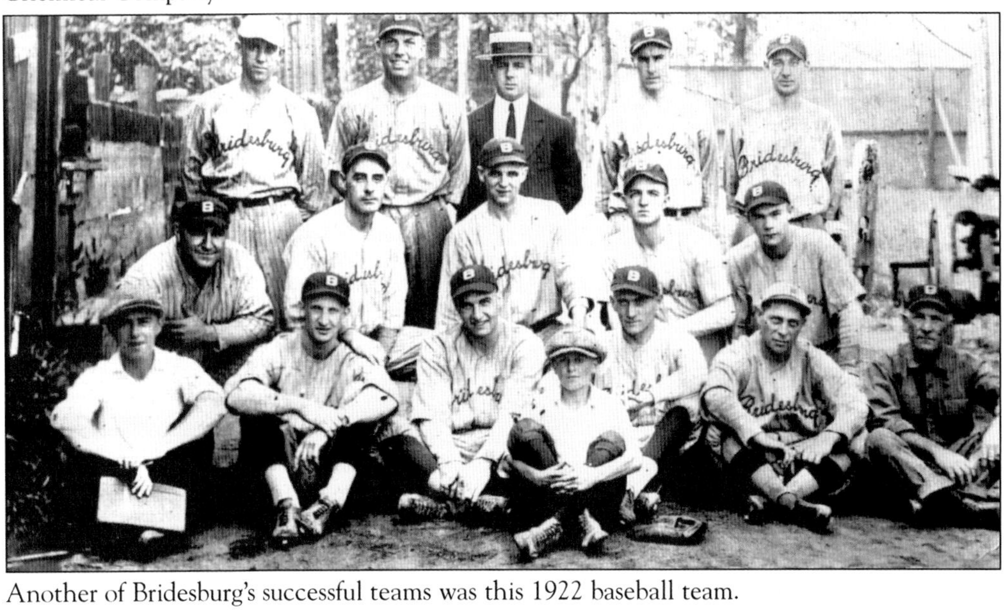

Another of Bridesburg's successful teams was this 1922 baseball team.

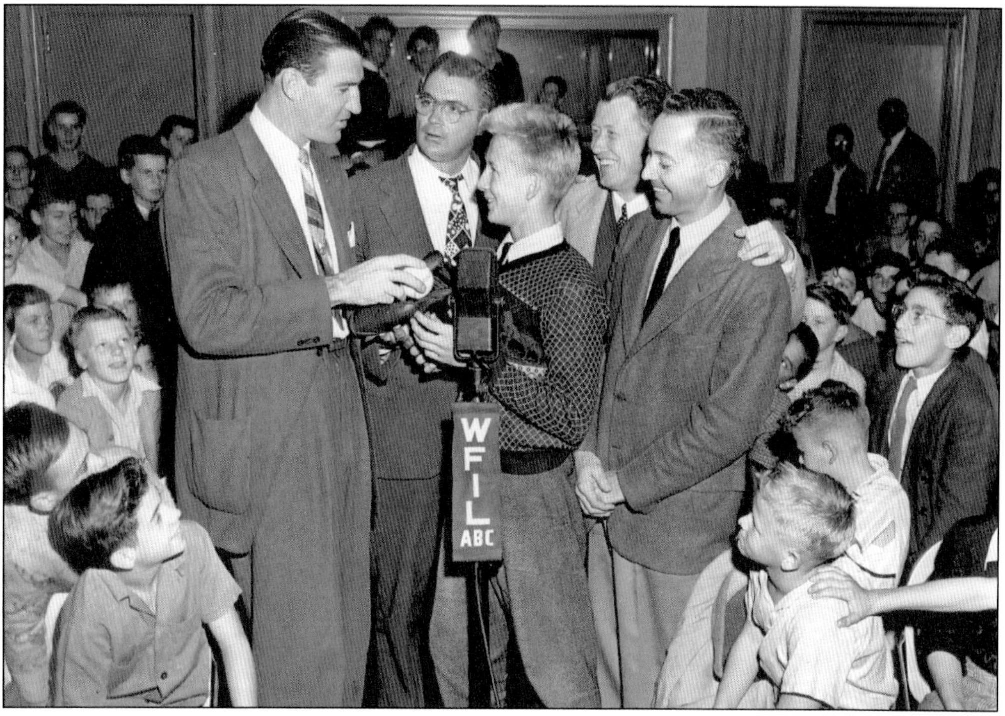

The Philadelphia Phillies pitcher presents a ball and glove to a young Raymond Parczewski, more widely known throughout Bridesburg as "Utki," in 1946.

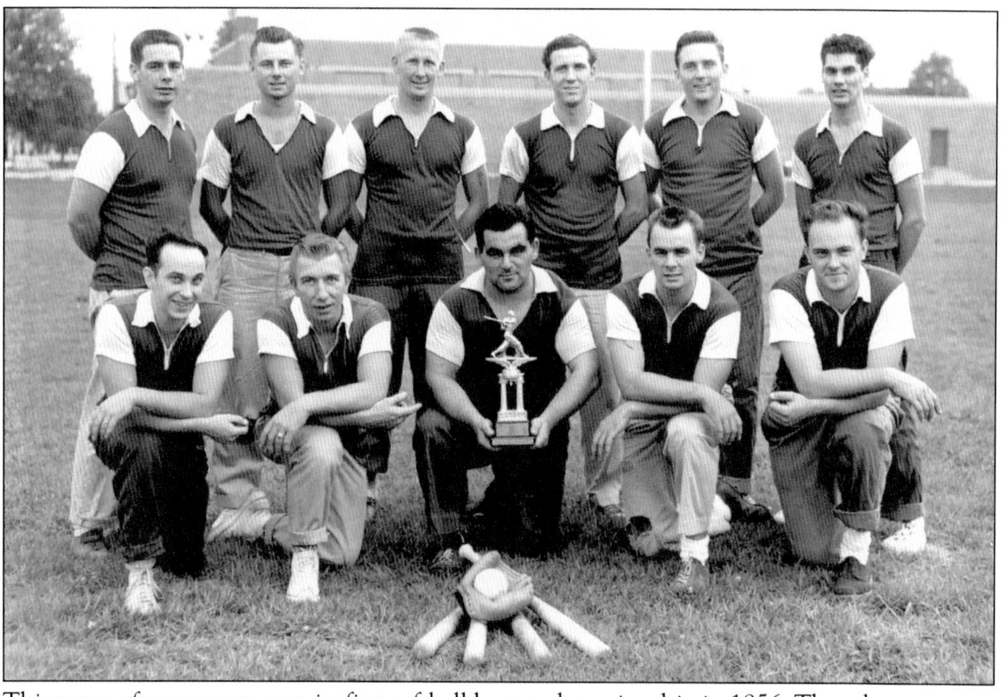

This group of young men won its first softball league championship in 1956. These boys grew up together, played ball together, and, now in their 70s, have lunch together three times a year.